The Biblical Seminar

22

A Translator's Freedom

D1424251

'You might say he was a little free with his originals. Yet in another sense he was entirely true to their spirit. They had challenged him into a new awareness of what they stood for, so that the challenge he had to meet was both technical and spiritual.' (Charles Tomlinson on the translation work of Abraham Cowley, the seventeenth-century poet and translator of Greek poetry.)

'Figures of speech and the liveliness of sentences and arguments can be rendered in a free translation only.' (Martin Luther, in a letter to a friend, 29 November 1520)

'Hwilum word be worde, hwilum andgit of andgite.'
('Sometimes word for word, sometimes meaning for meaning.')
(King Alfred's ninth-century description of his approach when translating parts of the Latin Bible into Anglo-Saxon)

'If one translates a verse literally, he is a liar; and if he adds thereto, he is a blasphemer and a libeler.' (Rabbi Judah, second century AD)

A TRANSLATOR'S FREEDOM

MODERN ENGLISH BIBLES
AND THEIR LANGUAGE

CECIL HARGREAVES

jst
1993
jsot press

Copyright © 1993 Sheffield Academic Press

Published by JSOT Press
JSOT Press is an imprint of
Sheffield Academic Press Ltd
343 Fulwood Road
Sheffield S10 3BP
England

Typeset by Sheffield Academic Press
and
Printed on acid-free paper in Great Britain
by Cromwell Press
Melksham, Wiltshire

British Library Cataloguing in Publication Data

Hargreaves, Cecil
    Translator's Freedom: Modern English
    Bibles and Their Language.—(Biblical
    Seminar; No. 22)
    I. Title II. Series
    220.5

    ISBN 1-85075-400-4

CONTENTS

PREFACE

The list of those to whom I wish to acknowledge a debt of gratitude is inevitably a long one. I put first, perhaps surprisingly, some of the critics of modern translations of the Bible. Though I disagree with many of their conclusions, it was they, more than anyone, who stimulated me to attempt to write this book, and I am grateful for that. One of these critics, Peter Mullen, has written, 'No one ever answers my criticisms'. As far as books are concerned, certainly British books, that seems to be true. The primary aim of the present book is not to try and answer the critics. It is less defensive than that. It tries, as the title says, to tackle the whole topic of freedom in translation. But sweeping criticisms of modern Bible translations and the comparative paucity of explicit replies are bound to be a spur to anyone like me who finds himself in considerable disagreement with the critics.

Influences and stimuli lying behind this book of course go further back. There have been many stimuli from colleagues with whom, at one time or another, I have shared tasks related to Bible translation, and from whom I have gained insight and inspiration. Teaching biblical studies in India led to such involvement. The demands of a teaching course on 'St Mark in Greek' led to the writing of a small book entitled *The Translation and Text of St Mark's Gospel in Greek*, and I learnt much from colleagues and students in that exercise and field of study. I was also lucky enough, while in Calcutta, to be a consultant on New Testament Greek to a committee preparing a fresh Bengali translation of the New Testament. While I was in Bangalore, I was fortunate to work alongside Dr Harold Moulton for a brief period—this was shortly after the completion of the Translator's New Testament, which owed so much to his leadership. His enthusiasm and skill were precious things to experience at first hand.

More recently I was part of the team, under the General Editor, Dom Henry Wansbrough, doing editorial work in connection with the preparation of the New Jerusalem Bible. Discussions and cooperative work during those years gave me many new insights, many occasions for discussing problems of translation, and much enjoyment.

I should also acknowledge here other, less academic factors. During the 1980s regular attendance at services in an English cathedral, combined with parish ministry in an English village, inevitably stimulated thought on practical, pastoral and aesthetic aspects of the language used in our modern reading and hearing of the Bible.

I am grateful to Professor David Clines and other staff of Sheffield Academic Press for all their recent help in preparing my typescript for publication; especially for an initial letter from David Clines which helped to make the presentation of the book clearer, and pointed out one important area of omission.

I record a debt of gratitude to my wife Catriona, not only for checking the proofs but for her encouragement throughout in the writing of this book. Also to my son Richard, for his help on the Index of Biblical References.

This book is dedicated to the memory of my grandfather, John Price Hargreaves of Birkenhead. In the early days of the twentieth century he was an intrepid campaigner for the introduction of the Revised Version of the Bible as a successor to the Authorised Version for common use. His academic training at Cambridge was, following a pattern of those days, both in mathematics and in classics. He was a keen student of the Greek New Testament and its translation. But, far beyond the bounds of family ties, this book is also dedicated to some of the great names in Cambridge biblical studies, not least that of Professor C.F.D. Moule, whose teaching and writings have been a continuing inspiration to me.

ABBREVIATIONS

AV	Authorized Version (or King James Version)
GNB	Good News Bible (Today's English Version)
JB	Jerusalem Bible
NAB	New American Bible
NEB	New English Bible
NIV	New International Version
NJB	New Jerusalem Bible
NKJV	New King James Version (or Revised Authorised Version)
NRSV	New Revised Standard Version
REB	Revised English Bible
RSV	Revised Standard Version
RV	Revised Version
TNT	Translator's New Testament

INTRODUCTION

Much of the discussion about modern versions of the Bible has, in one way or another, to do with freedom. The maxim of the New Revised Standard Version about what it aims to be, 'as literal as possible, as free as necessary', is just one example of how translators and revisers posit freedom and the use of the right sort of freedom as a central concern in biblical translation. Critics of the new versions certainly raise many questions about freedom. They often say that the new versions are 'too free' and that the free use of modern English idiom too easily deflects translators from paths of accuracy of translation and from scholarly integrity. At the same time critics tend to say that in another sense the modern versions are 'not free enough': their language is mostly too pedestrian and pedantic, it is said, to catch the imaginative spiritual cadences and poetic mystery of much biblical material. This latter complaint was voiced at a distinguished level when the Prince of Wales said publicly that the New English Bible had been written 'in the style of an internal office memo'. The remark came significantly at the end of the 1980s, a decade which had seen such a strong growth, in the literary and theological world, of a literary approach to the Bible.

This book attempts to explore two aspects of language that are very closely connected with issues of freedom and with charges of excessive freedom or insufficient freedom in translation. First, it looks at idiom and modern idiomatic English translation, especially in Chapter 1 and the first part of Chapter 2. Secondly, particularly in Chapters 3 to 7, it looks at depth of language, and the expressing of profundity, poetry and mystery in modern translations. The reader will notice that it is issues of style of translation, as distinct from issues of content, that are to the fore. This may suggest that among the complexity of considerations that have to be taken into account in any full discussion of biblical translation—textual, philological, literary, hermeneutical, semantic—too many considerations are going to be virtually ignored. But I hope that this will not prove to be so. Points concerning accuracy of translation are, of course, discussed as an underlying concern in every section of the book; and it is anyway barely possible, as we know, ever fully to treat style and content separately. Accuracy is the main topic in Chapter 8, and questions of accuracy are taken up at regular points in the notes that follow the more extended biblical passages quoted from one or other of the modern versions. The concerns of linguistic analysis are given some close attention in the second half of Chapter 2.

In the English tradition of religious translation freedom has always been valued. When Archbishop Thomas Cranmer was translating St Augustine's prayer, 'Deus, quem nosse vivere est; cui servire regnare est...', he was very free, not to say expansive, in his translation: 'O God...in knowledge of whom standeth our eternal life, whose service is perfect freedom...' (The Second Collect, for Peace, from the Order for Morning Prayer, *Book of Common Prayer*). And in the Authorized Version's preface from 'The Translators to the Reader', the importance of freedom in translation is emphasized at several points. The translators say that they resisted a policy of uniformity favoured by some people, whereby a Hebrew or Greek word would be translated by the same word in English on each occasion that it occurred. One particular word in the original language, they said, we sometimes translate by 'journeying' and sometimes by 'travelling'. (They might have added that they sometimes translated the Hebrew word *ḥesed* as 'mercy', sometimes as 'kindness', and sometimes as 'loving-kindness'). They spoke of the 'scrupulosity' or the 'obscurity' of some other translators who wanted to use sophisticated or over-precise words. 'Is the Kingdom of God', they said, 'become words and syllables? Why should we be in bondage to them, if we may be free?' But to quote such things is not, of course, to imply that the constraints of faithfulness to the original text have been ignored in the English tradition. It is simply to recall that the claims of freedom have always been seen as strong claims.

In the twentieth century the tradition of freedom has often been notably upheld in a number of fields of religious translation in English, such as hymnody and poetic mystical writing. Helen Waddell's acclaimed translation, in her *Mediaeval Latin Lyrics*, published in 1929, of Peter Abelard's famous twelfth century Latin hymn 'O quanta, qualia...' was an example of that. For Abelard's beautiful lines about the heavenly Jerusalem ('ubi non praevenit / rem desiderium, / nec desiderio / minus est praemium') Helen Waddell has the equally beautiful but very free translation:

> Where finds the dreamer waking
> Truth beyond dreaming far,
> Nor is the heart's possessing
> Less than the heart's desire.

To quote that example of free translation obviously raises questions about the relationship between translation and paraphrase, an issue discussed at various points in the pages of this book; but the quotation does illustrate the strength of traditions of freedom in religious translation in English.

Although, in the field of literary translation generally, there seems to have been considerable scholarly opinion preferring a more literalist approach to translation, Helen Waddell has not been alone in her exploration of the use of free translation in modern times. The distinguished poet and translator C.H. Sisson, who would, I think, describe himself as a traditionalist in his general outlook, has these fascinating words in his autobiography:

> Translation is the best of literary exercises, perhaps the only serious one. It is strictly impossible, and the scope for the apprentice's ingenuity is therefore unlimited. At the same time the translator can have before him a competent model, not to copy but to study and to make something of his own out of.[1]

Part of the meaning of free translation is translation that is imaginative. I have always been intrigued by the fact that both those who are traditionalists in the matter of English biblical versions and those who are innovators alike use the language of imagination. The traditionalists tend to talk about imaginative poetic nuance, and the innovators about imaginative idiomatic nuance. As I said above, traditionalists say that they too often miss in the new translations the sort of imaginative cadences by which William Tyndale and the AV in their day brought out deep meanings in the original text. But users of twentieth-century translations have also frequently described them in terms of the firing of the imagination; and they continue to do so, usually in relation to some sort of imaginative freshness coming to them in turns of phrase in the new versions. In the middle of the

---

1.   *On the Look-Out* (Manchester: Carcanet, 1989).

twentieth century the biblical scholar A.M. Hunter used this classic phrase about one new translation which he had been using: 'it was like looking through a new window at an old landscape'. Even so literary a figure as Stevie Smith the poet, though a lover of the language of the AV, and the author some years later of a scathing review of another, more radical modern version, found E.V. Rieu's modern translation of St Mark's Gospel in the 1940s so imaginative in its presentation that she wrote a notable poem about the figure of Christ that she saw portrayed. However rigid the dividing line between traditionalist and innovator may at times appear in the field of translations of the Bible, a longer perspective may reveal a common concern between them, with that which is imaginative and liberating. One of the issues explored in the following pages is the relationship between these two sorts of imaginative and liberating qualities in translation. Another theme is the distinction between the right sort of freedom and the wrong sort of freedom.

Many of these pages are taken up not with generalized comments about modern versions but with actual quotations from modern versions: the aim being to earth discussion in actual texts and to let the versions speak for themselves as far as possible. A good number of substantial 'readings' from one or other of the modern translations is given, spread over the various chapters, and each chapter is, of course, full of briefer quotations of phrases and verses. The longer passages quoted are given with the modern version printed alongside the AV (or in one case the Coverdale psalter) rendering of the same passage. The modern translations are taken from a variety of modern English versions, ranging from those most commonly used in churches to a modern translation of part of a psalm in the Penguin Classics series, a translation made by the modern poet Peter Levi. Most of the longer quotations, though not all, are taken from the more radically worded modern versions since it is these which have been most at the centre of modern debate and which best typify experiments in freedom of wording.

Chapter 1

THE FREEDOM OF NEW IDIOM

In Isaiah 43 the prophetic writer says that God, who blessed his people at the crossing of the Red Sea, has new blessings in store for them. He passes on God's word of encouragement. In the AV the passage is, 'Remember ye not the former things, neither consider the things of old. Behold, I will do a new thing: now it shall spring forth: shall ye not know it?' (Isa. 43.18, 19a). The translation in many modern versions is different. For example, the New Jerusalem Bible has,

> No need to remember past events,
> no need to think about what was done before.
> Look, I am doing something new,
> now it emerges: can you not see it?'

The differences between those two translations are almost entirely differences of idiom and style, and in some ways they may appear to be very tiny differences. In the NJB the slightly colloquial modern 'no need to remember' may be compared with the AV's 'remember ye not...'; the modern idiomatic word 'emerge' in the NJB, may be compared with the AV's 'spring forth'; 'can you not see it?', may be compared with 'shall ye not know it?' The original text of the passage presents the translator with no great problems of varying textual readings or of verbal meaning; nor indeed of interpretation, though any translation has to be careful to reflect the fact that it is good past events and not bad past events that are being spoken about in the context. Hence the emphasis is on idiomatic translation. It is likely that the modern translators would say that they found nothing inaccurate in the traditional version, but that they were striving to convey accurately, and with some impact for modern ears, what the original passage in Hebrew was saying, through modern idioms or phrases held to have an equivalent meaning to that in the original text. To those who take a traditional line, such modern translations as that of the NJB may appear in danger of adding some at least slightly distorting nuances to the original; and such detailed questions arising from a passage such as this, as to whether or not the precise imagery lying behind the verb translated 'spring forth' (AV) needs to be literally conveyed in English, are important questions for debate (a later chapter touches on this more fully). On the other hand, those who take an innovative line may find in the traditional wording something slightly distorting: for example, the purely generalized phrases in the AV such as 'remember ye not' and 'things' may be felt to have here for modern ears less impact than the original prophetic word would surely have carried.

It hardly needs to be said that much of the tension and suspicion about biblical translation done in modern idiomatic English centres round an anxious concern over free translation, colloquialism and paraphrase. The editors of modern versions themselves have sometimes changed their minds over the years on particular wordings. The NEB in its original forms (1961 or 1970) had some phrases in it which were, arguably, suitably free in conversational passages, but which seemed to the editors of the Revised English Bible (published in 1989) over-colloquial. In 2 Cor. 12.13 (AV) Paul writes to the Corinthian Christians, 'I myself was not burdensome to you...'; the NEB has 'I never sponged on you...'; the REB has 'I was never a charge on you'. Again, in 1 Cor. 15.20 the AV has, 'But now is Christ risen from the dead, and become the firstfruits of them that slept'. A free version such as the following from the Living Bible will seem to many people as a translation much too free, expansive and over-interpretative: 'But the fact is that Christ actually did rise from the dead, and has become the first of millions who will come back to life again some day'. It should be added that the Living Bible puts a footnote against the second part of the verse: 'Literally, "the first-fruits of them that are asleep"'.

Similar points will come up for discussion frequently in this book. But before going further we should first concentrate on some basic matters of idiom, syntax and grammar, if we are to take seriously the significance of the whole question of idiomatic translation. Discussion on translation in a modern idiom is not just concerned with sensational isolated instances of colloquialism and paraphrase (where mistakes are easily made), but with fundamental differences in the structure of languages. These differences make communication difficult and have to be tackled in some detail.

Should a Translation Always Reflect the Original's Idiom?

One issue that arises is that some languages have, say, more adverbs than others, or more nouns or adjectives: as a result, word for word translation runs into difficulties at a very basic level. In 1 Chron. 12.8 we find a simple example of how translators into English, a language with many adjectives, have dealt with idiom in Hebrew, a language with not so many adjectives. Describing some of David's warriors, the AV has the phrase 'men of might': this is changed by a modern translation such as the REB into 'valiant men' on the grounds that this is a natural idiomatic equivalent of the Hebrew idiom where two nouns are joined together by 'of'. The remit given in the 1940s to the panel of Old Testament translators for the NEB said that 'Hebraisms and other un-English expressions should be avoided'.[1] And one recommendation passed by the original 1946 conference which planned the NEB was that 'the translators should be free to employ a contemporary idiom rather than reproduce the traditional "biblical" English'. Some qualifications to those vigorous statements about idiom have been made in more recent years: the preface to the New International Version in 1978 said that the aim was to be 'idiomatic but not idiosyncratic, contemporary but not dated'. But most modern translators (including those of the NIV) have moved broadly along the lines of idiomatic freedom.

Naturally, criticism of this general policy has come not least from scholars of English literature. Gerald Hammond has pleaded for Hebrew idiom, syntax and phrase formation to be retained in modern versions, in the manner of the AV. He attacks as 'treacherous' what he calls 'idiom for idiom translation', that is, the attempt to translate Hebrew and Greek idioms by equivalent English idioms rather than literally. He writes, 'Idioms are even more embedded in language and culture systems than single words are'.[2] To remove an original idiom, he contends, is to remove an indispensable vehicle of meaning. Other scholars, taking up different types of idiomatic expression, have made a similar protest. In the middle of the twentieth century, T.R. Henn,

1. G. Hunt, *Introduction to the New English Bible* (Cambridge: Cambridge University Press, 1970), p. 21.
2. In R. Alter and F. Kermode (eds.), *The Literary Guide to the Bible* (London: Collins, 1987), p. 647.

the poet and English literary scholar, protested that the new versions of his day often discarded phrases in the AV that have not only become part of the English language but that remain valuable idiomatic phrases in modern English. In 'The Bible as Literature',[1] he instanced the phrase 'high time' in Rom. 13.11 (AV) ('And that, knowing the time, that now it is high time to awake out of sleep...') and regretted its absence from modern translations. He wrote, 'The idiom of AV is, except for a few obscure passages, much less antiquated than we might suppose'. In the case of that verse his plea has not gone unnoticed: it is significant that whereas in 1961 and 1970 the NEB had, 'In all this remember how critical the moment is. It is time for you to wake out of sleep...', in 1989 the REB has, 'Always remember that this is the hour of crisis: it is high time for you to wake out of sleep'. 'High time' has returned.

An example of an individual translator who was wholly convinced of the importance of translating into modern idiomatic English was E.V. Rieu, already mentioned in the Introduction. In the middle of the twentieth century he translated the Gospels into English after a career as a translator of Greek classics and as editor of the whole Penguin Classics series. He felt that he could not follow any different policy when translating the Gospels than he had when translating the Odyssey. In the Odyssey he replaced a very literal and traditionalist phrase about Eurycleia in the Loeb translation ('her word remained unwinged') by the very different rendering that she was 'too awestruck to argue'. He wrote in his introduction to his 1946 Penguin translation of the Odyssey, 'I have found it necessary, in fact my duty as translator, to abandon, or rather to transform, the idiom and syntax of the Greek'.[2] In the same way, when he encountered a piece of New Testament Greek in the Gospels that had a very Semitic sentence structure, he altered that too to fit in with English idiom. In Mk 7.3 the AV has, 'For the Pharisees, and all the Jews, except they wash their hands oft, eat not, holding the tradition of the elders...' In contrast to that version, with its Semitic sentence structure, E.V. Rieu, without using any larger number of words, put it into the structure of English idiom. He rendered it, 'The Pharisees, in fact the whole Jewish community, always wash their hands thoroughly before meals, in

---

1. In *Peake's Commentary* (London: Nelson, 1962), p. 15.
2. *The Odyssey* (Harmondsworth: Penguin, 1946), p. 18.

strict observance of ancient tradition'. In his introduction to his translation of the four Gospels, Rieu said that in general it was his duty as a translator to preserve the 'style' of the original but not the idiom. 'Style is one thing and idiom another', he wrote.[1]

1 Sam. 20.30 is one example of colourful idiomatic language in the original where there may well be considerable support among both traditionalists and innovators for a translation that gives English idiomatic equivalents. The AV renders it,

> Then Saul's anger was kindled against Jonathan, and he said unto him, Thou son of the perverse rebellious woman, do not I know that thou hast chosen the son of Jesse to thine own confusion, and unto the confusion of thy mother's nakedness?

It is a dramatic moment, and some lively language is called for: Saul has wanted to kill David and is enraged with Jonathan for what he sees as disloyalty to their royal line, in helping David to slip away to safety. A modern version, the NIV, translates it,

> Saul's anger flared up at Jonathan and he said to him, 'You son of a perverse and rebellious woman! Don't I know that you have sided with the son of Jesse to your own shame and to the shame of the mother who bore you?'

The NIV there puts three English idiomatic expressions where the AV has three literal Hebrew idiomatic expressions. Where the AV has 'anger was kindled', the NIV has 'anger flared up', though the same imagery is retained. Where the AV has 'thou hast chosen', the NIV has 'you have sided'. Where the AV has 'unto the confusion of thy mother's nakedness', the NIV has the clear and rhythmic 'to the shame of the mother who bore you'.

In Amos 1.3 we find a very distinctive Hebrew idiom with a good poetic ring about it: 'for three or for four transgressions' (AV). 'Thus saith the Lord; For three transgressions of Damascus and for four, I will not turn away the punishment thereof...' Here some modern translators retain the Hebrew idiom literally word for word: NRSV, NIV, NJB and the New American Bible do this. But others, interpreting the term 'three or four' to mean 'more than enough', put the claims of clarity before those of literal precision and still retain resonance. The REB has the more English idiom of 'for crime after crime

1. *The Four Gospels* (London: Lane, 1951).

of Damascus...' and the Good News Bible has, 'the people of Damascus have sinned again and again'. Eugene Nida, in his book about the GNB,[1] states the case for this type of translation here: 'in present day English "three or four times" implies something which is relatively infrequent... But in ancient Hebrew "for three...and for four" meant "over and over again".'[2]

In Eph. 2.3 we meet again, in a more doctrinal passage, the same sort of idiom in Hebrew (and in New Testament phrases with a Semitic flavour to them) that we met in relation to the Old Testament phrase literally translated 'men of might'. Eph. 2.3 says, 'we were by nature the children of wrath' (AV). This literal translation is retained in the NRSV, but not elsewhere in modern translations that I have seen. The NIV tries to catch the meaning through a comparable English idiomatic phrase: 'we were by nature objects of wrath'. The REB finds it necessary to go for a more radical reconstruction: 'in our natural condition...we lay under the condemnation of God...'

How remote from modern experience does an original biblical phrase have to become for there to be a change to a different English idiom? The translation of Jn 19.24 is a good example of a vivid narrative passage in the Gospels, where modern translators have on the whole felt it necessary not to retain an idiom literally. In this verse, part of the crucifixion story about Jesus' seamless tunic, the AV has, 'They said... Let us not rend it but cast lots for it, whose it shall be: that the scripture might be fulfilled, which saith, They parted my raiment among them, and for my vesture they did cast lots.' The phrase 'cast lots' is not entirely unused in modern versions: the REB retains it at the second point where it is used. But the first time it is used they put a more modern idiomatic, even colloquial, phrase: 'let us toss for it'. The GNB renders the verse, 'The soldiers said to one another, "Let's not tear it; let's throw dice to see who will get it". This happened in order to make the scripture come true: "They divided my clothes among themselves and gambled for my robe".'

---

1. *Good News for Everyone* (London: Collins, 1977), p. 68.
2. Some scholars have defined the precise meaning of the Hebrew phrase translated 'for three and for four...' as being 'more than enough'. And in Jer. 36.23, where Jeremiah's scroll is destroyed three or four leaves or columns at a time, 'three or four' seems to signify just 'several' (not necessarily 'few'). But in Amos 1 and in most contexts the effective meaning seems to be 'again and again'.

Since we are considering some of the small intricacies of idiomatic translation, a further word may be fitted in about T.R. Henn's comment on the AV's 'now it is high time...' (Rom. 13.11a). In addition to the point already noted, that the REB retains the AV phrase 'high time', it is worth noting that the REB also introduces a bold modern idiom 'the hour of crisis' in the first clause of 13.11a: it has, 'Always remember that this is the hour of crisis: it is high time for you to wake out of sleep' (cf. AV, 'And that, knowing the time, that now it is high time to awake out of sleep'). The REB's new and free translation seems not only to have strength and clarity in general, but also to bring out well the special meaning of the original word καιρός through the 'crisis' phrase.

Semitic Grammar and English Translation

Sometimes modern versions, far from ignoring subtlety in Hebrew or Greek idiom, go out of their way to reproduce them carefully, though in a modern way, often somewhat different from the usually literal and word for word method of the AV.

In Mt. 25.24, in the parable of the talents, the AV reproduces very literally the distinctive Greek idiom which has not 'Lord, I knew that thou art a hard man', but 'Lord, I knew thee, that thou art a hard man'. The Translator's New Testament still takes the subtle idiomatic point very seriously, with a slightly changed wording: 'Sir, I knew you; you are a hard man...', combining a good feel of modern English idiom with sensitivity to Greek idiom. Not all scholars or translators would allow such subtle significance to the precise Greek mode of expression here, but a strong case can be made for taking it as the TNT does. It is interesting to note that the philosopher R.M. Hare, in writing about Plato and his theory of knowledge, says that Plato's mystical or metaphysical side is related to the fact that his mother tongue was Greek, which, when speaking of knowing someone, most naturally uses the idiom of personal relationship, 'I know you who you are', rather than the simply factual and propositional, 'I know who you are'.[1]

As already mentioned, an English translation sometimes needs to turn an original phrase containing two nouns joined by 'of' in Hebrew

---

1. R.M. Hare, *Plato* (Oxford: Oxford University Press, 1982), p. 31.

into an English phrase containing a noun and an adjective. All translators, including the translators of the AV, have done it in a good number of passages. In Deut. 16.18 the Hebrew is literally 'laws of justice' or 'judgments of justice'. The AV translators changed the construction into 'just judgement', and subsequent English translators have either followed a similarly changed structure (REB: 'true justice') or used verb and adverb in place of noun and adjective (NIV: 'judge the people fairly'). But the question is: how often should the translator follow this course? Even the early translators were not agreed on this. In Ps. 48.1 the Hebrew may literally be translated, 'Great is the Lord, and greatly to be praised...in the mountain of his holiness'. For the last phrase Coverdale, more than half a century before the AV was published, put an adjective and a noun for Hebrew's two nouns, and rendered the phrase, 'even upon his holy hill'. But the AV translators decided to stay literal here and put, 'in the mountain of his holiness'. Modern versions have followed Coverdale, but pleas for a more completely Hebraic rendering of such phrases in English may sometimes be heard.

What does the translator do about the literal reproducing of frequent Semitic 'and's, which seems of great importance to some literary scholars? Modern translators in English have tended to put, in place of some of the Hebrew 'and's, an 'if' or an 'as' or a 'when'. In Neh. 4.18 the AV translates the Hebrew quite literally: 'For the builders, every one had his sword by his side, and so builded'. But the REB is typical of modern versions in putting, 'The builders had their swords attached to their belts as they built'. We find the same sort of Semitisms in New Testament Greek, especially in Mark's Gospel, where the Semitic, Palestinian, Aramaic origins show through most clearly in the linguistic pattern. In Mk 15.25 the AV gives the completely literal rendering, 'And it was the third hour, and they crucified him'. But the Revised Standard Version gives, 'And it was the third hour, when they crucified him'. We may say that the Hebrew 'and...and' idiom has passed into the English language through the AV and become English idiom, and that is true in a sense: but most people would agree that such wordings now lie on the fringes of real English idiom. (It may be noted in passing that in the first clause of the verse just quoted the NRSV is freer than the RSV: 'It was nine o'clock in the morning when they crucified him'.) Mt. 26.53 provides a further example of Semitic sentence structure in literal English translations, including an 'and'. The AV has, 'Thinkest thou that I cannot now pray to my Father, and he shall presently give me more than twelve legions of angels?' Many modern translators have found that the structures get too Semitic, and are therefore 'under-translated', in a simply literal translation. Perhaps it was Ronald Knox who first altered structures in this passage: he put, 'Dost thou doubt that if I call upon my Father even now, he will send more than twelve legions of angels to my side?'

More controversial, in these matters of minute detail, is the translation of Hebrew and Greek 'cognate' and emphatic constructions, where verbs and nouns with a similar root are piled up. The phrase about the wise men in the AV's literal rendering of Mt. 2.10 gives us both 'rejoiced' and 'joy': 'When they saw the star, they rejoiced with exceeding great joy...' This may be thought to be the only adequately poetic and dramatic rendering in English for a passage so often read at Christmas carol services. But some of the modern versions which alter the structure have strength and impact. The REB has, 'they were overjoyed at the sight of it', using a much-used modern term in idiomatic English. Or again, in Lk. 22.15, the AV has the literal 'With desire I have desired to eat this Passover with you before I suffer...', which the RSV puts into idiomatic English with 'I have earnestly desired...' (NRSV: 'I have eagerly desired').

Problems of Prophetic Overstatement

Much more difficult for the translator than any of the above is the rendering into English of Hebrew prophetic overstatement, or of the characteristic Semitic idiom whereby a preference for one thing rather than another is sometimes expressed in stark black-and-white terms, opposing them to each other. It is at least arguable that the Hebrew phrase and idiom 'and not' is often best translated into English as 'rather than'. There has been some scholarly support for this. In Mal. 1.2, 3 the words 'I loved Jacob, and I hated Esau' (AV), quoted in Rom. 9.13, may be held to mean, in effect, 'I loved Jacob rather than Esau'. I am not aware that any modern translation has departed from the word 'hate' in the Malachi passage. But a few have done so in translating the same Greek word when it comes in Lk. 14.26. In the AV this latter verse reads, 'If any man come to me, and hate not his father, and mother, and wife, and children, and brethren, and sisters, yea, and his own life also, he cannot be my disciple'. The GNB puts, 'Whoever comes to me cannot be my disciple unless he loves me more than he loves his father and his mother...'; and the NAB has, 'If anyone comes to me without turning his back on his father and his mother...' On the whole most modern translators retain 'hate' in Lk. 14.26, and would agree with George Caird[1] that the original starkness of the Palestinian expression should be retained.

A different type of oriental overstatement is encountered in Dan. 2.4 and in ensuing verses. The AV renders it, 'Then spake the Chaldeans to the king in Syriack, O king, live for ever...' Here again most modern translations give a literal translation of the original. But the NEB and REB have what they regard as the equivalent English idiom: 'long live the king!' Ronald Knox, who had something similar, explained his radical translation as follows:

> A biblical phrase like 'O king live for ever!' has got to be changed; nobody ever talked like that in English. But you must not change it into 'I hope that your Majesty's life may be spared indefinitely'. You must get back to the language of a period when palace etiquette was more formal, 'Long life to the King's majesty' or something like that.[2]

This latter comment reflects Knox's belief that idiomatic translation does not so much mean translation into modern English idiom, but rather into English idiom instead of Semitic idiom. His own aim being 'timeless' English, he said that the AV's English was often not timeless, but Hebrew idiom in English words.

Interchanges of Verb and Noun

Many passages could be quoted in which the use of a verb in English proves to be the best way of translating a Hebrew noun. The phrase 'weight of glory' (βάρος δόξης) in 2 Cor. 4.17 ('our light affliction, which is but for a moment, worketh for us a far more exceeding weight of glory' [AV]) can become a significant phrase for English readers, if they are prepared to put in some careful study on its background as a Semitic idiom, but it has little English idiomatic force

---

1. G.B. Caird, *The Language and Imagery of the Bible* (London: Gerald Duckworth, 1980), pp. 111-12.

2. R. Knox, *On Englishing the Bible* (London: Burns & Oates, 1949), pp. 71-72.

for a new reader of the Bible. It has been illuminated by the imaginative writing of C.S. Lewis on the subject of this phrase, but can still leave the ordinary reader puzzled.[1] For many of us the idiomatic meaning of the Semitic phrase is best caught in English when the verb 'outweighs' is used in English for the Greek noun 'weight', as is done in the NEB and REB. The REB gives, 'Our troubles are slight and short-lived; and their outcome is an eternal glory which far outweighs them'. This perhaps gets nearest to the original imagery underlying the Semitic idiom. The word for 'glory' in Hebrew had, early on in the history of the language, meant simply 'weight'; and then, through the association of weight with the weighing of gold and silver in the marketplace, came to mean 'value', 'magnitude', 'glory'. The noun 'weight' in modern English can certainly have a metaphorical sense, as when we say that the word of an experienced person carries weight; but it is not quite the same metaphorical sense that 'weight' has in Hebrew. The idea of 'outweighing' or the more common verb form 'outweighs' gets closer.

Sometimes it is the other way round, and English idiom is best served by the putting of a noun where Hebrew or Greek idiom has a verb. The literal, word for word translation of Paul's great statement in Rom. 11.32 (reputed to have been Karl Barth's favourite biblical verse) is translated in the AV as, 'For God hath concluded them all in unbelief, that he might have mercy upon all'. But the REB (as, similarly, TNT and GNB) turns the AV's verbal phrase 'concluded' (i.e. 'imprisoned') into a noun phrase ('prison of disobedience'): 'For, in shutting all mankind in the prison of their disobedience, God's purpose was to show mercy to all mankind'. A further idiomatic point in the REB's translation, not shared by the TNT or GNB, is that it turns the Greek main clause into a subordinate clause in English ('in shutting all mankind...'), and turns the Greek subordinate clause into a main clause ('God's purpose was...'). Does this weaken the force of Paul's strong phrase about putting both Jews and Greeks into imprisonment? I do not think so. It simply reflects the fact that in modern English we do not seem to use an 'in order that' type of wording very often: we express the same thing in a different way. It is arguable that this verse of Paul needs, in truly idiomatic English, to revolve around some word such as 'inevitable' or 'inevitably': we tend

---

1.   C.S. Lewis, *A Weight of Glory*, an Oxford Sermon.

to talk today about inevitability, where Christians of 400 years ago talked about predestination. (Paul's point may be taken to be this: that although by giving both Jew and Greek freedom, God made their sinning inevitable, yet [also inevitably] God's love, which gave the freedom, involved and also had as its purpose the giving of mercy to them both.) But to introduce the word 'inevitable' would lose Paul's particular imagery of the prison, and would only partly get the feel of his strong picture of all humankind being in a situation from which there is no exit except by God's grace.[1] In addition to the main points made above, one may notice that the REB also clarifies the meaning of the AV's now archaic word 'concluded' and of 'unbelief'.

Interjections and rhetorical questions are also idiomatic and grammatical features that are of particular importance for translators. The typically Semitic 'behold' as an interjection does not always need to be translated literally. In 2 Cor. 6.9 (AV) Paul describes himself and his fellow-Christians as people who, for all their humiliations, cannot easily be written off: to the world they are 'as dying, and, behold, we live'. The NJB uses an equivalent English idiom in place of the Semitic 'behold': 'dying, and yet here we are, alive'. Hebrew rhetorical questions can sometimes be transferred quite naturally into English in a literal, word for word translation, but may need a little idiomatic change. In 1 Kgs 21.7 (AV) Jezebel says to Ahab, urging him not to be timid in seizing Naboth's vineyard, 'Dost thou now govern the kingdom of Israel?' At this point the NEB and REB have the apt and slightly altered, 'Are you or are you not king in Israel?'

Rethinking the Translation of Other Characteristic Phrases

It may be appropriate to return here to more general and less purely grammatical matters: this time to various key Hebrew and Greek words, phrases and idioms, where, in modern English translation, a less entirely literal rendering than that found in the AV is helpful, if we are to get across the idiomatic meaning or nuance.

Hebrew sometimes uses the phrase 'many' when it really means what in English we might express as 'the many' or 'all'. In Mk 10.45 the AV has, 'the Son of man came...to give his life a ransom for many' and in Mk 14.24, 'This is my blood of the new testament,

---

1. See C.E.B. Cranfield, *Romans: A Shorter Commentary* (Edinburgh: T. & T. Clark, 1985), p. 287.

which is shed for many'. In English the word 'many' here can sound very limiting, as though it meant 'many in contrast to all', whereas in fact the Semitic idiom carries rather the meaning of 'many in contrast to one'. Behind that point lies the fact that Hebrew and Aramaic may be said to have no word for 'all' in the plural. As the *Jerome Biblical Commentary* says on Mk 14.24, 'The "many" should be understood in the Semitic sense as designating a great number without restriction'. The usage in Mark echoes such Old Testament phrases as 'he shall justify many' and 'he bare the sin of many' (Isa. 53.11, 12 [AV]). In such famous and oft-quoted verses modern translators have on the whole been hesitant to alter in any way the use of the single literal word 'many'. But the NAB tackles the issue and uses the phrase 'the many'. In Mk 10.45 it has, 'The Son of Man has not come to be served but to serve—to give his life in ransom for the many'. Also in Dan. 12.3 the NAB has, 'those who lead the many to justice shall be like the stars forever'. The NAB retains the single word 'many' in Isaiah 53 and in Mk 14.24. Some modern translators use the phrase 'the many' in Isa. 53.12 ('I shall give him a portion with the many' [NJB]), but in this instance we are dealing with the translation of a different Hebrew word *rab*, which can be variously translated 'the great' or 'the many'.

Difficulties also arise, at a less doctrinal level, over the English translation of resounding idiomatic Hebrew phrases such as that translated 'blow up the trumpet' in the AV. That is just one example of the use of an English verb which has various idiomatic meanings in English. In Ps. 81.3 the AV, reproducing Coverdale precisely, has, 'Blow up the trumpet in the new moon...' In some ways 'blow up' is more accurate than many modern translations which, in an effort to avoid phrases about 'blowing up', just put 'blow the trumpet', since the Hebrew verb here means something like 'strike up'. (The AV is less literal in the preceding verse, Ps. 81.2, with its 'Take a psalm...', where the Hebrew verb means 'lift up' or 'raise'.) But the phrase 'blow up' for musical instruments is not a very viable translation for today, unless one wants to sound exceptionally mediaeval or Shakespearian. The word translated 'trumpet' in the AV also makes for complication in the translation of the verse, since the Hebrew word used here (*šôpār*) probably refers to the curved horn of a cow or ram, of the sort still used today by Jews at festivals. Does the modern translator put 'horn' in place of 'trumpet'? Many have done so, sometimes landing themselves in difficulty with phrases about 'sounding the horn' which is also hardly viable today. The NIV gets over many of the difficulties skilfully with its 'Sound the ram's horn at the New Moon...' (*'Start up* the ram's horn *for* the New Moon...' might have been even better?), and in the preceding verse the NIV has the clear phrase, 'Begin the music...', where the AV has, 'Take a psalm...'

Many modern translators have tackled well the translation into idiomatic English of centrally important and profound Hebrew or Greek words such as, for example, the Greek words ἀληθής and ἀλήθεια, usually translated 'true' and 'truth'. These are words which have traditionally been too uniformly translated simply as 'true' and 'truth', and we have had to wait for the new movement of modern translation to get a more flexible and idiomatic translation in many contexts. Such idiomatic, strong and much-used English words as 'reality', 'integrity' and 'honesty' (with related adjectives) have long been under-used to translate these terms. Now they are being so used, and help English versions of the Bible to catch more of the many idiomatic nuances found in the original. In Mk 12.14 (AV) we find, 'Master, we know that thou art true (ἀληθής), and carest for no man, for thou regardest not the person of men, but teachest the way of God in truth (ἀλήθεια)'. The REB makes use of idiomatic English in new ways to help catch nuances in the original: 'Teacher, we know you are a sincere man and court no one's favour, whoever he may be; you teach in all sincerity the way of life that God requires'. Similarly the NIV has, 'Teacher, we know you are a man of integrity. You aren't swayed by men, because you pay no attention to who they are, but you teach the way of God in accordance with the truth'. We do not find there a discarding of the words 'true, truth', but we find an enrichment of vocabulary. I have no wish to give the impression that the AV translators were unaware of such words as 'integrity' and other such idiomatic resources at their disposal. In fact, in Ps. 7.8 the AV very beautifully uses 'integrity' to translate the Hebrew word *tōm*. Whereas Coverdale has, 'Give sentence with me, O Lord, according to my righteousness and according to the *innocency* that is in me', the AV translates it, 'Judge me, O Lord, according to my righteousness, and according to my integrity (*tōm*) that is in me'. But the point is that many modern translators have felt free to use idiomatic resources in English even more widely, which has surely been a great gain for our age.

Another example in the same semantic field may be briefly quoted. In Heb. 11.1 the AV had the fine wording, 'faith is...the evidence of things not seen' (πραγμάτων ἔλεγχος οὐ βλεπομένων). But the REB translation is, 'faith...convinces us of realities we do not see'; this use of 'realities' is a very idiomatic rendering for modern times.[1]

Radical translators have searched for better and more idiomatic modern English translations of many other major biblical and religious words. The word 'bless' ('Bless the Lord, O my soul...', Ps. 103.1 [AV]) is a case in point. Some have regarded this as a traditional, stereotyped, English translation word that is now outdated. One group of modern translators has declared that the word 'bless' is 'no longer very much alive in modern English'.[2] Certainly the word 'bless' has come to do service for an almost impossibly wide group of meanings, as we see in relation to its traditional use in the translating both of the Hebrew term *bārak* and of the Greek word εὐλογέω. 'To bless' in English has suffered probably from its long and complex history. Originally connected with the old term *blod*, and meaning 'to blood' or 'to mark or consecrate with blood', it was chosen eventually by many English translators to render the Latin *benedicere* in the sense of 'to praise' or 'to worship'. Within the very general meaning of 'to declare blessed', the precise meaning of 'to bless' in any given context is often confused in biblical translations. It is noticeable that alternatives to 'bless' were used in centuries long before modern times: although in Ps. 103.1 the AV has 'Bless the Lord, O my soul...' (Hebrew *bārak*, Latin Vulgate *benedicere*), Coverdale in the 1530s had put 'Praise the Lord, O my soul...' Many modern translators have retained 'bless' at that point and elsewhere in similar passages, but others (e.g. GNB and NIV) have put 'praise'. Some too have wanted a much more radical change to English idioms that seem to them to catch in English more of the flavour of the original. For example, where the AV has, 'Bless the Lord...' in Ps. 103.1, Harry Mowvley translates, '[Kneel...and] *adore* the Lord...';[3] and, where

1. There are of course, in English versions of the Bible, several different interpretations and translations of this sentence in Heb. 11.1. The words about faith and its basis are taken either in terms of 'conviction' or of 'proof'.

2. D. Smith *et al.* (eds.), *Fifty Psalms: An Attempt at a New Translation* (Burns & Oates, 1968 [1967]).

3. H. Mowvley, *The Psalms for Today's Readers* (London: Collins, 1989).

the full sentence in the AV is, 'Bless the Lord, bless his holy name...'
(though the verse in Hebrew has only one 'bless'), *Fifty Psalms* has, 'I
want to call him by his Name, the holy God...' Some may regard
those versions as falling into the category of 'unacceptable paraphrase'
in a translation, but they are attempts to catch the meaning in an
idiomatic way in a phrase that has challenged English translators for a
very long time.

A similar discussion has centred on the traditional English
translation 'soul' in that same verse. 'Soul' has been regarded by some
modern translators as another stereotyped English translation word
that has been worked too hard as the translation of the Hebrew word
nepeš. It has been said quite frequently that 'soul' can often be
misleading as a translation of *nepeš* since *nepeš* really means
something more like one's 'whole being'. The translators of *Fifty
Psalms* find 'soul' a weak term now in English, though they add the
important comment that 'heart and soul' is still a strong English idiom
with a great deal of meaning. In Ps. 103.1 many modern versions
have retained the word 'soul', though where the AV has in the second
clause 'and all that is within me (*beqereb*) bless his holy name', they
are likely to have brought in a fresh phrase such as 'and all my being,
bless his holy name' (NAB). But a number of modern translators have
tackled the translation of *nepeš* and not just *beqereb*, in a radical way:
for example Peter Levi has, 'My spirit, bless God; *everything in me*,
bless his name and holiness', and Harry Mowvley has, 'Kneel, *my true
self*, and adore the Lord'. Where the AV gives 'O my soul' and 'all
that is within me', *Fifty Psalms* has 'as truly as I live' and 'from the
bottom of my heart'.

Related points arise in connection with the translation of Lk. 1.46,
the first verse of the Song of Mary, a passage traditionally translated,
'My soul doth magnify the Lord, and my spirit, hath rejoiced in God
my Saviour' (AV). The original Greek words here are ψυχή (AV
'soul') and πνεῦμα (AV 'spirit'), though the Song of Mary and its
opening verse clearly go back to the Song of Hannah in 1 Samuel 2
and to a Semitic pattern of thinking in that passage. Hannah said that
her *lēb* ('heart') rejoiced in the Lord, and that her *qeren* ('horn') was
exalted in the Lord, which the Septuagint had translated by using the
Greek words καρδία ('heart') and κέρας ('horn'). So both 'soul' and
'heart' may come close to rendering the idiomatic sense in English of
the Semitic phrase used by Mary in her praise of God. Very many

modern translators retain the traditional translations 'soul' and 'spirit':
for example the NJB has, 'My soul proclaims the greatness of the
Lord, and my spirit rejoices in God my Saviour'. But a good number
of the new versions feel it necessary, against the background of
Hebrew idiom and vocabulary underlying the Greek terms in the
Gospel, to try and capture the meaning through fresh English
idiomatic terms or a fresh combination of terms. The NAB has, 'My
being proclaims the greatness of the Lord, my spirit finds joy in God
my Savior...' And the GNB uses the two words from the modern
'heart and soul' phrase (boldly putting 'heart' for ψυχή and 'soul' for
πνεῦμα): 'My heart praises the Lord; my soul is glad because of God
my Saviour'.

Changes in Translating Hebrew Poetic Rhythm

It will be useful now to look at the stylistic structure found in some of
the verses above, known as Hebrew poetic parallelism, that is, their
idiomatic poetic structure. In this one gets a poetic couplet of two
lines, in which a first line (e.g. 'Let the earth rejoice' near the
beginning of Ps. 97.1 [AV]) is paralleled or twinned by a second line
('Let the multitude of the isles be glad thereof'). The second line not
only echoes the first but is also by way of being a variation on it. This
type of parallelism has sometimes been called the equivalent in
Hebrew poetry of rhyme in English poetry. Most modern biblical
translators, as most traditional ones, have simply reproduced the
distinctive Hebrew structure and pattern of poetic expression, even if
they give an altered translation of particular words: for example, the
NRSV has in Ps. 97.1, 'let the earth rejoice; let the many coastlands be
glad!' But a few modern versions have attempted an interesting and
radical restructuring, aiming to produce a different, and what they
would regard as a distinctively English, idiom for this passage: that is,
something aimed to achieve a distinctively English way of expressing
coupling, twinning and matching here. The editors of *Fifty Psalms*, in
attempting such a restructuring, state the view that, although in
Hebrew and to the Jews their particular pattern of parallelism and
echoing couplets gave a fine sense of urgency and strength, yet when
translated literally into English it often had 'a disturbing and
enfeebling effect' and gave the feeling of a sort of 'marking time'.
They had searched, they said, for a change of structure or idiom in

English that would 'build up an English climax' in the second line of the couplet, and that would be the equivalent of 'the urgency and the fierceness of the original Hebrew'. Their solution was to put in the first line a twinning of the noun phrases (translated by the AV as 'the earth' and 'the multitude of the isles') and in the second line a twinning of the verb phrases (AV 'rejoice' and 'be glad thereof'). Their translation was,

> ... all shores on earth
> are laughing and shouting for joy.

This certainly achieves its climax in the second line. Perhaps an even more convincing experiment is the same translators' version of the first verse of Psalm 142. As compared with the AV's 'I cried unto the Lord with my voice; with my voice unto the Lord did I make my supplication', *Fifty Psalms* has,

> I am crying out, I cry to God—
> O God, I implore you and beg for mercy.

Those who have long used the AV's or Coverdale's version of this and similar verses in the Psalms will be able to use that traditional wording without embarrassment and indeed with delight. But it is evident, both from the productions of the mainline modern translations and from such radical experiments as we have just looked at, that there are other alternative ways of expressing in English what was referred to as 'the urgency and the fierceness' of the Hebrew Psalter than through literal Hebraic structures and idioms alone.

It is worth noting the radical way in which one major modern translation tackles the translating of the Semitic parallelism in a passage which we looked at previously. In Lk. 1.46 the TNT does not reproduce the strict pattern of the 'echoing' parallelism of the original by any echoing in a twinned 'my soul... my spirit...' structure. But it brings the substance of those two echoing and twinned nouns together in a repeated 'I' and in the phrase 'all my being'. It translates,

> With all my being I declare that the Lord is great,
> and I rejoice in God, my Saviour...

The translators of that version departed from the Hebraic structure and idiom, but, many would say, came as close as anyone to the Hebraic content.

A somewhat different emphasis is found in Peter Levi's translation of the Psalms, and in his account of how he has tried to catch the spirit and idiom of the Hebrew Psalter.[1] As a poet known for his strong rhythmical effects, there is naturally much emphasis on rhythmical strength in what he writes. He does not aim at so radical a restructuring of the original wording of the Psalms as do some of those whom I have mentioned above. He wants his language to reflect idiomatic Hebrew patterns of poetry. He does not seem primarily concerned to achieve a translation where the stresses and climaxes are of the sort that are natural in English. Although he mentions the need for unity and modernity of language in a biblical translation and the need for the true meaning of the Hebrew to be conveyed to the reader or hearer, he adds these words: 'I thought my first duty was to Hebrew, my second to the English language'.[2]

As I have said, for Levi the important idiomatic patterns of Hebrew poetry to be reflected in any translation are not only those to do with parallelism and with the skilful echoing and balancing of one clause by another, but particularly to do with rhythm and metre: what he describes as 'metre that is free but strong'. As he says, Hebrew poetry is not shaped by rhyme but by what has been called a loose sustaining rhythm; and the important role of assonance is stressed. He explains how Hebrew poetry achieves its effects (and its stresses in couplets and stanzas) particularly through a flexible echoing and balancing of little blocks of a few impressive composite words: the blocks are built up by the addition of the prefixes and suffixes common in Hebrew (corresponding to the use of pronouns, prepositions and conjunctions in English). 'Solid blocks of meaning are built up, each with one main stress', he writes. And again, 'There is relatively little formal structure, and the poetic effect is achieved primarily through the marshalling and deployment of images and ideas'. Levi contrasts this with English poetry and 'the familiar English structure of regular lines and verses'; he contrasts it also with 'the long strings of monosyllables' which are common in English poetry, and its many small pronouns, prepositions and conjunctions. Hebrew's metre, says Levi, works differently: according to the natural stresses of words

---

1. *The Psalms* (Harmondsworth: Penguin, 1976), Translator's Preface.
2. The quotations in this paragraph are from pp. ix, xi and xxiii of Levi, *The Psalms*.

rather than the syllables. And Hebrew poetry is seen to have rather compact structures.

Levi declares his aim as that of translating this sort of poetry into English 'through English words of passionate common speech'. He says that in their original form 'the language and form of most of the psalms, and some of their music, seem to be popular', in an age in which court and temple poetry would probably not differ greatly from what was sung by herdsmen in the desert. In some psalms Levi's translation uses fewer words than that of Coverdale, but he is keen to point out that there are far fewer words in the Hebrew original than in his own English translation, and he implies that an English translation has to aim to achieve some terseness or economy. (We may compare with this John Stek's account of one of the rules given to the translators of the NIV for translating Hebrew poetry: 'Keep the style tight, economical, but do not attempt to imitate the terseness of Hebrew'.[1] But the general approach is similar, in that comment and in Levi's view.)

I give below an example of Levi's translation, a passage in which his translation happens to be considerably shorter than Coverdale's (87 words to Coverdale's 120). It gives some idea of the generally more clipped and lively style in which Levi tries to capture the spirit and idiom of the original.[2]

Psalm 73.1-5, 11, 27

	Coverdale	Levi
73.1	Truly God is loving unto Israel: even unto such as are of a clean heart.	God is good to Israel, to the clean-hearted.
2	Nevertheless, my feet were almost gone: my treadings had well-nigh slipt.	I nearly turned away, I all but stumbled,
3	And why? I was grieved at the wicked: I do also see the ungodly in such prosperity.	because I was envious of boasters and I saw the peace of the wicked.

1. 'When The Spirit Was Poetic', in K. Barker (ed.), *The Making of a Contemporary Translation* (London: Hodder & Stoughton, 1987), p. 98.

2. In a similar type of modern translation by Robert Alter, of some verses from Isa. 40 (*The Literary Guide to the Bible*, p. 32), Alter's translation only has 270 words where the AV has 343 and the NEB 313. Alter, like Levi, is trying to catch the feel of the 'poetic compactness' of Hebrew poetry.

4	For they are in no peril of death: but are lusty and strong.	They are not hanged, they are strong and healthy.
5	They come in no misfortune like other folk: neither are they plagued like other men.	They are outside the sufferings of mankind, they are not whipped like other men.
11	Tush, say they, how should God perceive it: is there knowledge in the most High?	And they say, How does God know? Is there knowledge in heaven?
27	But it is good for me to hold me fast by God, to put my trust in the Lord God: and to speak of all thy works in the gates of the daughters of Sion.	But my good is to be close to God, my refuge is in God, and to speak of what he has done.

Notes

a. Levi's interpretations, reflecting a diversity of traditional interpretations, differ from Coverdale's at two points in vv. 4 and 5. A textual difference comes out in v. 27.

b. In v. 4 the word translated 'peril' by Coverdale (Hebrew *harṣubbot*) has been variously taken to mean 'bands', 'cords', 'fetters', 'pangs', 'pains'. The AV has, 'For there are no bands in their death'.

c. In v. 5 the word translated 'plagued' by Coverdale has long been translated *flagellantur* in translations of the Hebrew into Latin.

d. It may be noted that in v. 11 Coverdale's colourful introduction of 'Tush' does not correspond to any word in the original, but is simply an attempt to insert contempt into the translation. The later AV has, 'And they say, How does God know?'

e. In v. 27 Coverdale follows the Septuagint reading in adding 'in the gates of the daughter of Sion', whereas the AV, and Levi, follow the Masoretic text's shorter reading. The difference in the numbering of the last verse given above (27 in Coverdale, but 28 in the AV, the NRSV and Levi) is also due to the difference in whether Hebrew or Greek texts have been followed.

Liveliness without Eccentricity

The question of colloquialisms, and of some exceptionally free use of modern idiom in modern versions of the Bible, will have been raised in the mind of the reader at various points in this chapter. Some may conclude that all colloquialism should be ruled out. Peter Levi has used a phrase about avoiding 'colloquial eccentricity', although he is sometimes free in his translation. William Barclay advocated the use of colloquial language in suitable places but not 'slang'. Many would agree with a degree of 'acceptable colloquialism' in general, and especially in conversational parts of narratives, or in correspondence. Below are a few further examples of experiments in a more colloquial and free type of translation.

Acts 8.20 provides us with a classic example of the use of a colloquial phrase in a modern version, which was withdrawn in a revised edition. In translating the story of Peter and Simon Magus, the NEB, in its original 1961 New Testament publication, had the phrase, 'You and your money, may you come to a bad end...' But in the second edition of its New Testament translation in 1970, the phrase used was, 'Your money go with you to damnation...' (REB: 'Your money can go with you to damnation...').

But both the NEB and REB have surely a highly acceptable colloquial phrase in 1 Sam. 24.17, where Saul says to the rebel David, 'The right is on your side not mine; you have treated me so well; I have treated you so badly'. The AV has, 'Thou art more righteous than I; for thou hast rewarded me good, whereas I have rewarded thee evil'.

In 1 Sam. 17.28, 29, in another story about David, we find a phrase that is especially hard to translate well. The young David had been sent to take food to his brothers who were fighting against Goliath and the Philistines. He asked some of the men in the army what reward would be given to the man who killed Goliath. David's elder brother rebuked him for leaving his sheep and coming to ask impudent questions. The AV continues, 'And David said, What have I now done? Is there not a cause?' This last phrase is a literal translation of an idiomatic Hebrew phrase containing the word *dābār* ('word', 'matter'). Modern translations try to catch the Hebrew idiom through a common English idiom. The NIV has, 'Can't I even speak?' and the NEB has, 'I only asked a question'. Some may prefer to have the AV phrasing, giving the literal, old-world feel of the Hebrew phrase. Others will find reality in the new translations, which convey the feel of the boy's comment, one that can hardly alter much from age to age.

In the above examples I have concentrated on turns of phrase. Also important are single words with an idiomatic meaning. One modern version, the TNT, makes significant use of the English word 'suggestive' in the translation of Eph. 5.4, in what the *Shorter Oxford English*

Dictionary describes as the word's 'euphemistic' meaning of that which suggests something indecent. The TNT's idiomatic vocabulary here is a refreshing change from the corresponding word in the AV, 'jesting'. Single idiomatic words can clearly often give strong impact to passages in which the words used by the AV are not only now outdated or long-winded, but slightly off the main point in the context. Eph. 5.3-4 is a forceful passage and needs a strong translation. The AV gives, 'Fornication, and all uncleanness, or covetousness, let it not be once named among you, as becometh saints; neither filthiness, nor foolish talking, nor jesting, which are not convenient: but rather giving of thanks'. The TNT by contrast seems down-to-earth: 'God's people must not even mention sexual vice, impurity of any kind, or lust. Such talk is out of place. Nor is there any room for coarse, foolish or suggestive language. There is room only for thanksgiving.' It is not just a case of words like 'saints' and 'convenient' being spelled out more clearly, but of the original terms translated as 'covetousness' and 'jesting' by the AV being rendered in a more idiomatic way ('lust' and 'suggestive [language]' in the TNT). The original Greek word lying behind 'suggestive (language)', εὐτραπελία, is discussed by a TNT footnote in this way, 'it meant quick-witted repartee, not bad in itself but often leading to doubtful conversation, innocent-seeming words with underlying dirty meanings. Paul clearly has this in mind here.' Similarly with the Greek term underlying the AV's 'covetousness' and the TNT's 'lust', the TNT has this footnote:

> The Greek word 'pleonexia', here translated 'lust', is literally 'desire to have more'. This desire may take various forms. In Lk. 12.15 it is greed for material gain, and many translations use the word 'greed' here. It is also used of sexual desire, and this sense would seem to fit the context here. Hence the translation 'lust'.

Some modern translations have been criticized by those who prefer a completely common-language translation as containing too sophisticated a vocabulary: Alan Duthie, in his exhaustive survey of modern versions,[1] mentions the NEB's use of such words as 'parricide', 'felicity', 'contumely' as coming into that category. But, on the whole, modern translations (including the NEB) seem to have gone out of their way in all sorts of contexts and passages to use a strong and

---

1. A.S. Duthie, *The Bible Translations and how to Choose between them* (Exeter: Paternoster Press, 1985), p. 82.

idiomatic vocabulary, getting much of their undoubted impact from that fact.

By and large, the aim in much modern translation has undoubtedly been to achieve living and lively equivalents of the original, rather than to achieve, through exaggerated colloquialisms, a superficial sense of modernity. And since idiom, and that which is idiomatic, is a main creator of vitality in language (it has been described as the sap of language), it is good idiom that one surely looks for in any translation and not primarily good colloquialism: the colloquial may be part of the idiomatic, and may overlap with it, but it is idiomatic vitality that is entirely central. This is in line with the phrase quoted from Peter Levi about William Tyndale: 'he achieves liveliness without colloquial eccentricity'.[1] Not all of Tyndale's lively and idiomatic phrases can be used today. In Gen. 39.2, where Joseph's success in Egypt is being described, Tyndale uses the phrase 'he was a lucky fellow' ('And the Lord was with Joseph, and he was a lucky fellow'.) Coverdale puts 'a lucky man' and the AV 'a prosperous man'. But some of Tyndale's idiomatic phrases point the way to a liveliness of translation that has often wrongly got lost through the centuries. A phrase in his translation of 1 Kgs 19.5 is the simplest of examples, but quite significant. The angel, when he comes to Elijah under the juniper tree, says to him, in Tyndale's translation, 'Up and eat...', a more lively rendering than the AV's 'arise and eat'. The Hebrew, literally, is 'rise up and eat...' Several modern translations have returned to fitting in Tyndale's lively word 'up': for example, the NJB has 'Get up and eat...'

Peter Levi himself, as we have seen, has been among those modern translators who have used this quality of liveliness in biblical translations. Although his preference is clearly at times for a wording that is very formal and mannered, yet combined with this is a distinct use, at intervals, of modern vernacular phrasing. I like his bold translation of the last phrase in the following passage in Jn 18.4-5. In the AV this reads, 'Jesus went forth and said unto them, Whom seek ye? They answered him, Jesus of Nazareth. Jesus said unto them, I am he.' Levi renders it, 'Jesus went out to them and he said, Who are you looking for? They answered him, Jesus of Nazareth. Jesus says to

---

1.   P. Levi, *The English Bible* (Worthing: Churchman, 1985), p. 40. See also the mention, in Chapter 3, of other comments by Levi on Tyndale.

them, That is me.'[1] Though purists would like to see 'I' instead of 'me' in the final phrase, it is worth remembering that Shakespearian language sometimes transposed 'I' and 'me' in a lively way: for example, 'All debts are cleared between you and I'.

1. P. Levi, *The Holy Gospel of John: A New Translation* (Worthing: Churchman, 1985).

Chapter 2

THE PIONEERING OF MODERN FREEDOMS

There were a few attempts between 1611 and the mid-nineteenth century, especially in the eighteenth century, to translate parts of the Bible into contemporary English idiom. But they made little impact, in their day or later, and tended to be either very florid and diffuse or very traditional. It was only after the advances in biblical scholarship in the mid-nineteenth century that any real pioneer work in contemporary translation was tackled, of a sort that could be expected to achieve a good balance between sound and sense, style and scholarship. Among the pioneer movements in English biblical translation that started at the beginning of the twentieth century, or shortly before, two main ones are described in what follows.

A mainstream movement has clearly been that which began with such pioneers as James Moffatt and Edgar Goodspeed. It continued with other notable figures such as Ronald Knox, J.B. Phillips and William Barclay, and with official translations such as the NEB in Britain. The approach of this movement can fairly be summed up as 'a general idiomatic approach' with its use of modern English idiom.

Another, and distinct, pioneer movement began rather later in the twentieth century, emerging mainly from the work of the American Bible Society, and from the latter's 'common-language' translations of the Bible (or parts of the Bible) for use in Latin America and West Africa. From this there developed Today's English Version, later to be also called the Good News Bible. The approach here, while also being an idiomatic one, was more noticeably scientific, in the sense that the final translation was only worked out after a scientific linguistic analysis had been carried out on the structural differences between the original language (Hebrew or Greek) and the language into which the translation was being done, and only after certain linguistic theories about communication of meaning between one language and another had been applied to the whole process of translation. This approach may therefore be adequately described as 'a linguistic analysis approach'. It is not quite true to say that this approach had no beginnings in Britain at all. The now largely forgotten, though significant, experiment called *The Bible in Basic English*[1] was the work not only of biblical scholars and translators, but also of the linguistic scholar C.K. Ogden, of the Orthological Institute in Britain, and co-author with I.A. Richards of a seminal book of the 1930s called *The Meaning of Meaning*. However, the linguistic analysis approach to biblical translation in general, and certainly that lying behind most 'common-language' Bibles today, was worked out largely in the United States.

A third movement, described in more detail in Chapter 3, has been the whole Catholic translation movement in America and Britain. It has overlapped with the first movement mentioned above, in so far as it has included figures such as Ronald Knox and has followed a general idiomatic policy in translation. But it has been in a real sense a significant pioneer movement with its own distinctive characteristics, ever since the Papal Encyclical of 1943 and the start of a new age in Catholic biblical study. It has been represented by individual translators, by British translators in the two JB translations (stimulated by the original French *Bible de Jerusalem*), and by official new American translations such as *The New Confraternity Bible* or the NAB.

The reader may be surprised to see no mention in the above of versions of the Bible in the RSV and NRSV tradition. From 1946 onwards proponents of that tradition have certainly been among the pioneers in the provision of new biblical versions. Its authentic challenge suffered a similar fate to that of many other pioneering ventures when a copy of the RSV was publicly burned in at least one American pulpit in the 1950s. More importantly, the RSV has introduced changes of wording and notable examples of new scholarly accuracy that have been fed into the whole process of modern translation. But in spite of all that, it has always provided what its name says it does, a new revision rather than a new translation; and it has been particularly strictly confined to revision as far as style is concerned; its editors have never felt called to any free or radical

1.   Cambridge: Cambridge University Press, 1941, 1950.

re-structuring of the literal form of the original sentences and of units of language in the biblical material. Their pioneering work has not lain in the direction of experimenting with modern contemporary idiom. For that reason, the RSV and NRSV have not exactly fitted along with the versions mentioned in the above 'movements'.

James Moffatt and the Early Pioneers

We look now at what I have called 'the general idiomatic approach', and at those whose translation work may be said to fall within that category. First we shall look at James Moffatt, whose ground-breaking work as a translator at the very beginning of the twentieth century was a highly significant moment of change. Although the particular translation of the new Testament now associated with his name did not come out until 1913[1] (and his translation of the Old Testament did not appear until 1924) his book *Historical New Testament*, published in 1900, contained an early translation of the New Testament done by him.

Moffatt was a distinguished biblical scholar of his day. He brought to the task of translation a mind both scholarly and sensitive. He was no mere amateur, entering the delicate and dangerous field of biblical translation in brash and over-confident mood. He expressly said, in the preface to his 1913 translation, that for him some phrases and key-words in the Bible were virtually untranslatable into English. He cited the Greek words λόγος, μυστήριον and δικαιοσύνη as examples (translated in the AV as 'word', 'mystery' and 'righteousness'). In his version, he left the word λογός transliterated but not translated. μυστήριον he translated most often as 'open secret', but sometimes as 'secret truth', 'secret', 'divine secret' or 'secret purpose', according to the context. For δικαιοσύνη ('righteousness' in the AV) Moffatt kept 'righteousness' in nearly all instances in books such as Romans and Galatians; but he was clearly not too happy with the translation 'righteousness' in all passages in the New Testament, and at various points, according to the context, he rendered δικαιοσύνη as 'goodness', 'justice', 'integrity' or 'moral truth', or by other phrases. And in verses in the Old Testament such as Gen. 15.6 ('And he

---

1.   Moffatt's translation of the New Testament was first published in one volume in 1913 by Hodder & Stoughton.

believed in the Lord; and he counted it to him for righteousness', AV),
in relation to the translation of the corresponding word in Hebrew
($s^e\bar{d}\bar{a}q\hat{a}$), Moffatt boldly used the translation 'true religion': 'he
reckoned it to him as true religion'. All this shows his sensitivity, and
his sense of the importance, for the bringing out of the full meaning,
of combining the use of traditional English religious 'code-words' in
translation with the use of fresh English words. But when all that has
been said, he was among the very first of modern translators to plunge
into the use of modern contemporary idiom. The editors of the
Revised Version of the Bible in Britain in the 1880s had already taken
the plunge of departing from the traditional English translation of
many individual words, but had still followed the AV in its idiom and
general structure of language. Moffatt was foremost among those who
revolutionized the use of idiom in English translation, and produced
new modern alternative ways of approach.

As an example of his translation work, a few verses from his classic
version of 1 Corinthians 13 are given here:

	AV	Moffatt
13.4	Charity vaunteth not itself,	Love makes no parade,
	is not puffed up,	gives itself no airs;
5	doth not behave itself unseemly,	is never rude,
	seeketh not her own,	never selfish,
	is not easily provoked,	never irritated,
	thinketh no evil	never resentful...

Moffatt's translation 'never selfish' is fairly radical idiomatically. The
NRSV, eighty years after the publication of Moffatt's New Testament,
has, 'it does not insist on its own way' for that clause. But the REB and
GNB follow Moffatt. Moffatt's use of the word 'love' was a
revolutionary change from the AV's 'charity', but the Revised Version
of 1881 had of course made the same change, since 'charity' for all its
fine resonance had accumulated its own shades of meaning; 'love'
anyway was simply a return to what was there in Tyndale's New
Testament in the fifteenth century, altered by the AV to 'charity' in
1611.

Some of Moffatt's other new wordings were equally successful, and
urgently overdue. In Rom. 12.16 the AV had, after the phrase 'mind
not high things', the words 'but condescend to men of low estate',
which had become increasingly difficult to read in church.
'Condescend' had changed its meaning in English over the centuries

from something attractively to do with descent and humility to something pejorative, to do with superiority. For the 'condescend' phrase, Moffatt put 'but associate with humble folk'. By the end of the twentieth century, revisions of the AV have followed this. The New King James Version has, 'but associate with the humble'. In this verse the translator's job is complicated by the fact that the Greek word translated 'men of low estate' in the AV may be either masculine or neuter, so could mean either 'humble folk' or 'lowly service'.

It is hard to pinpoint exactly what lay behind the eagerness with which the modern translations have been greeted by large numbers of people in the twentieth century. The social upheaval of two world wars has clearly had a great deal to do with it.[1] There has also been a strong sense among many that such a movement was simply a continuation of what had been done by pioneer translators like Wyclif, Purvey and Tyndale in the centuries leading up to 1611, and was in line with the spirit of leaders such as Archbishop Thomas Cranmer. From what he wrote,[2] all the indications are that Cranmer was keen on periodic re-translation of the Scriptures, and saw the work of English biblical translation in his day, and his encouragement of it, as a natural follow-on from earlier translations of parts of the Bible into Anglo-Saxon and Anglo-Norman, and from the translation work of Caedmon, Aldhelm, Bede and King Alfred. He certainly warned people not to be put off by the fact that suggestions for periodic re-translation are always bound to be resisted by the natural human dislike of change.

Mid-Twentieth-Century Translators

It is worth looking at what some well-known British translators in the middle of the twentieth century wrote about their own work. J.B. Phillips started translating the letters of the New Testament into modern English during 1941 when wartime bombs were falling on the

1.   It is interesting to note that the beginnings, through John Wyclif, of the great biblical translation movement of the fifteenth and sixteenth centuries followed another huge social upheaval, that of the Black Death.

2.   See Cranmer's Preface to the second edition of the *Great Bible* of 1540 (otherwise called *Cranmer's Bible*): also D. Frost, *The Language of Series 3* (Nottingham: Grove Press, 1973); and C.S. Meyer, *Cranmer's Selected Writings* (London: SPCK, 1961).

inner-city parish in southeast London where he was vicar. It was a
time when the need to have the Bible in a form that could speak
directly to people was urgent and obvious. He later described the
situation in these words:

> I wrote primarily because, rather to my surprise, I found that the young
> people in my youth-club did not understand the English of the Authorized
> Version. For that matter neither did the bulk of my faithful churchpeople,
> and many of them had long ago given up the attempt to understand the
> Epistles. They regarded them as obscure and difficult as well as having
> little bearing on the sort of lives we were then living.[1]

> In those days of danger and emergency I was not overconcerned with
> minute accuracy; I wanted above all to convey the vitality and radiant
> faith, as well as the courage, of the early Church.[2]

Phillips started by translating the Letter to the Colossians; other
translations followed, resulting in what was later published as *Letters
to Young Churches*.[3] In his introduction he said that he wanted the
reader 'to forget that the words are a translation and to feel their
sense as if they were "written for today"'. Although he was, as he had
said, not 'overconcerned with minute accuracy', he worked directly
from the original Greek and was deeply concerned to be faithful to it.
As his work progressed he took advice from some distinguished
scholars known to him.

Phillips's translation of the last two verses of Romans 8, given
below, is perhaps typical of his style of translation. As for accuracy of
rendering, one point arises: 'monarch of earth' (8.38) is just possible
but extremely unusual as an interpretation of ἀρχαί. This word is,
admittedly, twice used in the New Testament of earthly rulers, but the
New Testament use of both ἄγγελοι (which Phillips takes as angelic
'messengers of heaven') and ἀρχαί (which Phillips takes as 'earthly
monarchs' or 'rulers') in such contexts is almost universally taken to
refer to cosmic spiritual powers, whether good or bad. On other
counts, Phillips's strengths will be apparent. When read aloud these
two verses come across very strongly in his version, and his use of

---

1. J.B. Phillips, 'Preface to Luke's Gospel', in J. Drury, *Luke* (Fontana
Religious Commentaries; London: Fontana 1973).
2. J.B. Phillips, *The Price of Success* (London: Hodder & Stoughton, 1984)
p. 94.
3. J.B. Phillips, *Letters to Young Churches* (London: Bles, 1947).

alliteration in the 'messenger-monarch' clause just mentioned is striking. His rendering is unashamedly modern in its idiom ('I have become absolutely convinced'). Above all, while having a certain simplicity about it, it seems to catch, fairly effortlessly, the passage's air of solemn mystery.

Romans 8.38-39

	AV	Phillips
8.38	For I am persuaded, that neither death, nor life, nor angels, nor principalities, nor powers, nor things present, nor things to come,	I have become absolutely convinced that neither Death nor Life, neither messenger of heaven nor monarch of earth, neither what happens today nor what may happen tomorrow,
39	Nor height, nor depth, nor any other creature, shall be able to separate us from the love of God, which is in Christ Jesus our Lord.	neither a power from on high nor a power from below, nor anything else in God's whole world has any power to separate us from the love of God in Jesus Christ our Lord!

During these wartime years Bishop William Wand was attempting something similar in Australia. A scholarly man, at that time Archbishop of Brisbane, he came from an ecclesiastical background different from Phillips's and belonged to a tradition that greatly valued dignified and traditional ritual. However, he had had experience as an army chaplain in the First World War, and had a concern for communicating the faith in language that the layperson could understand. He was finding, in the 1940s, that the language of the AV was totally unsuitable for use in his diocese. He wrote in 1943 that he found young people 'repelled by the archaisms of the AV or RV' and said that for older readers 'the language fails to bite, because it is already so familiar'.[1] He produced not a translation but a paraphrase of the New Testament letters. His aim was in general the same as that of J.B. Phillips.

Ronald Knox, who has already been mentioned briefly, did major translation work during the same period. Like J.B. Phillips, he experimented in the radical adoption of English idiom and English

---

1. J.W.C. Wand, *The New Testament Letters: Prefaced and Paraphrased* (Oxford: Oxford University Press, 1946), p. viii.

sentence structure as his style of translation.[1] He was concerned to
fashion English that had both dignity and liveliness. He was especially
successful in the New Testament letters and in the New Testament as a
whole. In the Old Testament he adopted a deliberately archaizing
style,[2] which many found unattractive. There was also the
complication that he belonged to an era when, for him as a Catholic,
the translation still had to be done from the Latin, and he could only
take account of the Hebrew and Greek original in his footnotes.
Nevertheless he was one of the pioneers in new idiom.

What such people felt impelled to produce was freshness of
meaning. For this they knew that three things were needed: accuracy,
clarity, and directness of impact (what Wand called 'bite'). New idiom
had to pass the test of accuracy, if it was to be used: then, as now, the
new idiomatic language inevitably came in for criticism on this score
from some quarters;[3] doubt was expressed as to how far some of the
idiom used represented the original sense. But the clarity and impact
that the new idiom brought was on the whole widely acclaimed.

It was not until 1961, with the publication of the NEB translation of
the New Testament, that there was any official biblical translation that
used modern English. The American RSV, published in 1952, was, as I
have said, a revision of older versions rather than an entirely new
translation. It brought to the Bible in English the results of a century
of modern biblical scholarship. It removed many obscurities,
inaccuracies and archaisms. Its up-to-date form is the NRSV.[4]

Translation, Paraphrase and Prophecy

Several of the translators mentioned above give detailed comments
on particular topics that are still much discussed. For example,
J.B. Phillips writes in some detail on the distinction between translation and paraphrase, and on the choice of different styles of language for different parts of the Bible. His own translation is of course
free translation, and undoubtedly uses paraphrase. It is sometimes

1. See his *On Englishing the Bible*.
2. The phrase is that of the *Jerome Biblical Commentary*.
3. The most substantial critique was T.R. Henn's ('The Bible as Literature', in
Peake's Commentary).
4. Oxford: Oxford University Press, 1990.

referred to by others as more a paraphrase than a translation, and as using excessive colloquialism. But he regarded himself as only occasionally resorting to paraphrase. In 1957 he wrote that in translating New Testament letters he had attempted to turn the original material into modern English by the use of 'imaginative insight, a little expansion,and occasionally a little paraphrase'.[1] He would no doubt have agreed with the thinking behind the clause in the Introduction to the NEB New Testament where it is said that, while the NEB was strictly a translation and not a paraphrase, yet 'every intelligent translation is in a sense a paraphrase' and that 'the line between translation and paraphrase is a fine one'. Some major, and more recent, translations than Phillips's have declared a policy of employing a minimum of paraphrase: they would no doubt differ from Phillips's assessment of his own work in this respect. Phillips's free method, whereby he felt free to depart from a strictly literal rendering, used 'expanded' translation, and would look for the word or phrase that was the closest natural equivalent in idiomatic English to the original phrase, made important advances in the understanding of translation. This has now become one of the foremost of several recognized approaches to biblical translation in Britain.

Phillips was not the first person to say that different books of the Bible need different styles of translation, but he wrote sensitively on this topic. Although he made his name through his initial work on the New Testament letters, he went on to translate the rest of the New Testament (work completed in 1958) and also four prophetic books in the Old Testament (1963). In his preface to the latter he discusses the difference between translating the prophetic books and translating most of the New Testament books. Most of these are 'human, non-literary documents', written in everyday language, matter-of-fact, conversational, colloquial, and should be translated accordingly. In his autobiography he writes of the importance of avoiding 'the style of legend' or the language of 'a beautiful story' when translating many passages in the New Testament where 'men were writing down things which were actual facts within the living memory of people...' There, 'we have to translate in a matter-of-fact style because these are matters

1. *The Book of Revelation (A New Translation of the Apocalypse) Translated by J.B. Phillips* (London: Bles, 1957).

of fact'.[1] On the other hand when it comes to the Old Testament prophets, clearly a modern translator cannot simply use 'the language of everyday experience'.[2] In some high prophetic passages Phillips believes that the modern translator will find the language little changed from the English translation of centuries ago, apart from the removal of those traditional phrases that have become obscure. Phillips reiterates these opinions in his preface to his translation of the book of Revelation. His translation of these books is far more conservative than some radical translations that have appeared since. However, when Phillips finally asks whether a modern translation of Old Testament prophetic books is necessary, his answer is an emphatic 'Yes'. In many prophetic passages, he says, there are not only obscurities in the wording of traditional translations, but also a lack of directness and sharpness to the modern ear. He uses the simile of a sword (taken from phrases about God's word in Eph. 6.17 and Heb. 4.12), saying that if only the AV is used, there is a danger that 'the sharp edge of what the prophets had to say is blunted by being enclosed in so beautiful a scabbard'.[3]

Most translations today distinguish carefully between the different styles needed for different scriptural books. One of the difficulties when using the AV regularly is its use of uniformly fine and measured language (or language that sounds so to us today) for every part of the Bible. Northropp Frye, a writer who cannot be said to have been averse to the use of noble language in the right place, cites Eccl. 2.3, 'I sought in mine heart to give myself unto wine, yet acquainting mine heart with wisdom' (AV). Frye says that the meaning here is that the author, in enjoying the drinking of wine, has aimed at moderation, but that the language used by the AV does not convey this. A translation is needed that catches more of the 'shrewd, humorous, toughminded attitude' of the person who wrote that verse.[4]

The search for freshness and impact in words and meaning based on the real needs of real people and real churches has marked not only those early individual pioneers mentioned in this chapter. More

---

1. Phillips, *The Price of Success*.

2. J.B. Phillips, *Four Prophets* (London: Bles, 1963), p. xv.

3. Phillips, *Four Prophets*, p. x.

4. N. Frye, *The Great Code: The Bible as Literature* (London: Routledge & Kegan Paul, 1982), p. 215.

recent, well-known collective ventures in new translation such as the NEB, the REB and many others have also adopted a general idiomatic approach. It is worth remembering that the origins of the NEB lie in a request from the Presbytery of Stirling and Dunblane to the General Assembly of the Church of Scotland in 1946 that a translation of the Bible be made in present-day language. The historic translations which resulted from this, with the New Testament produced in 1961 and the whole Bible in 1970, originated from popular demand, not just scholars' fancies.

Two New Versions and their Style

Here follow more examples from this same category of the general idiomatic approach and taken from two of the major versions of recent times: the NIV (1978) and the NJB (1985). The passages have been chosen for their directness of impact and freshness of wording. The NIV translation of Deut. 15.7 is simple and effective:

> If there is a poor man among your brothers in any of the towns of the land that the Lord your God is giving you, do not be hard-hearted or tight-fisted towards your poor brother.

This has more direct impact for a modern hearer or reader than the measured words of the AV:

> If there be among you a poor man of one of thy brethren within any of thy gates in thy land which the Lord thy God giveth thee, thou shalt not harden thine heart, nor shut thine hand from thy poor brother.

The NIV does not give a literal translation of the Hebrew word translated 'gates' in the AV, but its 'hard-hearted' and 'tight-fisted' remain true to the original imagery, as well as delivering, through a modern term, that slight shock which may be suitable in this context.

Again, in Exod. 16.2, the NIV has,

> In the desert the whole community grumbled against Moses and Aaron.

This may seem strong modern wording to place alongside the AV words:

> And the whole congregation murmured against Moses and Aaron in the wilderness.

But both words, 'grumbled' and 'murmured', have been around in the English language for a long time: 'grumbled' is not a fancy modern colloquial word, it is Shakespearian and has an appropriately down-to-earth quality while 'murmured' has become less direct.

A longer passage from the New Testament, the beginning of Romans 8 taken from the NJB, may be studied now. The content of the letter to the Romans has many theological profundities in it which will and should always be present in any translation. Unfortunately, in the traditional English translations it has for the modern ear many unnecessary obscurities of language. In this letter some of the AV's literal translations of Paul's phrases have left many a reader unnecessarily puzzled or misled (for example, 'condemning sin in the flesh' [Rom. 8.3], or 'the carnal mind' [Rom. 8.7]). Modern translations such as the NJB are less baldly literal in the translation of such key phrases. Although in the NJB version there is no major alteration of the original word order or sentence structure, each of the NJB verses contains more words than the AV.

The attempt to get an idiomatic English translation of Paul's use of the Greek word σάρξ (AV 'flesh') is a major characteristic of the NJB translation here. To translate Paul's use of σάρξ here, the NJB employs various phrases, according to context, such as 'human nature', 'natural inclinations' and 'disordered human nature'. This reflects the way in which many modern scholars understand the meaning of Paul's writings and the way in which the words have directness of meaning. The AV's translation of σάρξ throughout as 'flesh' (for example, Rom. 8.8, 'they that are in the flesh cannot please God') is of course a main point of discussion. The NRSV follows the AV in this, making 'flesh' a sort of reiterated code word. George Caird expressed the difficulties about this approach, saying that only 'percipient and studious readers' can cope with the complexities and apparent narrowness of the meaning of σάρξ if it is translated indiscriminately in this way throughout. Caird wrote that when Paul used σάρξ he is referring to the whole of sinful human nature, including what one may call sins of the spirit such as envy and selfish ambition:

> for the popular understanding of Christian ethics, this indiscriminate rendering has proved disastrous, since it has given the impression that Christians ought to adopt a negative and disapproving attitude to the body and its passions.[1]

1.   G.B. Caird, *The Language and Imagery of the Bible* (London: Gerald Duckworth, 1980), pp. 11 and 44.

Romans 8.1-13

AV

NJB

8.1 There is therefore now no condemnation to them which are in Christ Jesus, who walk not after the flesh, but after the Spirit.

Thus, condemnation will never come to those who are in Christ Jesus,

2 For the law of the Spirit of life in Christ Jesus hath made me free from the law of sin and death.

because the law of the Spirit which gives life in Christ Jesus has set you free from the law of sin and death.

3 For what the law could not do, in that it was weak through the flesh, God sending his own Son in the likeness of sinful flesh, and for sin, condemned sin in the flesh:

What the law could not do because of the weakness of human nature, God did, sending his own Son in the same human nature as any sinner to be a sacrifice for sin, and condemning sin in that human nature.

4 That the righteousness of the law might be fulfilled in us, who walk not after the flesh, but after the Spirit.

This was so that the Law's requirements might be fully satisfied in us as we direct our lives not by our natural inclinations but by the spirit.

5 For they that are after the flesh do mind the things of the flesh; but they that are after the Spirit the things of the Spirit.

Those who are living by their natural inclinations have their minds on the things human nature desires; those who live in the spirit have their minds on spiritual things.

6 For to be carnally minded is death; but to be spiritually minded is life and peace.

And human nature has nothing to look forward to but death, while the spirit looks forward to life and peace,

7 Because the carnal mind is enmity against God: for it is not subject to the law of God, neither indeed can be.

because the outlook of disordered human nature is opposed to God, since it does not submit to God's Law, and indeed it cannot,

8 So then they that are in the flesh cannot please God.

and those who live by their natural inclinations can never be pleasing to God.

9 But ye are not in the flesh, but in the Spirit, if so be that the Spirit of God dwell in you. Now if any man have not the Spirit of Christ, he is none of his.

You, however, live not by your natural inclinations, but by the spirit, since the Spirit of God has made a home in you. Indeed, anyone who does not have the Spirit of Christ does not belong to him.

10	And if Christ be in you, the body is dead because of sin; but the Spirit is life because of righteousness.	But when Christ is in you, the body is dead because of sin but the spirit is alive because you have been justified;
11	But if the Spirit of him that raised up Jesus from the dead dwell in you, he that raised up Christ from the dead shall also quicken your mortal bodies by his Spirit that dwelleth in you.	and if the Spirit of him who raised Jesus from the dead has made his home in you, then he who raised Christ Jesus from the dead will give life to your own mortal bodies through his Spirit living in you.
12	Therefore, brethren, we are debtors, not to the flesh, to live after the flesh.	So then, my brothers, we have no obligation to human nature to be dominated by it.
13	For if ye live after the flesh, ye shall die: but if ye through the Spirit do mortify the deeds of the body, ye shall live.	If you do live in that way, you are doomed to die; but if by the Spirit you put to death the habits originating in the body, you will have life.

Notes

8.1. Few modern translations retain what the AV has as the second half of this verse, which appears only in later Greek manuscripts of the letter and which has almost certainly crept in from 8.4.

8.2. A textual point arises: 'set you free' is chosen on balance as the best reading by most modern scholars; it is backed by better manuscript evidence, though 'set me free' or 'set us free' are alternatives found in some manuscripts.

8.6. The NJB's 'look forward to' is a translation of the idea of aim, striving and aspiration contained in one of the Greek nouns for 'mind' used here by Paul; the AV translation turned it into the verb 'minded'.

8.10. The NJB puts some clarity into a difficult clause at the end of the verse by translating Paul's Greek noun δικαιοσύνη (the AV 'righteousness') by an English verb, 'justified', even though this is a somewhat technical theological word.

It should be emphasized that the verses of the translations given above are set out for convenience of comparison and not as printed in each publication.

The Linguistic Analysis Approach

I come now to those who have pioneered the approach to translation through linguistic analysis. It has been described as a more noticeably scientific approach. Eugene Nida, the American biblical and linguistic scholar, was for many years secretary for translation work in the American Bible Society and the United Bible Societies. He had a close connection with the translation of the Good News Bible (the contemporary English version) and put the heading 'Science Comes to the Aid of the Translators' to one of the chapters in his book about the GNB.[1] He was referring to the range of problems experienced by biblical translators when trying to convey the original scriptures in language suitable for modern readers or hearers.

The GNB, in its Preface, declared its aim of trying to 'use language that is natural, clear, simple, and unambiguous'. The version emerged out of various experiments. In the 1950s parts of the Bible were translated into the everyday Spanish spoken in various parts of Latin America or into the everyday English spoken in Liberia; following this, a translation was made into the colloquial English spoken throughout the English-speaking world (GNB/TEV). Nida wrote that, 'the science of semantics...has been providing us with totally new insights as to the real nature of translation'.[2] He and others drew particularly on some aspects of communication theory in Noam Chomsky's system of 'transformational grammar' and in Chomsky's linguistic concern with the distinction between the meaning of an expression and its form.[3] Chomsky was, among other things, concerned to examine what he saw as 'the deep structure' of the 'semantic components' behind each surface structure and sentence used; he was concerned also to clarify the logical subject and object of each verb in a sentence. Words were seen as the important, formal and explicit vehicle to carry the meaning, but the key element to be identified and conveyed in any clear and full communication was seen to be the meaning itself, or 'semantic content', including that implicit or underlying meaning behind the surface words.

Nida and others developed this approach in relation to biblical translation, going far beyond previous 'word-for-word' methods.

1. E. Nida, *Good News for Everyone* (London: Collins, 1967).

2. Nida, *Good News*, p. 101.

3. Chomsky's seminal book was *Syntactic Structures* (The Hague: Mouton 1957). For an article that includes a summary and a critical evaluation of the 'Chomskian' linguistic approach of the Good News Bible translators, see S.E. Porter, 'Greek Language and Linguistics', *Expository Times* (April 1992).

They explored the idea of arriving at the deep structure of a biblical sentence or passage by breaking it down initially into a simple sentence or sentences, called 'kernel' constructions or core-constructions. This pioneering of 'kernel-analysis' has been described as being not 'a standard linguistics approach to analysis' but an offshoot from Chomsky's work.[1] Nida's team acted on the semantic principle that words are not adequately described simply as points of meaning, but should be seen as territories of meaning ('semantic domains'), having 'associative fields of meaning' to be explored. These have already been encountered with the fields of meaning of the Greek word σάρξ which cannot always be satisfactorily translated simply as 'flesh' in English.

This approach was a considerable change from former emphases in linguistic study and translation work. Formerly the etymological side of linguistics (Greek and Hebrew word origins) had predominated; now the emphasis came from the grammatical and semantic aspects of linguistics. Another major feature of the new approach was that it put stress on the criterion of reader response, with the translator asking, 'What will be the reader/hearer's response to this translation?' rather than simply, 'What was the original author's intended meaning?' The second question obviously remained valid and central, but was seen to be not the only criterion for any translation that aimed to be a communicative translation.[2]

Associative Fields of Meaning

Peter Cotterell and Max Turner substantiate the claim that modern linguistics can 'afford new precision, system and depth to older

1. See P. Cotterell and M. Turner, *Linguistics and Biblical Interpretation* (London: SPCK, 1989), p. 197.

2. Though in this section I am dealing mainly with the writings of Eugene Nida and his colleagues in the United States and with the GNB, similar writings elsewhere on related themes, linguistic or hermeneutical, should not be forgotten: for example, G. Ebeling's *Introduction to a Theological Theory of Language* (ET; London: Collins, 1973); and A.C. Thiselton's, *Language, Liturgy and Meaning* (Nottingham: Grove Press, 1975) and *The Two Horizons* (Exeter: Paternoster Press, 1980). Such writing followed on Heidegger's and Wittgenstein's emphasis on the fact that the problem of communication cannot be solved in terms of vocabulary alone (cf. also Wittgenstein's distinction between 'surface-grammar' and 'depth grammar').

disciplines such as word-study'.[1] It is clear that attempts to identify and analyse deeper and broader meanings of words are undertaken as one of several preliminary stages when producing a final wording and translation, providing a picture of the whole meaning implicit in the original word. But it is a vitally important stage if the translation is going to have clarity, impact and accuracy. As a further example, the Hebrew word *šālôm* may be looked at. The GNB, like other modern Bibles, nearly always translates the word as 'peace', as have the traditional English translations. However, the word has what could be described as both a basic general meaning of 'well-being' and associated meanings of 'health' and 'abundance'; that broader meaning has been recognized in every age, by traditional and modern translations, and has, in certain contexts, affected the translation into English. The translators of 1611 were well aware of the idea of an associative field of meaning for a word; modern translators have simply explored the idea much further, and in many cases let it take their translation into less literal wording.

In Gen. 29.6, where Jacob asks about Laban, the AV has, 'Is he well?' as does the GNB; the literal Hebrew reads, 'Is there *šālôm* to him?' A Hebrew verb plus noun is translated by an English verb plus adverb. And the AV sometimes translates *šālôm* as 'prosperity', 'prosperous'. So there is nothing new there, and it can be seen that many modern translators (for example, the NJB translators in Rom. 8) who do not follow the tradition of linguistic analysis have also brought out much breadth of verbal meaning in their versions. However, as may be seen from the excerpt of the GNB translation in Isaiah 58 printed at the end of this chapter, the GNB has explored this area of translation especially vigorously and implemented the results in its renderings.

Deep Structure and Kernel Structures
Linguistic translators have also tried to analyse and identify below-surface structures of meaning and areas of meaning in units larger than single words, such as phrases, clauses and sentences. Nida examines the phrase 'the baptism of repentance for the remission of sins' in the AV of Mk 1.4 ('John did baptize in the wilderness, and preach the baptism of repentance for the remission of sins') and

---

1. Cotterell and Turner, *Linguistics*, p. 31.

explains why the GNB renders this in such a radically different way:
'So John appeared in the desert, baptizing and preaching. "Turn away
from your sins and be baptized", he told them, "and God will forgive
your sins".'[1] Using the language of linguistic analysis about deep
structure, Nida says that the phrase 'baptism of repentance' is really
'only a noun form of an underlying verb expression "repent and be
baptized".' In any biblical passage, say Nida and Taber, such underlying deep structure or 'kernel-constructions' are to be found as 'the
basic structural elements out of which the language builds its elaborate
surface structures'.[2] The authors explain that the GNB translators
found that the four Greek nouns in Mk 1.4 in particular, hung
together as they are only by prepositions, were a somewhat artificial
grammatical form for conveying the meaning in English with any
clarity or impact. Hence the need for freedom to alter the form of the
original, so as to communicate the full meaning.

Practically speaking, in the linguistic analysis approach translators
are encouraged, before they begin their actual translation, to break
down the original material into a simple sentence or a list of simple
sentences ('kernel' expressions), summarizing the content of the
material and the core of meaning. Translators are advised, when
writing down these brief sentences, to use only the basic constructions
of most human language and to pay attention to the following four
factors, identified as helping to achieve that end:

1. To use verbs when recording events and actions rather than
    using a large number of abstract nouns; and to turn nouns
    into verbs when a noun expresses an event or an activity
    (behind this policy lies the conviction that all languages have
    more available equivalent expressions and find more common
    ground in the verb area than in the noun area).
2. To make clear mention of who the participants are in any
    event, action or situation, through nouns or pronouns; in the
    case of Mk 1.4 the GNB translators must have included in
    their brief sentences or 'kernel-constructions' the word
    'your' ('your sins' and not just 'sins' as in the AV) and that

---

1. Nida, *Good News*, p. 105.
2. E. Nida and C. Taber, *The Theory and Practice of Translation* (Leiden: Brill,
1969), p. 39.

point was included when making their final translation after the 'kernel-construction' exercise.

3. To ensure the recording of all necessary qualifying factors through adjectives and adverbs.
4. To ensure the inclusion of all necessary connecting links and transition marker words between the different parts of the material by the correct use of conjunctions and other marker words.

The aim of this is to ensure that the final translation is structured along the lines of the basic components of human language and expression, and to help the translator achieve the best correspondence between one language and another.

In the past many teachers of biblical exegesis and translators (such as J.B. Lightfoot and other more recent biblical scholars unconnected with the world of modern linguistic analysis) have insisted on the importance of the breaking down or breaking up of biblical material into a paraphrase, before arriving at the meaning of the passage or translating it into English. Their disciplines were entirely different from those of the linguistic analysts, but one may catch an echo of what they said when linguistic analysts insist on the importance of a preliminary breaking down of material into short 'kernel-constructions' as a way of arriving at meaning before translation.

The comparative role of nouns and verbs in different languages was under discussion in the twentieth century well before modern scientific analysis in biblical translation emerged into prominence. And the conclusions sometimes were opposite to those arrived at in modern linguistic analysis. Ronald Knox, while no doubt accepting that a Hebrew noun may sometimes be best translated by a verb in English, wrote this tentative but clear sentence in his book on biblical translation: 'I suppose we should all admit that English is a language of nouns rather than verbs'.[1] There is more than a suggestion here that, this being so, the best and most natural English translation is likely to be one that uses plenty of nouns. Knox bases the claim that English is a 'language of nouns' on the point that the Oxford English Dictionary always gives the noun first. His Hebrew dictionary gives precedence to the verb unless it is a case of obvious back formation.

---

1. Knox, *On Englishing the Bible*, p. 50.

His main argument is based on the following examples: to say in English 'they *gave* him a gold watch' (using a simple verb) has much less impact and colour than to say 'they *made him a presentation* of a gold watch' (with the major role given to the inclusion of the noun in the verbal phrase). For that reason Knox himself, in his translation, often used the phrase, 'he *made answer* to him' rather than 'he *answered* him'. He goes on to state that a sermon could well be preached on the probable greater depth found in words concerned with process (evidently seen by Knox as the category into which nouns fall) than in words concerned merely with results. Other comments on the priority of nouns have not necessarily quoted Knox's type of example, with an elaborative noun plus a verb seen as a useful strengthening of language in English. (In Chapter 1, criticisms of Knox's rather formal and sometimes archaic translation of the Old Testament were mentioned, though the distinction between his Old Testament and his New Testament work may be noted.)

Whatever views may be held among linguists, literary folk and the general public, the modern linguistic approach's emphasis, in biblical translation, on the fundamental importance of 'event-words' in all human language and in all true human communication, will be seen by many people as a factor worthy of serious consideration. That is not to say that translators are being urged by the linguists to use as few nouns as possible in their final surface translations. But they are being urged, before finalizing a translation, to analyse underlying constructs of meaning in terms that reflect fundamental components of meaning.

Paragraph-to-Paragraph Translation
Linguistic translation in recent years has aimed to look at the material before it in terms of large blocks, whether that be two verses, whole paragraphs or whole passages, rather than just single words or sentences.[1] Writing about the translation of Eph. 1.3-10, Nida and Taber comment,

> One must not translate this passage a clause at a time. The entire passage must be dealt with as a unit and its essential structure analyzed, transferred, and then restructured, so that it will preserve something of the same grandeur it has in the original text.[2]

1. See Cotterell and Turner, *Linguistics*, p. 18.
2. Nida and Taber, *Translation*, pp. 155-56.

Here is the text of the passage:

Ephesians 1.3-10

	AV	GNB
1.3	Blessed be the God and Father of our Lord Jesus Christ, who hath blessed us with all spiritual blessings in heavenly places in Christ:	Let us give thanks to the God and Father of our Lord Jesus Christ! For in our union with Christ he has blessed us by giving us every spiritual blessing in the heavenly world.
4	According as he hath chosen us in him before the foundation of the world, that we should be holy and without blame before him in love:	Even before the world was made, God had already chosen us to be his through our union with Christ, so that we would be holy and without fault before him.
5	Having predestinated us unto the adoption of children by Jesus Christ to himself, according to the good pleasure of his will,	Because of his love God had already decided that through Jesus Christ he would make us his sons—this was his pleasure and purpose.
6	To the praise of the glory of his grace, wherein he hath made us accepted in the beloved.	Let us praise God for his glorious grace, for the free gift he gave us in his dear Son!
7	In whom we have redemption through his blood, the forgiveness of sins, according to the riches of his grace;	For by the death of Christ we are set free, that is, our sins are forgiven. How great is the grace of God,
8	Wherein he hath abounded toward us in all wisdom and prudence;	which he gave to us in such measure! In all his wisdom and insight
9	Having made known unto us the mystery of his will, according to his good pleasure which he hath purposed in himself:	God did what he had purposed, and made known to us the secret plan he had already decided to complete by means of Christ.
10	That in the dispensation of the fulness of times he might gather together in one all things in Christ, both which are in heaven, and which are on earth; even in him...	This plan, which God will complete when the time is right, is to bring all creation together, everything in heaven and on earth, with Christ as head.

There are a number of well-known surface difficulties in this passage. First, the fact that its 132 words in Greek are given in just two long and highly complex sentences. This pattern of two sentences is literally followed in the AV, with only two full stops used. In the GNB version there are nine sentences and nine full closes (stops or exclamation marks). Secondly, there are a number of points of interpretation needing special attention: for example, the phrase translated 'in love' in the AV at the end of 1.4 is taken, in many modern translations (including the GNB), to refer to 1.5, though the AV took the phrase as referring backwards to the rest of 1.4. The distinctive concerns of linguistic analysis in this passage are not only those, but also the striving for clarity in communication in English by identifying the core constructions or deep structure underlying the passage's surface structure. Fourteen such core constructions or simple 'kernel' sentences are discerned by Nida and Taber:

Verse			*Core Constructions*	
1.3	we thank	God		
1.3		God	blessed	us
1.4		God	chose	us
1.4			we would be holy	
1.4		God	loved	us
1.5		God	destined	us	through Christ
1.6	we praise	God's	grace	
1.6		God	gave	us	in his Son
1.7		God	set	us free	in Christ
1.7		God	forgave	our sins	in Christ
1.8		God	gave	us grace	
1.9		God	revealed to	us	
1.9		God	plans		by Christ
1.10		God	unites all		with Christ as head

Nida and Taber emphasize that what has been done here is simply to lay bare a pattern and structure of thought that is implicit in the original. In the original Greek, they say, 'it is instructive to discover just how much organisation there is, and how subtly this organisation has been structured...there is a very considerable and largely unsuspected parallelism of structure'. The GNB acting on such an analysis, has centred its rendering of the whole passage on the two large phrases, 'Let us give thanks to the God and Father' in 1.3 and 'Let us praise God for his glorious grace' in 1.6; the latter echoing the former, giving a strong framework and clarity to the whole passage in English. The corresponding phrases in the AV are undoubtedly also strong, as well as noble and historic in their resonance: 'Blessed be the God and Father' (1.3) and 'to the praise and glory of his grace' (1.6).

But the GNB gives stronger impact and a clarion phrase that picks up an earlier phrase in 1.3 when it translates 'Let us praise God' in 1.6, compared with what in the AV is an auxiliary clause at the end of a very long sentence ('to the praise of'). It may be seen that in these verses, where the keywords are either an adjective in the A V ('blessed') or nouns ('praise', 'glory'), which literally follow the form of the original Greek, the GNB puts verbs ('Let us give thanks', 'Let us praise God').

In some parts of the Bible the concern of the GNB that a phrase or a verse should be seen in the context[1] of what precedes and follows leads to bold restructuring of the verbal form of the original. Isa. 11.1 is a case in point:

	AV	GNB
11.1	And there shall come forth a rod out of the stem of Jesse, and a Branch shall grow out of his roots...	The royal line of David is like a tree that has been cut down; but just as new branches sprout from a stump, so a new king will arise from among David's descendants.

The disappearance of the name of Jesse from the GNB translation has been criticized, since the name is a reminder of David's humble and unexpected origins; and that is certainly lost here. But there are gains. The GNB's determination that the reader gets a chance to understand the verse's place within the whole story of the Davidic dynasty makes its point. Underlying 'kernel' elements in this part of the prophetic material evidently indicated to the GNB translators that some radical restructuring was necessary if the full meaning was to come out in English.

---

1.   Through linguistic analysis, context has obviously become an increasingly important issue, and often in ways less straightforward than so far mentioned in this chapter. Some biblical scholars have (with obvious relevance for biblical translation) applied to Hebrew texts and grammar a linguistic theory that the meaning of verbal forms lies not so much in themselves as in the contexts in which they are found. Or the well-known fact that Hebrew verb forms do not signify the tense of an event but an aspect of it (completeness or incompleteness, and so on) has been seen by some scholars, in the light of modern linguistics, to indicate more nuances and expression of meaning than previously thought. See the book review headed 'Hebrew and Modern Linguistics' by John Gibson in *Expository Times* 102.10 (July 1991).

Linguistic Translation and Issues of Freedom

After studying these two passages and what went before, two points should be made about the linguistic-analysis approach. First, although its proponents maintain that attempts to preserve the structural form of the original material lead 'in most cases' either to awkwardness or unintelligibility in English, a basic maxim of the approach is still that 'one endeavours to keep the structural form if it is possible'.[1] Not all the Greek nouns in Eph. 1.3-10 have been turned by the GNB into verbs: 'faith', 'love', 'purpose', 'grace', 'wisdom' are some prominent parts of the GNB translation that remain nouns.

Secondly, for all the freedom that it uses and claims, linguistic translation may rule out what is called 'cultural translation', a translation that uses freedom of a wrong sort. It may be defined as 'a translation in which the content of the message is changed to conform to the receptor culture in some way' (perhaps the culture of the language into which the translation is being made) 'and/or in which information is introduced which is not linguistically implicit in the original'.[2] It follows that 'only a linguistic translation can be considered faithful'; and linguistic translation is defined as 'a translation in which only information which is linguistically implicit in the original is made explicit...'[3] Nida and Taber give the following examples of 'cultural translation' or cultural modernization. 'One cannot remake the Pharisees and Sadducees into present-day religious parties, nor does one want to, for one respects too much the historical setting of the incarnation'. And again, there is repudiation of the 'cultural re-interpretation' that would take place if suggestions for translating 'demon-possessed' as 'mentally distressed' were accepted.[4] J.B. Phillips's translation of Mt. 7.12, 'This is the essence of all true religion...', is criticized (the AV reads, literally, 'This is the law and the prophets') for containing something absent from the original, and missing the culture of the original. The GNB in Mt. 7.12 reads, 'This is the meaning of the Law of Moses and the teaching of the prophets'.[5]

---

1. Nida and Taber, *Translation*, p. 112.
2. Nida and Taber, *Translation*, p. 199.
3. Nida and Taber, *Translation*, p. 203.
4. Nida and Taber, *Translation*, p. 13.
5. Nida and Taber, *Translation*, p. 134.

Linguistic considerations are singlemindedly emphasized at every stage in the linguistic-analysis approach.

  This disciplined stand on certain issues does not stop linguistic translators from returning, in the end, to talking about freedom of expression, new patterns of wording, and from being aware of poetic and literary considerations. Using the word 'cultural' in a different sense from the definitions in the last paragraph, one could say that literary and cultural considerations are not excluded from the attitudes of linguistic translators. This point will be taken up again later, but it is interesting to note that Nida and Taber, in the middle of writing about verbal structures, put forward the idea that 'much poetic language is in kernel or near-kernel form', and suggest links between kernel and poetic expressions of meaning.[1] Moisés Silva writes, 'literary scholars are often critical of the approach taken by linguists because the latter allegedly see translation as merely the transmission of data rather than as the process of literary creation'.[2] While accepting that the fact of the debate is neatly summed up by this, one may accept the proposition that the linguistic approach has been closer to certain aspects of the literary approach than would appear on the surface. Certainly, the journal *The Bible Translator*, in which the concerns and implications of linguistic translation in relation to the translating of the Bible into many different languages are aired and discussed, contains regular pleas for the use of creativity as well as efficiency in translation, and for emphasis on the word 'dynamic' as well as the word 'equivalence' in the key linguistic phrase 'dynamic equivalence'.[3]

A Linguistic Translation of a Prophetic Passage

To match the GNB translation of the passage from Ephesians given above, here is a GNB rendering of an Old Testament passage, Isa. 58.6-10. This prophetic passage is chosen for reading in many churches at the beginning of Lent. The GNB version of it is often

---

1. Nida and Taber, *Translation*, p. 133.

2. M. Silva, *God, Language and Scripture* (Grand Rapids: Zondervan, 1990), p. 135.

3. See, for example, H. Salevsky, 'Theory of Bible Translation and General Theory of Translation', *The Bible Translator* 42.1 (January, 1991), pp. 101ff.; also E. Wendland, 'Receptor Language Style and Bible Translation', *The Bible Translator* 32.1 (January 1981), pp. 107-24.

thought to catch the ruggedness of the original particularly well.

There are few major points of difficulty in the Hebrew text of this passage: the differences in the two English versions shown here in parallel columns are mainly differences in style rather than interpretation. At the few points where there is a difference of interpretation, mention is made in notes following the translations.

The passage, dating probably from the fifth century BC, follows verses about fasting among the Jews after the Exile. Having fasted regularly and in special ways for 70 years, particularly to commemorate the fall of Jerusalem at the beginning of the Exile, many of the Jews were asking that the special fasting be allowed to stop. The prophetic writer reminds the Jews that, whether or not special ceremonial fasting is allowed to stop, the sort of fasting and self-denial that God really wants to see is an inner commitment that continues; the giving of time and caring to the needy and the oppressed.

For easy comparison the passage has here been 'lined out' as though it were in verse form; it is actually printed as prose in both versions:

Isaiah 58.6-10

	AV	GNB
58.6	Is not this the fast that I have chosen? to loose the bands of wickedness, to undo the heavy burdens, and to let the oppressed go free, and that ye break every yoke?	The kind of fasting I want is this: Remove the chains of oppression and the yoke of injustice, and let the oppressed go free.
7	Is it not to deal thy bread to the hungry, and that thou bring the poor that are cast out to thy house? when thou seest the naked, that thou cover him; and that thou hide not thyself from thine own flesh?	Share your food with the hungry and open your houses to the homeless poor. give clothes to those who have nothing to wear, and do not refuse to help your own relatives.
8	Then shall thy light break forth as the morning, and thine health shall spring forth speedily: and thy righteousness shall go before thee; the glory of the Lord shall be thy rereward	Then my favour will shine on you like the morning sun, and your wounds will be quickly healed. I will always be with you to save you; my presence will protect you on every side.

9	Then shalt thou call, and the Lord shall answer;	When you pray, I will answer you.
	thou shalt cry and he shall say, Here I am.	When you call to me, I will respond.
	If thou take away from the midst of thee the yoke,	If you put an end to oppression,
	the putting forth of the finger, and speaking vanity;	to every gesture of contempt and to every evil word;
10	And if thou draw out thy soul to the hungry,	if you give food to the hungry
	and satisfy the afflicted soul;	and satisfy those who are in need,
	then shall thy light rise in obscurity, and thy darkness be as the noonday.	then the darkness around you will turn to the brightness of noon.

Notes

Simplification in the GNB

There are 25 words fewer, overall, as compared with the AV.

58.6. Two 'yoke' clauses are compressed into one.

58.7. Several long rhetorical questions ('Is it not to deal thy bread...' AV) are turned into imperatives ('Share your food...' GNB).

Throughout, in the GNB, it is the Lord speaking, whereas the AV gives the wording literally as in the Hebrew, with the Lord speaking in vv. 6-8, but the prophet speaking from v. 9 onwards and saying, 'The Lord shall answer...'

Less Vague Terms Used in the GNB

58.6. There is the use of 'chains' instead of the archaic 'bands'.

58.6. The strong phrase 'remove the chains of oppression' is used (cf. REB 'Loose the fetters of injustice') instead of AV's more vague and general wording: 'loose the bands of wickedness'. Probably the Hebrew phrase is the equivalent of 'release those bound unjustly and wickedly'.

58.7. The modern term 'homeless' is used instead of the more general term 'cast out'. The literal meaning of the Hebrew is 'vagrant', 'wanderer'.

Beauty of Phrasing in the GNB

58.10. There is a simple rhythmic beauty about 'then the darkness around you will turn to the brightness of noon', alongside AV's own special type of poetic beauty.

Losses in the GNB Version

58.7. We lose the AV's haunting phrase 'that thou hide not thyself from thine own flesh', in the interests of clear meaning.

58.6. In connection with injustice, three things are mentioned in the Hebrew: chains, cords (or knots), and yoke. The GNB has nothing explicit about the second of those.

58.8. Another piece of the original imagery is absent: 'vanguard' and 'rearguard'. It is a characteristic of the GNB's methods that, in the interests of clarity, the Hebrew imagery is sometimes lost or compressed into condensed phrasing. But chapter 7 gives a more adequate discussion of the translation of imagery, including the GNB's.

Other Points of Interest

58.8. The GNB has the phrase 'my presence', where the AV and most translators have God's 'glory'. This is no doubt an attempt to get at the accurate meaning of the Hebrew word *kābôd* which, when applied to God, may basically be said to mean 'radiant presence'.

58.8. The GNB's 'I will always be with you to save you' is a free English translation of the Hebrew, taking the latter to mean literally 'saving righteousness for you will go before you' or something similar.

58.9. The GNB has 'every gesture of contempt': it is possible that the meaning may rather be 'gesture of accusation' (the REB has phrases here about 'the accusing finger', followed by 'false charges').

58.10. The AV rendering is 'if thou draw out thy soul to the hungry'. Behind this lies a difficult Hebrew expression, recognized as such since the days of the Septuagint (LXX). Some scholars think that the real meaning is, 'if you bestow your bread on the hungry', much as in the GNB. The NJB has 'if you deprive yourself for the hungry'.

Chapter 3

THE MANY MODERN VERSIONS AND THEIR CRITICS

The new translations and their language have been criticized along the following lines: first, 'they have eroded our cultural heritage, nationally and for all English-speaking people; we no longer have a single uniform version of the Bible held in common and much of it known by heart'; secondly, 'they have lost the spirituality of the Authorized Version language'; thirdly, 'they have lost the beauty of the Authorized Version language'. The first part of this chapter considers the general question of the diversity, multiplicity and pluralism of modern English versions of the Bible. Later the three types of criticism mentioned above are examined. In this chapter the first type of criticism is looked at in detail with a brief preliminary description and discussion of criticisms of the second and third types which are given fuller treatment in Chapters 4 to 7.

Modern versions of the Bible in English have certainly multiplied in the second half of the twentieth century, one undoubted aspect of what freedom has meant in English biblical translation. In its Preface 'To the Reader', the NRSV of 1989 reads,

> During the years following the publication of the Revised Standard Version, 26 other English translations and revisions of the Bible were produced by committees and by individual scholars: not to mention 25 other translations and revisions of the New Testament alone.

For some major modern translations (the NEB and the JB for example) revised editions have appeared within 20 years of the original, increasing the complexity of the modern scene. Critics of the new translations are oppressed by this pluralism of translation and see the situation mainly as one of confusion. Others feel enriched by it.

The Complexities of Pluralism

There has been loss in what some Christians have called 'the squeezing out' of the AV and its wording from its traditional, exclusive and central place in English national life and religious worship. Every language needs icon phrases around which its thinking and values can revolve. The AV not only contributed hugely to the development of English as a language, but also to the verbal patterns and images that nurtured and sustained the faith of countless people. Many, particularly those who know the AV well, emphasize the pastoral confusion that can occur when congregations or individual readers of the Bible have to cope with different versions and wordings. Some have wanted to see the AV (or at least the New King James Version, as a slightly updated revision) continue as the one uniform Bible in English for regular use in churches. Others, also stressing the continuing need for a single common Bible in English, have hoped that one of the modern translations or revisions would fill this position. A strong claim has been put forward at various points in the twentieth century for the RSV (or now the NRSV) to be the new common Bible. In the middle of this century many Christians, Protestant, Catholic and Orthodox, backed this idea; the production of a Catholic edition of the RSV in 1965, slightly modified from the original, gave the movement impetus. In 1973 the Common Bible (RSV) was produced, again slightly modified from the original and accepted by the main Protestant Churches, the Roman Catholic Church and the Orthodox Churches. In a similar way claims have been put forward for the GNB as best able to fill the role of a common Bible for modern times; in this case, the word 'common' has been stressed not just in the sense of 'held in common' but of 'translated into the English of common usage and suitable for all levels of readership'.

In the 1990s the chances of the NRSV, the GNB or any other version becoming the universally accepted modern Bible in English for all purposes seem slender. While existing achievements in cooperation remain valuable, the differences of approach between those who want a very literal ('formal correspondence') version such as the NRSV and those who want other, less literal types of version such as the GNB are too great to allow of any simple solution at the moment. There is wide support for retaining, at least provisionally, the present pluralism of versions. The editor of *The Expository Times*, in an editorial written just after the publication of the NRSV argued that this position was right and inevitable, summing up the present situation as follows:

> What has happened in practice, if not wholly by design, is that we no longer have 'Protestant' and 'Roman Catholic' Bibles (the Authorized Version and Douai, the New English Bible and the Jerusalem Bible), but instead have conservative evangelical, academic and popular ones (the New International Version, the Revised Standard Version and the Good News Bible)... [1]

Writing of the desire for a single common Bible, the article continues,

> Much as we might wish to possess a translation which has been 'authorized' by all the churches, large tracts of which we could come to know by heart as we once did the Authorized Version (or, with some of us, the Revised Version, for which I retain an affection as the translation closest to the original text), the different aims and methods of the various translations, and a greater awareness of the uncertainties surrounding the biblical text, mean that none should now attain to that place. To make any one of them *the* Bible is to possess a sectarian spirit... We must place the translations side by side, neither abandoning the older translations nor limiting our reading to our own favourite version.

Many will agree with that conclusion and position, implying as it does that to try and fix on one common Bible in English at the moment would be to try and tidy up and make neat a complex situation in which there can be no neatness for the present. The above mention of several different versions and types of version could, in the space of a short editorial, cover only part of the modern translation field. The complexity is much wider, and the classification of particular versions is itself a complex matter. Although there is, quite correctly, a distinction between versions with a study emphasis which are useful for students, versions that are designed to be more popular for a wider readership, versions that are more literary in style, versions that have a more Protestant or more Catholic background, versions designed to be particularly suitable for liturgical use, and so on, it is always hard to classify and label precisely in a single word or phrase a particular translation. There are complex diversities within a translation itself, few modern translations being entirely consistent throughout to general principles enunciated in a preface.

1. *Expository Times* 102.3 (December 1990), p. 67.

For example the NIV may at first glance look simply traditional in style. On further inspection it is seen to be a fairly intricate combination of traditional phrasing and fresh phrasing, as may be noticed even from the brief extracts from the NIV (verses from Exodus and Deuteronomy) already given in Chapter 2. Moisés Silva writes, 'The New International Version adopts a moderate dynamic equivalent approach...'[1] A Bible Society catalogue describes it as follows: the New International Version is more than a word-for-word, formal correspondence translation; idiomatic but not idiosyncratic...' (this last phrase is taken from the NIV's Preface) and 'the NIV is designed to have clarity and literary quality'. To grasp fully the NIV's attitude to 'formal correspondence' policies (that is, policies that follow the grammatical form of the original text as closely as possible) or to 'dynamic equivalence' policies (that is, policies that are prepared, where it is considered necessary, to change the grammatical form of the original), it is necessary to read what Herbert Wolf, in a companion volume about the NIV,[2] writes, 'sometimes it is necessary to change one or more grammatical forms in order to translate a sentence properly'. He takes as the simplest of examples the translation of part of Isa. 1.13. It is given in literal form, he says, in the RSV: 'I cannot endure iniquity and solemn assembly' (NRSV, 'I cannot endure solemn assemblies with iniquity'); but in the NIV the original two nouns are translated by an adjective and a noun in English: 'I cannot bear your evil assemblies...' Wolf continues,

> Granted, no version that aims at accuracy is eager to depart from a literal translation too often. But at times it is necessary to move away from a literal translation, so that the message of the scriptures can be clearly communicated. The NIV has been cautious when it has departed from a 'literal' rendering, but its willingness to do so has markedly enhanced its overall accuracy.

Many modern versions, like the NIV, constitute a complex new mixture of language, form and style in biblical translation.

---

1. *God, Language and Scripture*, p. 136.
2. 'When "Literal" Is not Accurate', in *The Making of a Contemporary Translation* (London: Hodder & Stoughton, 1987), pp. 183, 188.

The Richness of Pluralism

In spite of criticisms mentioned earlier, the modern age of experimentation and diversity in translation is seen by a great many people as not only one of confusion, but, predominantly, as one of enrichment. The complex new mixtures of language and form in modern Bibles can also be enriching. It is at least arguable that there is an important role in history for some spells of intense periodical retranslation and revision, of pluralism of versions, and that our age is one such spell, not necessarily yet ended.

It is worth recalling that in the sixteenth century there was a similar long and major break-up of earlier uniformity of the (Latin) Bible as heard and read by British Christians. The period of break-up and transition lasted, at least, from 1525 to 1611, and much longer if one takes John Wyclif's work as a starting point. There were many different translations produced during that time, some of them along Puritan, others along more Catholic lines. Following William Tyndale's English New Testament of the 1520s (revised edition 1534), there was Coverdale's Bible of 1535, and the Great Bible (or 'Cranmer's Bible') of 1539. These were followed by the Geneva Bible of 1560 which has been described as 'the household Bible of the sixteenth century', and as a popular Bible for the common populace. It was also the form of the English Bible used by William Shakespeare and John Bunyan. Later, in 1572, came the Bishops' Bible, a revision of the Great Bible and a reaction against some of the Puritan and Calvinist influences in the Geneva Bible. And finally there was the King James Bible or Authorized Version of 1611, with the aim of 'making out of many good versions one principal good one' and of bringing together the various approaches. It was organized particularly at the request of the Puritans, who disliked the official authority given to the Bishops' Bible. But that was far from being the end of the great spell of transition. After 1611 came a long period of fifty years when parallel versions were still used alongside one another, and, in particular, when the new AV had to struggle hard to replace the Geneva Bible in popularity. The former age of pluralism in translation was unlike our present age in many ways: the number of new biblical translations and versions was smaller than today, not least because printing and channels of communication were less advanced. However, the parallels are real parallels.

During the Elizabethan and Stuart periods, the importance of using a variety of translations of the Bible was stressed. Dr Myles Coverdale, the translator and former Augustinian monk who became the first Protestant bishop of Exeter during the Reformation, subscribed to this view. He said, provocatively, that the use of various translations was of more value than all the commentaries: 'there cometh more understanding of the Scriptures by sundry translations than by all the glosses of sophistical doctors'. And the introduction to the AV of 1611 explicitly quotes St Augustine of Hippo as having declared that 'variety of translations is profitable for the finding out of the sense of the Scriptures'. That echoes the discussions about freedom and variety of biblical translation in early Christian centuries. Augustine is known to have had an interest in, and concern for, biblical translation; although as a bishop he is on record as saying that some of Jerome's new translations (Vulgate version) upset his congregations.[1] He is also on record as praising the LXX for its inspired rendering of many passages and for 'its freedom of the Spirit' in translation, and its avoidance of 'mere human servitude to words'.[2] In every age voices have been raised to point to the richness that comes from a variety of versions.

At the very least, one may say that the people of 1611 were not dismayed by the many versions, the pluralism of versions, of those times. While contemporary readers may not envisage our pluralist situation continuing indefinitely, and will surely look forward to some sort of emerging unity in the form of the English Bible, many people today are far from dismayed by modern diversities. For they know that those diversities have sprung, not just from some detached drawing-boards of the translators, but from the real-life experience and concerns of those who use the Bible. If one looks into the origins and characteristics of particular modern versions, one finds that one version emerged from a group of translators who had the life of ordinary parishes and church-members in mind; another version had as one of its translators a member of a religious community who

---

1. H. Chadwick, *Augustine* (Oxford: Oxford University Press, 1986), p. 36.

2. Modern scholars tend to agree that the LXX gives quite an accurate translation of the Hebrew in the historical books of the Old Testament, but not so adequately in the poetic books. Some modern translators have depended considerably on LXX renderings in passages where the Hebrew is obscure.

tested a version of the Psalms to see how it met the real needs of the community in the saying of the psalms; another version emerged from a group of translators with particular evangelistic concerns and commitments; yet another version owes some of its best characteristics to the fact that its translation was hammered out by those who lived and worked among the disciplines and needs of life in a university or theological college. Translators have their limitations and idiosyncracies, but the diversity of their own backgrounds and of the groups to which they belong can greatly enrich biblical translation.

One important aspect of the new richness found in the world of biblical translation in the twentieth century (already briefly mentioned in Chapter 2) has been the freshness brought in by the new age of Roman Catholic biblical study and biblical translation, especially since the Papal Encyclical of 1943 gave permission for the unrestricted use of ancient manuscripts and other material in study and translation. Matching the distinctive freshness and excitement of twentieth-century translators in churches that have largely used the AV for the previous three centuries has been the freshness and excitement of those twentieth-century translators whose church had previously used only the Latin Vulgate or the Douai–Rheims English Bible. The particular characteristics of translations in the JB tradition (springing from the initiative of modern French translators in the Dominican Ecole Biblique in Jerusalem) and in the tradition currently represented by the NAB are well known. Here I examine an individual Catholic translator, Peter Levi, already mentioned in Chapter 1 in connection with the translation of poetic metre. He brings to his translation work an unusual combination of viewpoints. He is a distinguished English poet, and has combined a desire to see preserved the best of sixteenth-century patterns of language in English biblical translation with a strong disapproval of the characteristic style of the AV. His strong commitment to working for a new idiomatic English wording for Bibles in our day is combined with a highly critical assessment of most well-known modern translations of the Bible in English. All this gives a freshness and a distinctive quality to his translation.

He writes that his aim is to achieve what he regards as 'a neglected quality' in much biblical translation and to produce translations that will 'speak with immediacy', and will, as far as possible, catch the sense and precise tone of the original. Of his translation of St John's Gospel, he writes, 'my only hope is that this version will...speak with immediacy as the Gospel was intended to speak and did speak to its first readers'.[1] He has looked back to the classic English translations of past centuries, and salutes the influence on English literature and the English language which those versions have. But it is to William Tyndale in the early sixteenth century that Levi looks back especially, not to the AV of 1611. He praises Tyndale's liveliness and directness of language and expression, grounded in the spoken English of his time. Tyndale's New Testament translations, says Levi, in some degree 'embody the handsomeness of the plain English of his time, and of an inevitably country habit of speech in the mouth of a learned and passionate man'.[2] Levi reminds us that Tyndale was basically a Gloucestershire man and lived there during some of his years of translating. In the AV Levi finds 'solemn learning and majestic prose', but he castigates its well-rounded style and 'smooth texture' and 'mellow voice' as 'harmonious honey' (strength of expression, he says, in the AV 'is drowned in harmonious honey').[3] Levi's translations are written by someone looking back over his shoulder to Tyndale, but not looking back too much to the AV. This gives them an air of some traditional dignities of expression as well as freedom and liveliness of language.[4] In his criticism of the language used by most modern, English translations of the Bible, Levi says that they tend to be written in the style of middle-class written English. 'The modern English Bibles are written in the language, or non-language, of a class, and of a class that has no authority in spoken English...'[5]

It is not without significance that Levi has one paragraph in his book *The English Bible* on Hugh Broughton in the late sixteenth and early seventeenth century, who strongly criticized the AV of 1611 when it was first published. Broughton was a noted Hebrew scholar,

1.   Levi, *John*, p. 5.
2.   Levi, *The English Bible*, p. 37.
3.   *The English Bible*, p. 37.
4.   Alongside Peter Levi's comments on the language of the AV, we may place some phrases from the 1968 edition of the *Jerome Biblical Commentary*, II, p. 587. It acknowledges the important place that the AV has had in English literature and national life, but has a somewhat qualified statement about its language: 'Gradually the language [of the AV] came to be thought of as classically beautiful...' And this sentence was added: 'Among many Protestants the Authorized Version became so sacrosanct that they felt it blasphemy to change it...'
5.   *The English Bible*, p. 12.

who might have been one of the 1611 translators if he had not been out of favour with the establishment over his book which attempted to reconcile the chronology of Scripture with what was known from secular historians. Broughton wrote of the AV, 'The late Bible...was sent to me to censure: which bred in me a sadness that will grieve me while I breathe, it is so ill done... The new edition crosseth me. I require it to be burnt'. Levi describes him as 'a powerful scholar and a brilliant writer in English', whose presence among the 1611 translators was badly needed, for his passionate liveliness of expression, and the 'verbal texture of thunder and lightning' that he could command.[1]

Whatever views there may be on these precise issues, many people will conclude that it is a healthy sign in any century when there is a forum for a wide variety of passionate convictions on important issues in biblical translation, and when a well-known poet such as Peter Levi is willing to voice his convictions and to be involved in producing his own biblical translations.

Heritage, Culture and their Modern Erosion?

I now consider in more detail the criticism of the new versions listed at the beginning of this chapter. Peter Mullen has voiced this type of criticism clearly. He has pleaded for a retention of the language of the AV, and for the AV to continue to be regularly used for church services and for individuals, among English-speaking people. In *The New Babel*[2] he writes of the confusion of language brought in by modern Bibles, and of what he sees as a disastrous erosion, by modern translators and liturgists, of the heritage and cultural riches of the AV and the Book of Common Prayer. 'To change one's language is to change everything, the whole system of perceiving the world, for language is what creates our world.'[3] In Mullen's view, historical continuity is central, and the biblical word for us to use in the modern age must not depart from the wording of the historic translation and cultural form of the AV through which it has been so long known and cherished. Nothing modern can penetrate deep enough. He emphasizes

1. *The English Bible*, pp. 35-37.
2. P. Mullen, *The New Babel* (London: SPCK, 1987).
3. Mullen, *The New Babel*, p. 65.

the great importance in British life of the political and ecclesiastical Acts of Settlement in the sixteenth and seventeenth centuries (the Elizabethan Settlement or first Act of Uniformity in 1559 and the new Act of Uniformity in 1662). By those settlements between sovereign, parliament and people, the AV and the Book of Common Prayer, at a supremely important moment in the development of British civilization, came to be, in Mullen's words, a sort of national epic. Like the sacred texts of which they were translations, they became 'sacred texts of that culture' of which they were a part. The Settlements are described as political solutions, 'envied throughout the world', but also as moments when a deep-rooted spirit of 'commonwealth and solidarity' was created in the nation.[1]

This thesis relies greatly on the correctness or desirability of close links between religion and culture; one of Mullen's central statements is 'religion is cultural'.[2] He writes that the AV and the Book of Common Prayer, through their uniform text, 'produced a common religious sensibility' in the nation, and created a common public language, culture and way of living, for

> texts create communities and whole cultures... each civilisation produces its epics near its beginning. Words do possess numinous power and this power is intensified by time and use... Sacred texts are like sacred buildings: they are hallowed by the repeated visits and hallowed prayers of succeeding generations.[3]

Mullen's book is a plea for the British nation, and what he describes as our divided society, to return to this pattern of English and British life and to this root of English and British culture. It is a plea for the AV (and the Book of Common Prayer) to occupy its former place as the original creative element of our pattern of life and culture. He says,

> the choice of a text is not a trivial matter. It must, in order to be an effective vehicle for religion, be one that is known to succeeding generations, or else we lose continuity with both past and future and the experience referred to as 'religious' becomes ephemeral—which is to say not religious at all but secular.

---

1. Mullen, *The New Babel*, p. 66, 115.
2. *The New Babel*, p. 36.
3. *The New Babel*, p. 60, for this and the next two quotations.

He goes on to use even stronger statements about the Bible in its AV form and about the Book of Common Prayer. He says that in them we have 'a veritable incarnation language', and adds that, since religion is cultural, 'we must re-learn the language of our culture, for it is the Word made flesh, the language of God'.[1] So the modern translations are seen as having lost the living language of 400 years ago, which was made up of words, phrases and universal images that have come to us through the AV and the Book of Common Prayer. Since we are losing these texts from common use, says Mullen, and losing their type of language, which was one that 'referred to reality', we can today only go deep and find God's cultural forms of truth for us in other types of literary and artistic richness in our heritage.

The Charge of Cultural Banality

Mullen describes the language of modern biblical versions as 'banal'. He sees the influence of supermarket language when the AV words 'this corruptible must put on incorruption' (1 Cor. 15.53) become in the NEB 'this perishable being must be clothed with what is imperishable'. And he has instanced Jn 11.39 as a verse in which the new versions have lost the direct and down-to-earth language of the AV. He says that whereas the AV had the strong 'by this time he stinketh', the RSV could only manage 'by this time there will be an odour'. Mullen goes on to speak of instances of other 'aesthetically vulgar' language in the modern versions as due to a link with modern charismatic or apocalyptist movements or with the Campaign for Nuclear Disarmament. The modern versions are seen as part of a modern craze for 'manic salesmanship'; the modern age,

> cannot provide the personal and psychological means for the putting into words and actions of those deep feelings of love and death, of suffering, awe, loss and redemption. It can give no meaning beyond what is trivial to those archetypal experiences which created the art and literature of Christian tradition.[2]

We have, he maintains, lost the language both of a national culture and of a national church. Mullen falls back, in the present climate, not

---

1.   Mullen, *The New Babel*, p. 120.
2.   In this paragraph, references are to Mullen, *The New Babel*, pp. 27, 89, 37, 85, 86, 106.

only on the AV and the Book of Common Prayer, but also on great works of literature and art from the past and of the present day, which still provide ways of expressing what is transcendent and deep. He mentions Dante, Donne, Bach, Mozart and, more recently, Alban Berg, D.H. Lawrence, James Joyce, Wyndham Lewis, Samuel Beckett, Olivier Messiaen and C.H. Sisson. He finds Samuel Beckett's sensitive language, and his 'spirituality of the void' (rather than some modern wording of the Psalms) to be the true modern successor to the traditional English wording in the Psalms about 'going heavily in sadness'.[1] How sad, says Mullen, that the traditional wording of the AV and the Book of Common Prayer is squeezed out of sight and out of use these days. We need to get back to their use, to appropriate 'the creative centrality of English Christianity'. It is in them that spiritual realities for us in Britain and in the English-speaking world have become incarnated in a practical available way, and proved effective in real life through many generations.

Mullen's book refers frequently to what T.S. Eliot wrote about religion, culture and tradition. It sees Eliot's *Waste Land* satire on the secularized society of the 1920s (like Dante's arena of despair) as prophesying an even more alarming situation at the end of the twentieth century. He quotes Eliot's remarks in *The Waste Land* about the fragmented culture of modern society, with 'hollow men, headpiece filled with straw', and no 'roots that clutch'.[2] Mullen echoes this sentiment, and his central phrase is 'religion and faith can only be mediated by a living culture'.[3] Eliot believed that without a renascence of that English cultural tradition in which inherited culture and religion were combined, there could be no remaking of modern society. He wrote of the culture of a people as 'an incarnation of its religion',[4] and that culture and religion were 'different aspects of the same thing'.[5] In his own way, in the middle of the twentieth century, he was echoing the warnings and clarion calls of other Christian voices earlier in the century, such as G.K. Chesterton and Dean Inge.

---

1. Mullen, *The New Babel*, pp. 53, 120.
2. *The New Babel*, p. 71.
3. *The New Babel*.
4. T.S. Eliot, *Notes towards the Definition of Culture* (London: Faber & Faber, 1948), p. 28.
5. 'Notes', p. 28.

(Inge once remarked that the theologian who marries the spirit of the age is soon left bereaved.) Eliot was undoubtedly convinced of the superficiality of the modern age and its language. He wrote,

> Contemporary literature as a whole tends to be degrading... there never was a time, I believe, when the reading public was so large, or so helplessly exposed to the influences of its own time... there never was a time so completely parochial, so shut off from the past.[1]

He looked with expectation to words from the past, not words of the present. Poetically, this issued in the statement 'we begin with the dead' and 'the communication of the dead is tongued with fire beyond the language of the living'.[2] Eliot's words are quoted by Mullen as a call to go back to the past, on whose language and convictions we cannot hope to improve; 'we must', says Mullen, 're-learn the language of God from tradition'.[3]

These salutary warnings should not be ignored; they point to some dangers and failures in modern translation and it is clear that in the case of many passages of Scripture the splendid phrasing of past translators cannot be improved on. The warnings are also a reminder to modern translators that they should at the very least read some of the AV as a preparation to fashioning new translations using modern methods. Nor should the convictions of an English poet of the eminence of T.S. Eliot be treated lightly. Apart from anything else, he lived through two world wars and the call to depth through his poetry is a timeless part of modern British spirituality. However, three questions arise as one examines these arguments, and may be very briefly listed here.

---

1.   *Selected Prose of T.S. Eliot* (London: Faber & Faber 1975), pp. 103, 104.

2.   Quoted in Mullen, *The New Babel*, pp. 96, 60.

3.   It is well known that Eliot in the 1930s was deeply disturbed over what he saw as the break-up of 'Christendom' or Western civilization in Britain and Europe, and was pessimistic about the new democratic 'levelling down' in the world. As Daniel Jenkins states in *The British: Their Identity and Religion* (London: SCM Press, 1975), p. 137, Eliot's extreme British and European conservatism and authoritarian viewpoint seemed partly to be a reaction on his part to the Nonconformist and Puritan type of tradition in which he had been brought up in New England. But Jenkins reminds his readers that later in his life Eliot's outlook on some of the matters mentioned above was less rigidly expressed.

Three Reflections on the Criticism

The first question relates to Mullen's use of the phrase 'living culture': 'religion and faith can only be mediated by a living culture'. What is meant by a 'living culture' in this connection? As Professor David Frost, a Shakespearian scholar, wrote some years ago, 'for the majority of English people the language of the Authorized Version and the Book of Common Prayer has, through the changes in vocabulary and syntax, ceased to be an entirely living word'.[1] On more detailed matters, as Frost again remarks, T.S. Eliot himself in the great writings of his later years wrote about God and the life of the spirit through metaphors taken, not from the old biblical images of shepherd or warrior, but from the world of his own living experience, the world of the social relationships and environment of the twentieth century. A passage in *Four Quartets* is cited, where Eliot writes about the divine compassion, made known in Christ, through the metaphor of a modern hospital and the work of a surgeon and nurse: 'the whole earth is our hospital'. Frost writes of how Eliot 'endured the loss of the old images, the thought patterns, the spiritual talismans to which we cling'.[2] In modern-day communication and translation translators can hardly avoid bearing in mind, as a background, the worlds of at least four levels of culture: the 'two cultures' of the arts and the sciences articulated by C.P. Snow; modern popular culture in all its senses; and modern international, inter-racial and cosmopolitan culture. This is not to say that each sentence in a biblical translation will use cultural resources from each of those levels, but it is certain that translators in modern times will not be unaware of those levels.[3]

A second question enquires into how far criticism about a poverty of resources in modern English (allowing some force in Mullen's

1. *The Language of Series 3*, p. 5.
2. *The Language of Series 3*, p. 16. The reference to *Four Quartets* is to *East Coker*, ll. 147-56.
3. No attempt is made in this chapter to discuss the large question of religion and culture, except to quote a sometimes forgotten sentence about the communication of faith, by David Paton. In the journal *Frontier* (17.3 [1974], p. 187), he wrote, 'The Christian mystery brought holiness and glory to Greeks and Romans for centuries before it produced for them satisfying cultural expression; and how many of the Churches of the "third world" today have liturgies with the evocative quality of Cranmer's company?'

comments about infelicitous modern supermarket language) stands up
to being tested against actual biblical verses and their translation?
Writing early in the twentieth century about words (many of them of
Latin origin) introduced into the English language since 1611 for use
in modern scientific, social and political discussion, the social historian
G.M. Trevelyan cited the word 'organisation' which, he said, the folk
of 1611 would not have understood.[1] Is that word or type of word to
be avoided in modern translation? Not at all: it is introduced
strikingly by one of the earliest modern biblical translators in English,
R.F. Weymouth, in relation to 1 Cor. 12.28. He translates as 'powers
of organisation' what stood awkwardly as 'governments' in the AV. In
the passage Paul is describing some of the gifts of the Spirit; in the AV
these include 'gifts of healings, helps, governments': Weymouth
translates this as 'ability to cure diseases or render assistance, or
powers of organisation'.[2] Similarly, in Eccl. 1.13, the words 'investigation' and 'exploration' are used in some modern translations. In the
AV the author (philosopher and teacher) says, 'I gave my heart to seek
and search out by wisdom concerning all things that are done under
heaven', a straightforward and classic rendering. But the NJB has a
useful modern phrasing when it puts, 'Wisely I have applied myself to
investigation and exploration of everything that happens under
heaven'. The Hebrew word behind the AV's 'seek' and the NJB's
'investigation' refers both to search and enquiry; the Hebrew word
behind the AV's 'search out' and the NJB's 'exploration' means 'to spy
out, to go around searching'.

A third question concerns the type or types of theology that underlie the language used in an English translation of the Bible. Mullen
uses terms from a theology of incarnation to describe the translation
language of the AV and the traditional language of worship in English,
describing them as the Word made flesh in language. Such descrip-
tions are a reminder that in reading, hearing or translating Scripture
we are on hallowed ground. But, should not the modern translator
also want to base new translations on a theology of God's providence

---

1. *English Social History* (London: Longmans, Green, 1941), p. 572.

2. The Greek word (κυβερνήσεις) lying behind the translations 'governments'
and 'powers of organization' (literally meaning 'steerings', 'pilotings') has frequently been interpreted in Weymouth's way, though an alternative interpretation is
'guidings': e.g. 'the power to guide people' (as NEB and REB) or 'guidance' (NJB).

and of the Holy Spirit as the issues of development in translation language and of the provision of new language for changed historical situations are tackled? After all, talk of incarnation in St John's Gospel, used of Jesus the living Word, is nearly always followed immediately by talk of the Holy Spirit. For example, in Jn 6.53, 'except ye eat the flesh of the Son of Man, and drink his blood, ye have no life in you' is followed by Jn 6.63, 'it is the spirit that quickeneth; the flesh profiteth nothing'. Modern theologies of God's providence and of God's incarnation must both undergird the thinking about biblical translation. Relevant to many of the issues encountered in biblical translation is a theology of divine providence such as that of the community of Taizé, with its emphasis on God's provision for each stage in history and for each present moment, and with its 'principle of the provisional'. Such a theology does not ignore the importance of what has gone before and fits in well with Mullen's highlighting of Eliot's phrase 'We begin with the dead'. Roger Schutz, prior of Taizé, has used the phrase 'Do not forget yesterday'.[1] Wrestling with problems of human unity and ecclesiastical unity for modern times, the Taizé community seems to have urged people to hold on to the wonder of God's provision already given. It has also urged people to look for God's new provision for the present and the future, another notable phrase of Roger Schutz's (found in a prayer of his) being, 'Let us hasten forwards to meet mankind's tomorrow'.[2] Knowing and acknowledging that both Catholic and Protestant institutional Christianity in Europe has in some sense 'grown weary through time' (as many young people who have flocked to Taizé have felt), Schutz seems keen to emphasize both the importance of traditions springing from God's provisional and providential provision for his people in the past, and the importance of present experimentings whereby that same providing for today and for the future may be taken hold of. The relevance of this type of theological thought to biblical translation is apparent to many people today.[3]

1.   R. Schutz, *The Power of the Provisional* (London: Hodder & Stoughton, 1969), p. 22 (original French title *Dynamique du provisoire*).

2.   Schutz, *The Power of the Provisional*, p. 79.

3.   Mullen's book and its title are concerned with the admitted confusion that new wordings have brought. The ancient Jews certainly interpreted the name 'Babel' as meaning 'confusion', and as taken from the root *bll* or *bālal*; and the Bible so uses the word. But it is intriguing to remember that the name 'Babel' was originally an

A Loss of Spiritual Resonance?

I turn now to a criticism that is closely related to Peter Mullen's criticisms, but which articulates clearly, and in a different way, the charge that the new versions have lost the AV's spirituality of language (the second charge listed at the beginning of the chapter). I refer to Professor Stephen Prickett's comments on the new versions in his important book *Words and the Word*.[1] Perhaps the most substantial and powerful criticism of the language of modern translations in English is Prickett's claim that the translations, so far, are not spiritual enough, and that the language that they use does not have spiritual resonance. The sub-title of the book, *Language, Poetics and Biblical Interpretation*, shows the breadth of the book's literary approach. Prickett, a Professor of English Literature, pleads with us not to turn our backs on the insights and the language of poets and writers in recent centuries who applied a poetic imagination to Scripture and its understanding. In particular he exhorts biblical translators to consider the issue of how mystery, wonder, spirituality and the supernatural can be best reflected in English in biblical translation.

Early on in his book Prickett puts forward, as a test-case and talking-point about biblical translation, the well-known phrase, 'a still small voice' from the AV translation of 1 Kgs 19.12 in the story of Elijah on Mount Horeb ('and after the earthquake a fire: and after the fire a still small voice'). He notes that although this phrase has reverberated through the English language and the pages of European literature for many years, modern translations such as 'and after the fire a low murmuring sound' (NEB) now replace the AV translation. Prickett finds this incredible, calling the NEB rendering, and other modern renderings, 'secularised' and 'naturalistic'. He regards the AV phrase as the true translation, having spiritual depth and resonance. His viewpoint is a literary one not because he makes great play with factors such as alliteration ('still small voice'), but because he wants

Akkadian word meaning 'the gate of the god' or 'gate of God'. Perhaps modern translations, for all the confusion they cause in some ways, can often truely be seen as God's gateways for us into new scriptural discovery.

1. S. Prickett, *Words and the Word: Language, Poetics and Biblical Interpretation* (Cambridge: Cambridge University Press, 1986).

the understanding of the phrase, cherished by the poetic imagination of a long line of figures in the world of literature, to be taken seriously. This takes us, of course, into the world of modern hermeneutics. Prickett points out that the phrase 'a still small voice' has long passed out of its original context into that of European literature and has thus grown and achieved a life of its own. It is a phrase originally belonging to a Hebrew context which has subsequently passed into new cultural contexts. This fact, says Prickett, makes concentration simply on original word meanings (including authors' meanings) a limited approach. However, Prickett does not ignore details about original word meanings; he expounds the meaning of the original Hebrew words as given by one Old Testament scholar, but his main approach spreads far wider than that. He laments the fact that 'contemporary biblical criticism has become separated from its own historical roots in the 18th and 19th centuries, and from the parallel and cognate discipline of literary criticism'.[1] He reminds the reader of Coleridge's plea to allow poetic imagination to work on the divine Word in Scripture, and Coleridge's strong sense of the centrality of the divine Word. While the book draws attention to the poets and 'poet-theologians' of the eighteenth and nineteenth centuries in Britain, it ranges widely, from Dante to modern writers.

It may be seen that Prickett's concern about the direction in which much modern biblical translation has gone is not caused simply by his own preference for particular types of wording, but by literary considerations about particular pieces of biblical material, and by considerations about the subjective insights (more technically and precisely described sometimes as the 'pre-understandings') in the minds of hearers or readers who have pondered on the passage. His concern is motivated by an interpretative conviction about the way in which the mysteries of God and of the Word should be approached, understood and translated. It is a concern that the written words of translation and the Bible which we use should reflect the deep underlying reality of the word, the Logos.[2] He declares himself

1. Prickett, *Words and the Word*, p. 241.
2. See also Prickett's 'On Reading Nature as a Romantic', in D. Jasper (ed.), *The Interpretation of Belief* (London: Macmillan, 1986); and his 'What Do the Translators Think they Are up to?', *Theology* 80.678 (November 1977), pp. 410-403.

unconvinced that modern translations can, on the whole, transmit the central biblical images and imaginative nuances.

The Question of Literary Style

By far the commonest criticism levelled at the modern translations (and the third criticism listed at the beginning of the chapter) comes from those who say that they miss the beauty and rhythm of language that the AV possesses. This type of comment again overlaps with the other two types of criticism already looked at. But it needs to be listed separately and has its own fields of literary concern. In Chapter 6 this topic is explored in more detail.

The politician and writer Roy Hattersley sums up well the sentiments expressed by many people, including those in public life, when he wrote in a national newspaper about 'the hideous English of the currently fashionable Bible'. In 1986, after describing how moved he had been at a memorial service in Westminster Abbey when the great words from the AV were read, 'I am the resurrection and the life, saith the Lord: he that believeth in me, though he were dead, yet shall he live', Hattersley said how thankful he had been that the words were not read from a modern translation. He continued, 'I believe in the language that modern translation cannot destroy... I need the sights and sounds of the Church Beautiful to make me believe in the Church Triumphant'.[1] Along similar lines, the public petition to the General Synod of the Church of England in 1979 was signed by 600 people prominent in public life and in the arts, and organized by David Martin, then Professor of Sociology at the London School of Economics.[2] This was a protest against modern religious language, from well-known poets (including Ted Hughes, subsequently Poet Laureate), literary critics, university professors of English literature, politicians, service-chiefs, judges, sociologists, journalists and many others. The Foreign Secretary and the Home Secretary were among the signatories. Their criticisms were levelled at both the Alternative Service Book of the Church of England and against new versions of the Bible. Feelings were strong; one noted signatory offered to sign in blood. The petition described the new religious language as being, 'no

---

1. Article in *The Guardian*, 29 March 1986.
2. This public petition was printed in *Poetry Nation Review* (November 1979).

man's English, neither popular nor elevated, neither ancient nor modern' as leading to 'weak, disposable, temporary texts' and as a sort of genteel middle-class style without roots either in the true vernacular or in the literary traditions of the language. David Martin said that the new language, 'strapped the relics of great invocations in the confines of contemporary middle-class grammar', and that its rhythms would not wear, in contrast to those of the AV and the Book of Common Prayer which, with splendour and dignity had carried the freshness and simplicity of the nation's language through the centuries. The petition pleaded for a restoring of the AV and the Book of Common Prayer to the central places of honour in the mainstream of worship and use, instead of pushing them into ecclesiastical corners.

National newspapers joined in the protest, not least those often labelled as 'progressive'. *The Guardian*, in a leader,[1] referred to new and experimental forms of service, saying that 'the unhappy experiments of the last decade have torn at the anchors of English speech'. The poet Philip Larkin was quoted as having felt totally frustrated during a brief spell as a literary adviser to the NEB, saying,

> The whole text seemed to me lacking in vitality, distinction, and above all memorability, and I found myself revising almost every sentence—not, I hasten to say, in the direction of poetic prose, but simply, as I thought, into something more powerful... After a year they quietly stopped sending me anything.

The Guardian leader praised real vernacular translations and described as 'blunt' and 'felicitous' an old Yorkshire translation of the well-known words in the first chapter of Genesis: 'First on, there were nobbut God...He said, Eh up, let's turn t' bloody light on'. But other modern translations on offer were held to be weak and colourless.

Another great poet, W.H. Auden, was cited as being against the new versions. David Martin quoted him as saying that we should not 'spit on our luck', but should recognize how lucky we are to have had our liturgy and Bible put into English at a high point in English literature, and should keep it as our main style of church language.[2] Perhaps the most articulate literary critic to have voiced strong dissatisfaction with

1. 6 November 1979.
2. D. Martin, 'A Plea for our Common Prayer', in B. Morris (ed.), *Ritual Murder* (Manchester: Carcanet, 1980), p. 22.

the new versions is Martin Fagg. In an enthusiastic review[1] of a chapter by Peter Mullen, entitled 'The Religious Speak-Easy' in the book *Fair of Speech*,[2] he contrasted the 'strength and directness' of the language of the AV and the Book of Common Prayer to what he called the 'unevocative literalism and pedestrian daintiness' of many modern versions of the Bible and modern forms of service. He described new versions as having 'a reductive banality...a softening of language...a sheer limpness of language'. He also described obscurity in the AV as only 'occasional'.

David Martin, writing on the language of worship and biblical translation, said, 'the question of absolute intelligibility and clarity is not the first question. The mind begins in incantation, and then approaches comprehension.'[3] He also has a phrase about the dangerous tendency of modern liturgies and translations to 'smooth out the suggestive edges of meaning'.[4] What he describes as 'occasional oddities' in the AV (the retaining of the word 'prevent' in its old sense of 'go before', as in Ps. 59.10, 'The God of my mercy shall prevent me', for example) are said to have the useful function of 'egging us on to comprehension'.[5]

This brief description of this type of criticism is merely an introduction to the topic of beauty of language in translation, which is discussed at greater length in Chapter 6.

---

1. *Church Times*, 6 April, 1985.
2. Ed. D.J. Enright; Oxford: Oxford University Press, 1985.
3. Quoted in Mullen, *The New Babel*, p. 97; cf. also recent statements found in 'canonical' or 'inter-textual' approaches to biblical study which argue that Scripture is not really translatable into extra-scriptural categories but should be read only in its own, as it were, coded forms.
4. Martin, 'A Plea for our Common Prayer', p. 13.
5. *Ritual Murder*, p. 28.

Chapter 4

THE LANGUAGE OF MYSTERY AND ITS FREEDOMS

The next two chapters take up more fully the whole issue of depth, or breadth, of language in biblical translation. The arguments, introduced briefly in the last chapter, of those literary scholars and others who have been concerned for the use of a language in translation that can adequately and imaginatively express the divine mysteries of the biblical Word are examined in more detail here. Chapter 5 carries the discussion further, and gives a chance for some modern translators to respond with their case for language in translation that is natural and clear.

Emphasis on the need for a translation language that has mystery and spirituality in it is one aspect of an emphasis on freedom. It is an emphasis demanding language that can freely and imaginatively soar upwards and plunge deeply. This emphasis has in general, and not just with reference to biblical translation, been at the forefront of theological and literary circles from the mid 1970s and throughout the 1980s. In 1987 alone three important books were published, all with the word 'imagination' or 'mystery' in their title: John McIntyre's *Faith, Theology and Imagination*,[1] Edward Robinson's *The Language of Mystery*,[2] and *The New Testament and Literary Imagination* edited by David Jasper.[3] Recently there has been considerable theological interest in those areas of European thought that have, in the past, stressed the centrality of the sense of the numinous. In an article

---

1. Edinburgh: Handsel Press, 1987.
2. London: SCM Press, 1987; cf. also the more recent book by Paul Fiddes, *Freedom and Limit: A Dialogue between Christian Literature and Theology* (London: Macmillan, 1992), which describes what is seen as the tendency of theology to hedge meaning around with more limits and less mystery than literature does, and yet asserts that both literature and theology can assist each other in creative dialogue.
3. London: Macmillan, 1987.

entitled 'The Theology of Schleiermacher',[1] John Kent pointed out that one reason for the modern interest in Schleiermacher lies in his concern with a sense of the numinous, not least because during the nineteenth century, as today, there was a marked crisis of faith, and Schleiermacher saw the approach through the numinous as crucial to the re-introduction of religion to thinking people.[2] This trend, and other more recent trends in theological thinking, have influenced the demand for the use of religious language and translation language that can express transcendental realities.

Edward Robinson's book is of particular interest for the present discussion. He writes as an artist and a theologian. The book is not primarily concerned with biblical translation, but many of its sections, such as that concerning symbolism in art, literature and religion, and on the relationship between freedom and tradition, are relevant to the concerns in this chapter. Robinson argues that symbols and images, whether verbal or artistic, are central in providing any creative communicator with essential freedoms and breadths of expression. He also says much about that communication of the transcendental realities in biblical material with which the biblical translator is concerned. In a Preface to the book, Bishop J.V. Taylor writes that for many people today who have a real sense of transcendence and a capacity for worship, traditional statements of belief have become dead: 'their annual participation in Bach's St Matthew Passion may be the most religious experience of the year'.[3] Those who ask for a due sense of mystery to be a feature of Bibles and religious language are sometimes thought to be concerned only with preservation (of traditional wordings). But it is often true that they are as much concerned with communication as with preservation; with communication of the biblical Word through language that is on the same wavelength as many people of sensitivity and depth of religious feeling.

1.   *Theology* 87.715 (January 1984), pp. 54-56.

2.   In relation to Schleiermacher's influential encouragement of biblical study at that time, it is of particular interest to note his insistence both on the importance of an objective study of the biblical text and also on a subjective, imaginative approach that would enable the meaning to be received in terms of living experience.

3.   Robinson, *The Language of Mystery*, p. vii.

The Importance of Wording that has Spaciousness

Interestingly, it is in terms of freedom and breadth that Robinson describes the imaginative symbolism for which he looks in the language of communication. He writes that, just as architecture 'at its best creates imaginative space' and 'can lead to a freeing of the spirit, an awareness of new possibilities, an enlarging of life', so verbal and artistic symbols can do the same. He says that, unlike signs which give clear and unambiguous information, symbols are part of a deeper, more spacious language of mystery. A symbol has the function of being 'the focus of a whole cluster of meanings, all related in some way to one another, but varying with the different interpretations of different people', as those people bring faith and understanding to bear on them. Again, a good symbol is seen as 'a focus for a variety of possible meanings or associations'; it has 'the power to open new doors in the mind'. A living symbol, including a verbal symbol, says Robinson, 'appeals to our freedom'[1] and to our creativity. In writing about freedom and tradition, he does not underrate the value of tradition. It is a precious 'learning from the past', but tradition, he writes, always needs renewing by creative imagination.[2]

Robinson disapproves of much of modern religious language, seeing it as unable to provide an acceptable language for transcendent experience. Writing about modern forms of worship and scriptural readings, he says, 'It is nothing less than tragic that those who have stood for renewal appear to have taken as their highest priority the literal intelligibility of all forms of worship'. For him, as far as modern expression is concerned, the imaginative freedom and breadth is to be found in art (especially abstract art).[3] Whether or not one agrees with these conclusions and unenthusiastic comments about modern religious language, one can hardly fail to catch the urgency of the plea and the importance of what is said about symbolism. For biblical translation, it is a plea for vivid, telling symbols and images through the phrases and wordings used, and a reiteration of the importance of that aspect of freedom.

1. *The Language of Mystery*, pp. 51-55.
2. *The Language of Mystery*, pp. 30, 31.
3. *The Language of Mystery*, pp. 66-69, 111.

This emphasis on symbolism in modern thinking is closely related to emphasis on metaphor and to metaphorical theology. Robinson's 'rich complexity of symbolism' ties up in many ways with Sally McFague's earlier writing on the rich complexity of metaphor (even allowing for some distinctions between symbol and metaphor). In her book *Speaking in Parables*[1] she reminded the reader of the importance of metaphorical thinking and parable form in communication, saying that 'the theological temper of our time is such that the form which holds the mystery in solution is more needed than the one that confronts it directly'.

The biblical structuralist movement is also allied to this whole line of thought. The structuralist stress on the importance of catching recurring and echoing motifs in a biblical passage is akin to Robinson's stress on the importance of having vivid, telling symbols and images built into the language used in worship and translation. John Drury has described biblical structuralism as 'treating a text very much as if it were music, noticing the development and inter-twining of themes, letting a pure attention to the text uncover the inward resonance of its shapes'.[2] Although the biblical structuralist approach as a whole may not seem entirely convincing to many biblical scholars, the value of its concentration on the importance for communication of that which goes beyond mere precision of meaning in words should be accepted.

Translating Mystery in Particular Biblical Verses

To relate this background practically to the translation of the Bible, I return in rather more detail to the phrase highlighted by Stephen Prickett, 'and after the fire a still small voice', a notable piece of

1. (Philadelphia: Fortress Press, 1975), p. 81. See also J.Soskice, *Metaphors and Religious Language* (Oxford: Clarendon Press, 1985), pp. 133-34, where the importance of the use of metaphor not only in religious but also in scientific language is stressed: e.g. for referring to 'little understood features of the natural world without laying claims to unrevisable knowledge about them': note also the further point made that 'the vagueness of metaphorical terms, rather than rendering metaphors unsuitable to scientific language, is just what makes them indispensable to it'.

2. Editorial in *Theology* 88.724 (July 1985), p. 254. See also Drury's chapters on passages in the Gospels of Mark and Luke, in Alter and Kermode (eds.), *A Literary Guide to the Bible*.

'verbal symbolism' with huge and wide appeal. I also look at some comments by other literary scholars on particular pieces of modern translation, and their pleas for a more spiritually imaginative translation.

Prickett goes carefully into the phrase as given in Hebrew: *qôl d^emāmâ daqqâ*. He gives as a literal translation, 'a voice of thin silence'. He stresses the depth of the dimensions of meaning to be seen in this phrase, a phrase full of mystery and of the ambiguities of an event both natural and supernatural. He considers that those dimensions would still be best caught in English by the AV's 'a still small voice', where the literal 'thin' (*daqqâ*) becomes 'small', the noun 'silence' (*d^emāmâ*) becomes an English adjective 'still', and *qôl* is translated 'voice'.

Prickett quotes Aharon Wiener[1] as saying that, whereas the Hebrew phrase is usually interpreted or translated as referring to a 'quiet voice' or a 'gentle breeze' or occasionally a 'shrill whistling', yet he prefers to be more literal and to bring out the sense of 'the nothingness of silence'. Wiener also says that the three Hebrew words are taken in the Talmud as meaning, in effect, 'soundless stillness'. Wiener comments that for Elijah 'in the nothingness of silence God's will becomes audible'. In phrases that echo Rudolf Otto and Søren Kierkegaard, Prickett quotes Wiener as speaking of the 'mysterium tremendum et fascinans' of Elijah's theophany that comes through in the Hebrew phrase.[2] The phrase in 1 Kgs 19.12 is taken to suggest a tension of opposites confronting Elijah, and a mystery in which the eternal depth and vastness of the divine otherness on the one hand, and of the intimacy of divine personal nearness on the other, are both present. The symbolism of the three-word phrase in Hebrew is seen as nothing less than that. In addition to what Prickett quotes from Wiener, the whole Hebrew phrase in question is found in one of the Qumran scrolls describing the divine presence and the divine word experienced in worship. This gives us another glimpse of the deeper dimensions of the phrase.

As implied earlier, Prickett sees modern translators as too easily gliding over the deep, subtle patterns of coded words, symbols and

---

1. The quotations are from Wiener's book *The Prophet Elijah in the Development of Judaism* (London: Routledge & Kegan Paul, 1978), p. 14.

2. *Words and the Word*, p. 7.

images which run through Scripture, and settling for what he regards
as merely secularized and naturalistic interpretations and translations.
Prickett makes clear how translations in the past, other than the AV,
translated the Hebrew phrase. The LXX has φωνὴ αὔρας λεπτής:
φωνή, like the Hebrew *qôl*, means either 'voice' or 'sound', but the
Greek phrase is probably to be taken in 1 Kgs 19.12 as 'the sound of a
gentle breeze'. The Vulgate has *sibilus aurae tenuis*, 'the whisper of a
gentle breeze'. Prickett takes these to be mistranslations, and dislikes
the modern renderings that follow such interpretations. Although he
admits that any translation which contains 'breeze' or 'air' catches
some sense of the Holy Spirit's presence, since in the ages of belief
'breeze' was associated with the Holy Spirit, and although he regards
the GNB phrase in 19.12 ('the sound of a gentle whisper') as better
than other modern translations, yet he sees all these renderings as
leaning too far towards the natural.[1] He feels that, in dealing with all
the images of wind, earthquake and fire as well as with the three-word
Hebrew phrase, modern interpreters and translators tend to concentrate too much on the outward natural meaning, and allow this to
become separated from the inward spiritual meaning. As a result, he
says, there is no adequate language for the spiritual dimension. He
writes of how, in the use of words, 'wind' has got separated from
'spirit', '"natural fire" from "Pentecostal"', and the "shaking of the
earth" from the "shaking of the foundations"'.[2] The biblical phrases,
he argues, should not be 'decoded' into ordinary language but left and
allowed to signify the reality.

Prickett finds Coleridge's approach (and that of Blake and others) to
be a deeper basis for theories of translation than modern approaches.
The latter, he says, work on the idea of being able to know objectively
and simply what the original author meant, in a way unrelated to the
insights that come from poetic imagination and literary tradition.
Prickett is distressed by what seem to him presumptuous attempts by
modern translators at intellectual 'mastery' over the original text. In
his view, the true attitude of translators should be one of submission
before the otherness, and possibly the inscrutability, of the original.
Through submission, he believes, the translator not so much becomes
master of the text but undergoes a real experience of newness and

1. Prickett, *Words and the Word*, p. 12.
2. *Words and the Word*, p. 175.

challenge; so creative change passes into the language into which he is translating. Translators' attempts at unambiguous language must give way before the biblical images which are more than ephemeral. At the end of his book Prickett distinguishes between two systems of interpretation and translation: 'those which claim to possess the Word, and those which are capable of being translated by it'.[1] For him a piece of biblical phrasing is like an icon in which we explore mystery as well as meaning. To demand from a translation that it should render the original phrase in terms of straight unambiguous meaning is, in his view, to rule out any possibility of growing meaning, or new meanings, coming out of biblical phrases. Prickett describes as 'an idea whose time has come' the application of 'the notion of the poetic' to the understanding of the Bible.[2] He reminds us that the poets of eighteenth-century Britain rediscovered the Bible as 'the source of the poetic sublime',[3] that this resulted in the flowing of creative biblical images into English literature and culture, and that the same secret waits to be rediscovered by us today. Undoubtedly these criticisms and reminders constitute the most substantial reactions and criticisms that the new versions have faced.

Prickett has not been alone in seeing mystery in the phrase in 1 Kgs 19.12. All interpreters and translators have asked themselves the question, 'Is the mystery and symbolism here the mystery and symbolism of an almost imperceptible voice speaking, or is it the mystery and symbolism of an almost imperceptible hushed sound before some great event or utterance, or is it the mystery and symbolism of an almost imperceptible sound of movement in the air?' Nor do Prickett's comments mean that the interpreter or translator should give up all interest in original word meanings or necessarily agree with Prickett that the AV alone has approached the spiritual meaning of the phrase. On the contrary, since Prickett does not attempt any wide examination of different interpretations of the passage, one can hardly avoid mentioning a number of issues that arise.

---

1. *Words and the Word*, p. 242; cf. Ernst Fuchs's 'new hermeneutic', with its demand that the interpreter of the biblical text must be engaged by the text and 'acted upon', rather than approach it as an outside objective observer.

2. *Words and the Word*, pp. 225, 242.

3. *Words and the Word*, p. 202.

1. The word *qôl* comes twice in 19.12 and the following verse. In 19.13 it certainly means 'voice', being followed by the actual words spoken. But in 19.12 the translation 'sound' (i.e. a sound preliminary to the voice and speaking in the next verse) is a possible option, as *qôl* can mean either 'voice' or 'sound' in Hebrew.

2. *dᵉmāmâ*, as used in the Bible, has a wide range of meanings. It can mean 'silence', but it can also mean a murmuring or moaning sound such as a breeze makes.[1] In relation to 'silence', it has the meaning 'hush' or 'calm' (Ps. 107.29, for example); it sometimes refers to a hushed moment before an utterance (e.g. Job 4.16 'there was silence [*dᵉmāmâ*] and I heard a voice saying' in the AV). So, in 1 Kgs 19.12, a modern translation such as 'after the fire, a faint hushed sound' is a possible option.

3. The question of the way in which *dᵉmāmâ* relates to other words in the phrase is important. Not only is there the question of whether it means (literally) 'a voice of thin silence', or 'a sound of thin silence' but also the question of whether the 'silence' word is part of the character of the sound or the voice (e.g. 'a still small voice') or is a silence preceding the voice mentioned in the following verse?

4. The question of whether there are any other verses in the Old Testament that shed light on the meaning of 1 Kgs 19.12 is important. What has traditionally been called Bengel's Canon, according to which one interprets scripture by scripture, does not fulfil every requirement in interpretation, but it has its uses. 2 Sam. 5.24 and the meaning of *qôl* there may help us to interpret our present verse. In it *qôl* means a hushed sound in a movement in the trees for which David is told to listen, indicating a divine supernatural presence and movement: 'when thou hearest the sound [*qôl*] of a going in the tops of the mulberry trees...thou shalt bestir thyself: for then shall the Lord go out before thee [AV]; that may offer a parallel and clue to the *qôl* and its nature as experienced by Elijah. If some similarity between the verses is accepted, translations of the 1 Kgs 19.12 phrases that use the word 'sound' rather than 'voice' do not necessarily need to be seen as predominantly 'secularized' interpretations, but rather as having a supernatural reference. The fact that English culture has known and cherished 1 Kgs 19.12 through several centuries in a translation

1. L.H. Brockington, *Theological Wordbook of the Bible* (London: SCM Press, 1947).

containing 'voice' rather than 'sound' (and that that translation has helped to unlock truths of God for many people) may be taken to mean that it must remain the only used translation for all time. But that is not necessarily so, and arguments for keeping the options open are strong.

However, when all that is said, the force and importance of Prickett's emphasis and thesis in relation to 1 Kgs 19.12 and other biblical translation should be recorded. His reinforcing emphasis on the importance of the translator catching the sense of mystery in the biblical phrasing is badly needed. In relation to translating 19.12, some modern English phrasings in the use of the word 'murmur' (for *dᵉmāmâ*) have not been strong or resonant, partly because 'murmur' is a word with several meanings in English. Prickett has forcibly reminded translators that this verse is to do with silence. It is interesting that the NRSV in 1989 gives the translation, 'and after the fire a sound of sheer silence'. That may not prove to be a definitive modern translation, but, like the rather more rhythmic 'faint hushed sound', it takes us deep into some of the mystery and the symbolism contained in the original phrase.

Other Champions of Depth of Language

We need at this point to broaden the discussion beyond the single example in 1 Kings, and look at what has been written by other literary scholars concerning the translation of other biblical passages. A classic article written by the poet and scholar T.R. Henn and published in 1962[1] constitutes one of the earliest substantial critiques of twentieth-century styles of biblical translation, though at its time of writing most major modern translations had not been completed or published. Henn's approach was a temperate and sensitive one. He said that there were both gains and losses in the modern versions that he knew. But, like Prickett, he emphasized the importance of the imaginative overtones attached to traditional scriptural phrases over the centuries. He quotes, with approval, some words of David Daiches, 'The Bible is not only what modern scholarship holds the text to mean: it is also what the text has meant to many generations of devout readers'.[2] Henn

1. 'The Bible as Literature', in *Peakes Commentary* (London: Nelson, 1962).
2. D. Daiches, *Literary Essays* (1956).

compares the text of the AV with some rich antique bronze that has
acquired, over the years, a patina of treasured colour and character;
he says that much of the English of the AV has acquired 'a patina of
meaning, penumbral or multiplex in character' and that when the
necessary work of discovering the original meaning has been done,
'much that is mysterious, much that is irrational is left: and (for
poetry may rightly be prophecy too) the penumbral meaning may
extend, to our mind, far beyond an "accurate" modern version'.

Henn cites the phrase 'the Ancient of days', in the AV of Dan. 7.9 as
a phrase whose full meaning is no longer only its original meaning of
'old', but 'is born of man's imagination, striving to picture that God
that answered Job out of the whirlwind, perhaps as Blake saw him'.
Henn would not have liked the phrase, 'one who had been living for
ever' which corresponds to 'the Ancient of days' in one modern
version published since his day. Henn also cites the phrase, 'works of
darkness' in the AV translation of Rom. 13.12, 'let us...cast off the
works of darkness', and compares it with J.B. Phillips's version, 'the
things that men do in the dark'. He believes that there are gains for the
modern reader in some of Phillips's other phrases in this passage, but
that in this case there is loss. He likes the 'width of reference' of the
AV here, and what he calls its 'deliberate imprecision'; the phrase
'works of darkness' carrying with it 'an accepted set of references'.
Paul, says Henn, is not only talking literally of things that people often
do in the dark such as murder and adultery, but (within the whole
night–day contrast in the passage) 'of everything that proceeds,
positively or negatively, from the unenlightened soul'.

Discussing the words of the Book of Common Prayer, including its
biblical material, John Betjeman wrote, 'where the words are a bit
vague and archaic, that makes them grand and historic. The words
give me time to meditate and pray: they are so familiar, they are like
my birthplace, and I don't want them pulled down.'[1] That statement
goes further than simply saying that old words must be retained on the
grounds of familiarity, though there is an honest admission of that
too. The phrase 'time to meditate and pray' represents the feeling
expressed by many people in reaction to policies of modernization in
liturgical and biblical language; the feeling that what matters is not

---

1.   Quoted in Morris (ed.), *Ritual Murder.*

only the biblical or liturgical words themselves but the thoughts that they trigger off in the hearer or reader.[1]

Dr Gerald Hammond, in his book *The Making of the Bible*,[2] pleads that what he calls the 'cultivated ambiguity and evocative vagueness' of many Hebrew poetic phrases should be retained in the form translated by the AV. He protests against the 'fixed and unreverberative meaning' which the NEB usually provides. He is critical of what he describes as the 'narrowly interpretative' approach of modern translators. In 1 Sam. 25.37, a passage about Nabal, he prefers the phrase 'his heart died within him' (AV) to the translation 'he had a seizure' (NEB/REB). In Prov. 14.13 he prefers 'Even in laughter the heart is sorrowful, and the end of that mirth is heaviness', as given in the AV, to the NEB's 'Even in laughter the heart may grieve, and mirth may end in sorrow', commenting that the NEB rendering 'has begun to interpret away the inconsolability of the original'. In Mt. 5.5, about the meek, he prefers the AV 'for they shall inherit the earth' to the NEB's 'they shall have the earth for a possession', saying that the latter is 'aridly scholarly'. In general, Hammond endorses the view that only those who are rooted in the poetic tradition of English literature can really catch the breadth of meaning contained in many passages of Scripture. In his contribution to *A Literary Guide to the Bible*[3] he writes, 'we have learned to prize ambiguity in poetry, and we see its roots in the English tradition largely in the work of John Donne and the metaphysical poets who followed him'. He also gives considerable attention to what he sees as the significance of the AV's literal retaining of some of the oddness of Hebrew syntax (the latter phrase is his own

---

1. There is of course something comparable here to St Augustine of Hippo's phrase about dogmas being 'fences round a mystery'. Something comparable also with T.S. Eliot's well-known words from *Four Quartets*, where he speaks of 'being occupied with frontiers of consciousness beyond which words fail, though meanings still exist'. The limitations of the actual words is the point. T.S. Eliot also speaks of the provisional nature of meanings. In *Little Gidding*, in the context of reflection on his favourite topic of the mystery of time and eternity and of ends and beginnings, he says that from inside 'the husk of meaning' we shall find in the moment of ultimate fulfilment that the real thing will break out: namely, the 'purpose' behind words and meaning.

2. Manchester: Carcanet, 1980.

3. 'English Translations of the Bible', in Alter and Kermode (eds.), *A Literary Guide to the Bible*, pp. 647-66.

description). This refers to Hebrew's repeated 'and's (*waw*) and various other formula-phrases and techniques of repetition which, as discussed in Chapter 1, are omitted or not taken over into modern translations. He finds these points of syntax to be often, in the context, 'expressive', 'prophetic' and 'evocative'. He writes, 'more important than the translation of words is the translation of syntax'.

There are important protests and positive points being made in these quotations from different writers. T.R. Henn was right to argue for the retention of something like the AV's width of reference in Rom. 13.12, 'let us cast off the works of darkness'. In contrast to J.B. Phillips, more recent modern translators, while spelling out the Greek phrase literally (e.g. 'the things that belong to the dark', or similar, in the GNB and the NJB), retain a considerable breadth of reference.

Gerald Hammond's point about 1 Sam. 25.37 is a reminder that it is dangerous for translators to try to leave behind altogether some of the AV's poetic and literal phrases, however imprecise and vague they may be in one sense. The NIV with 'his heart failed him', the NAB with 'his courage died within him', and the NEB and REB with 'he had a seizure', all give clear versions, distinguishing for the reader the dying of Nabal's heart in 25.37 from mention of what is usually called death in the next verse, 25.38. But Hammond's plea for 'his heart died within him' to be retained, though raising problems of clarity, is a healthy challenge. The NJB's phrasing is the same as that of the AV.

Another writer from the world of literature, Andor Gomme,[1] made his plea for a sense of mystery in the language of translation in terms that uncompromisingly call for the retaining of a special language for religious talk and biblical translation, different from the language of the world. He defines this as 'a religious language within English',[2] using the traditional English translation of the important religious words. He further defines this special language as 'the language of belief', and as a language with some 'triumphant strangeness' in it, to get across the triumphant strangeness of what the Bible says. He makes a distinction between that type of special language and another, bad type of special language which he calls 'pulpitese' and which he says modern translators use. An example of this is a phrase such as the

---

1.   In 'The New Religious English', in Morris (ed.), *Ritual Murder*, pp. 75-98.
2.   Gomme, 'The New Religious English', p. 77.

modern versions' 'my dear people' or 'dear friends' instead of the
AV's 'beloved' (see 1 Jn 4.7). Gomme's special language will retain the
important old words in English like 'righteousness', 'soul', 'blessed',
'pious', 'devout'. He describes these as 'essentially religious words'[1]
that are indispensable in that precise form. They are God-related
words and not humanistic words, he says. They 'bring promises' and
inspiration, not just information; 'blessed' brings more promises than
the modern 'happy' in biblical contexts. If these words are lost, the
Word loses its power among us. Contemporary language, Gomme
considers, often has no words for the timeless concepts of eternity,
righteousness and sin, since our age has lost faith in those concepts.[2]
Secular language is inadequate language for the translation of the
Bible, and has an inadequate theology behind it.

His examples of modern translation are taken, in the main, from the
1966 unrevised edition of the JB. Writing about Gen. 1.2, he expresses
his dislike of the JB's phrase 'God's spirit hovered over the water'. He
comments, 'hovering is what kestrels and helicopters do, and the
ludicrous impression is given that God might be trying to peer
through the darkness to see what was in the water; so the creation of
light which follows has the air of a pantomime trick'. Gomme sees
such modern translations as 'an attempt to reduce God to the language
of commonsense'. He prefers the AV's wording, 'the Spirit of God
moved upon the face of the waters'. He says, 'I do not know whether
this is a more or less "accurate" translation than the other; and I know
that I cannot understand it with my rational mind, for there is in the
language itself that which shares in the unfathomable mystery of
creation'.

On 1 Thess. 5.14 Gomme criticizes the Jerusalem Bible's 'warn the
idlers' preferring the AV's 'warn them that are unruly', saying that in
the JB here 'everything is weakened' and Paul's words made merely
'tentative' and 'unconfident', whereas the AV 'keeps closely to the
Greek' and 'gives firm injunctions'.

On Jer. 17.9 he says that the JB's 'the heart is more devious than
any other thing, perverse too' misses 'the grim and stark view of the
human heart' found in the original which is reflected well in the AV's
'the heart is deceitful above all things, and desperately wicked'. He

1. 'The New Religious English', p. 92.
2. 'The New Religious English', p. 84.

comments that 'perverse' in the JB appears as a sort of mild afterthought.

These last comments of Gomme on Jer. 17.9 have some force. Leaving aside his implication that behind the JB's choice of words lies a theologically weak view of human sin, many would agree that he is right to suggest that the word 'perverse' gives too weak a meaning in modern English, the term is now often used of behaviour that is simply 'contrary' or 'wayward'. *naš*, the original Hebrew word, is a strong word, meaning either 'in a desperate, hopeless state' (cf. the AV 'desperately wicked', the RSV 'desperately corrupt', and the REB 'desperately sick') or 'incorrigibly bad' (as the NJB) or 'incurable' (as the NIV and the GNB). The AV uses 'incurable' to translate *naš* in five out of seven usages in the Old Testament. Although 'perverse' has a strong sense when used by the AV in such verses as Mt. 17.17 ('O faithless and perverse generation'), and the Shorter Oxford English Dictionary gives as the first two meanings of 'perverse' the strong terms 'perverted', 'wicked'; and although the NRSV in 1989 moved from the RSV's 'desperately corrupt' to this very word 'perverse' in Jer. 17.9, yet it may be true that 'perverse' in modern usage has lost too much of its original meaning to be the right word here.

In Gomme's other criticisms, one can only say that his case is undoubtedly weakened for many people by his throwaway remark, in relation to 'hovered over the water' in Gen. 1.2: 'I do not know whether this' (the JB translation) 'is a more or less accurate translation than the other' (the AV translation). Such a remark seems, provocatively, to give no place at all to considerations of accuracy. Gomme does not even mention that the Hebrew verb used in the original of Gen. 1.2 is the same word used in Deut. 32.11 of an eagle hovering over its young to protect them, or that this piece of poetic imagery has, in some people's view, a claim to be brought out in the translation of Gen. 1.2. I happen to prefer the translation 'moved over the water' (given by the AV, the RSV and the GNB) with the solemnity of its long 'o' vowel in 'moved'. I am also attracted to the translation 'swept over the water' (given by the NEB, the NAB, the NJB, and the NRSV). But I think that the translation 'hovered over the water' deserves serious consideration and discussion and cannot be merely laughed out of court by comments about helicopters. The NIV and the REB, both published some years after Andor Gomme's comments, settle for the translation 'hovered over the water'.

The same point applies to his comments about 1 Thess. 5.14. I agree that the translation 'warn the unruly' may be the right one; of recent translations, the NJB follows that line with its 'admonish those who are undisciplined'. But I find it difficult to accept Gomme's lack of any acknowledgment that the original Greek word (ἄτακτος) has two other meanings besides 'unruly': 'careless' (as the NEB) and 'idle' (used either in the form 'idle' or 'idler' by the REB, the NRSV, the GNB, the TNT, and the NIV, in addition to the JB). I find it difficult that Gomme attributes the JB's choice of 'warn the idlers' (rather than 'warn the unruly') to a 'modish' desire for weaker and more tentative words rather than to a genuine exploration of word meanings.

However, to end this discussion, with all its detailed controversial points, the central importance of the general emphasis underlying all that has been quoted in this chapter from the 'poet-theologians' and the literary scholars needs to be reaffirmed. It is, as the title of this chapter has tried to indicate, an emphasis on freedom from all that is merely pedestrian or pedantic, and an emphasis positively on the use of poetic imagination in the use of language.

A Modern Translation of Psalm 63 and of the Opening of the Letter to the Hebrews

Some of these points may be tested out here against the REB's rendering of Ps. 63.1-8 and against the NIV's translation of Heb. 1.1-4, two passages of profound and meditative scriptural writing.

Psalm 63.1-8

		AV	REB
63.1		O God, thou art my God; early will I seek thee: my soul thirsteth for thee, my flesh longeth for thee in a dry and thirsty land, where no water is;	God, you are my God; I seek you eagerly with a heart that thirsts for you and a body wasted with longing for you, like a dry land, parched and devoid of water.
	2	To see thy power and thy glory, so as I have seen thee in the sanctuary.	With such longing, I see you in the sanctuary and behold your power and glory.
	3	Because thy loving kindness is better than life, my lips shall praise thee.	Your unfailing love is better than life; therefore I shall sing your praises.

4	Thus will I bless thee while I live: I will lift up my hands in thy name.	Thus all my life I bless you; in your name I lift my hands in prayer.
5	My soul shall be satisfied as with marrow and fatness; and my mouth shall praise thee with joyful lips:	I am satisfied as with a rich feast and there is a shout of praise on my lips.
6	When I remember thee upon my bed, and meditate on thee in the night watches.	I call you to mind on my bed and meditate on you in the night watches,
7	Because thou hast been my help, therefore in the shadow of thy wings will I rejoice.	for you have been my help and I am safe in the shadow of your wings.
8	My soul followeth hard after thee: thy right hand upholdeth me.	I follow you closely and your right hand upholds me.

Notes

63.1. The AV has, in effect, 'I will seek'; the REB has, 'I seek'. Why the difference? The same issue over the tenses of verbs arises in vv. 2, 4, 5, 8, where different tenses are given in the various English translations. The reason is that in the original Hebrew verb forms (which are more forms than tenses), it is often an open question whether the time of the action is past, present or future. As mentioned in Chapter 2, Hebrew verb forms are concerned with the type of the action (completed or uncompleted) rather than with the time of the action. A Hebrew 'perfect' verb form is concerned with completed action and, for example in the case of the verb 'to do', includes the sense 'I will have done' as well as 'I have done', 'I did', or 'I am in a state of having done'. A Hebrew 'imperfect' verb form is concerned with uncompleted action and includes the sense of not only 'I was doing', but also 'I will do', 'I may do', or 'I am doing'. Translators since the early centuries have been guided in reaching the meaning of the verb forms by how the ancient translations of the Old Testament, for example into Greek or Latin, interpreted the meaning. For 63.1, both the LXX translators in the last two centuries before Christ, and the Vulgate in the late fourth century AD, put a Greek or Latin present tense, followed by the REB's 'I seek', and in most modern translators similarly. However, some translators have taken the Hebrew to signify what is in English a future tense, and this is reflected in the AV's translation.

The AV has 'seek thee early'. The REB puts 'seek you eagerly'. The original Hebrew verb is connected with the word for 'dawn'. The use of the verb in this verse may be literally tied to the idea of 'seeking at dawn' or may mean more generally 'seeking eagerly, at the first opportunity, with longing'. The verb perhaps implies a mixture of both. The LXX translates the Hebrew verb with a phrase that, judging from its use elsewhere in the LXX, either means, 'I get up very early in the morning to be with you' or, more generally, 'I seek you diligently'. In the Taizé Community version of the Psalms in English[1] one finds the splendid phrase here 'I seek your face at dawn'.

63.2. The reasons for the variation between the AV perfect tense ('have seen') and the REB present tense ('behold') have already been mentioned. A modern Jewish translation[2] brings in the future tense here: 'I shall behold'. The Vulgate gave roughly the same sense as the AV, and most modern translations have something similar such as 'I have gazed on you' (NJB). But the LXX translated the Hebrew by a phrase meaning 'I have appeared before you'.

63.3. The AV has 'loving kindness'; the REB has 'unfailing love'. The basic meaning of the Hebrew word here used (*hesed*) is 'faithful, loyal love'.

63.5 The AV has 'marrow and fatness'; the REB has 'a rich feast'. The Jewish Publication Society Version gives a marginal note that the literal meaning is 'suet and fat'.

63.5. The AV has 'my mouth shall praise thee with joyful lips'; the REB has 'there is a shout of praise on my lips'. The Hebrew word translated as 'joyful' by the AV literally means 'singing' or 'shouting aloud'. The NEB 'I wake the echoes with thy praise', uses a phrase used in Middle English for making a place echo with great shouts of joy. Peter Levi's translation of the Psalms has the same exuberant type of phrasing: 'my mouth is full of praises and shouts of gladness'. The original Hebrew literally says, 'my mouth shall praise', not 'my mouth shall praise thee'.

1.   Taizé Community, *Psalms from Taizé* (London: Mowbrays, 1983).

2.   *The Book of Psalms: A New Translation according to the Traditional Hebrew Text* (Philadelphia: Jewish Publication Society of America, 1972).

63.7. The AV has 'in the shadow of thy wings will I rejoice'; the REB has 'I am safe in the shadow of your wings'. The Hebrew verb translated as 'rejoice' in the AV is literally, 'sing, cry aloud'. In the NEB/REB one misses this. The NIV has 'Because you are my help, I sing in the shadow of your wings'. The NRSV has 'in the shadow of your wings I sing for joy'. But the NEB/REB, evidently trying to maintain the emphasis in the first clause of the verse about God's protection, sees the central meaning of the sense of joy as a sense of safety. Knox had a similar idea, adding 'gladly', rendering it, 'gladly I take shelter under thy wings'.

63.8. The AV has 'my soul followeth hard after thee'; the REB has 'I follow you closely'. The LXX wording was more similar to 'my soul has been clasped to your back, your right hand has come to my aid', with the pictorial imagery being very strong. But the REB follows rather the line of the Hebrew and the AV (the Hebrew verb means literally 'to cleave to, to keep close to'), and sees the central meaning as one of spiritual closeness, dependence and following.

Hebrews 1.1-4

AV	NIV
1.1 God, who at sundry times and in divers manners spake in time past unto the fathers by the prophets,	In the past God spoke to our forefathers through the prophets at many times and in various ways,
2 Hath in these last days spoken unto us by his Son, whom he hath appointed heir of all things, by whom also he made the worlds;	but in these last days he has spoken to us by his Son whom he appointed heir of all things, and through whom he made the universe.
3 Who being the brightness of his glory, and the express image of his person, and upholding all things by the word of his power, when he had by himself purged our sins, sat down on the right hand of the Majesty on high;	The Son is the radiance of God's glory and the exact representation of his being, sustaining all things by his powerful word. After he had provided purification for sins, he sat down at the right hand of the Majesty in heaven.
4 Being made so much better than the angels, as he hath by inheritance obtained a more excellent name than they.	So he became as much superior to the angels as the name he has inherited is superior to theirs.

Notes

This passage is the beginning of one of the great traditional readings for Christmas Day and the Festival of the Nativity. Some scholars think that vv. 3 and 4 contain an early liturgical hymn, or strong traces of it. The whole passage is one long sentence in Greek, with many subsidiary clauses, a structure reproduced precisely by the AV. This makes the passage in the AV hard to read well aloud, which is a pity for one of the great classic pieces of AV wording.

1.3. The AV has 'brightness'; the NIV has 'radiance'. The original Greek word signifies either radiance (glory radiating out) or reflection (glory reflecting back). Many modern translations take the second sense (NRSV, GNB, NJB, NAB).

The AV has 'the express image'; the NIV has 'the exact representation'. The NIV's full phrase 'the exact representation of his being' is found in the modern age as far back as Weymouth's New Testament translation, and is happily retained here. The Greek word translated 'express image' in the AV literally means 'imprint' or 'impress', and the imagery is that of a seal pressed onto wax or clay.

The AV has 'of his person'; the NIV has 'of his being'. The Greek word is ὑπόστασις and means 'being'. In Latin it was translated by the word for 'substance'. Since early Greek theologians used it to describe the being of the three 'persons' of the Trinity, it came to be translated as 'person'.

Chapter 5

THE FREEDOM OF NATURAL LANGUAGE

The GNB states in the Preface to the 1976 edition that its policy as a 'common-language Bible' is to try and use language that is 'natural, clear, simple, and unambiguous'. The challenge to that statement by S. Prickett and others, as we have seen, has been a strong one, expressed most succinctly in Prickett's well-known dictum that 'religion is not about things that are natural, clear, simple and unambiguous'.[1] However, attempts to get the Bible read and heard in language that is natural and readily intelligible continue to be made, and not only from the so-called area of GNB readership. In 1991 BBC radio started a series of daily ten-minute readings from the Bible. In the planning of the series and the discussions of the responsible religious advisory committee, there seems to have been a good deal of controversy as to whether such readings should be from the AV or from one of the modern translations. Reportedly, during these discussions, a Roman Catholic bishop said bluntly, 'I personally think that the King James Version is unintelligible'.[2] Are the positions incompatible? Is Prickett's plea for a language of transcendence that can take wing incompatible with the GNB's and Roman Catholic bishop's pleas for a natural language that can move with freedom among its hearers?

Most of the translators in the mid-twentieth century would have agreed with Prickett that biblical translators have to take seriously the sense of poetry, mystery and awe in much biblical material and not just ride roughshod over it. J.B. Phillips, as mentioned in an earlier

---

1. 'What Do the Translators Think they Are up to?', *Theology* (November, 1977).

2. The radio correspondent of the *Church Times* (2 August 1991) wrote of the committee, 'one member, the Roman Catholic Bishop of Portsmouth, Crispian Hollis, is reported to have said, "I personally..."' The bishop was reported as acknowledging the 'sonority and beauty' of the AV.

chapter, changed his style of language when he had finished translating the New Testament letters and began translating some of the Old Testament prophets and the book of Revelation. He wrote, 'if the (biblical) author intends a mystery, then the translator must transmit a mystery'. C.H. Dodd, director of the whole NEB venture, spoke a great deal about both the transcendent biblical mysteries that the translator encounters and about the whole strangeness of the ancient world whose words had to be translated. In a noted university lecture he said that the New Testament interpreter and translator must be someone who has 'entered into that strange first-century world, and has felt the whole strangeness', and who will then 'return to our world, and give to the truth he has discerned a body out of the stuff of our own thought'. And the GNB itself would surely declare that its aim was never to reduce everything in the biblical material to a bland simplicity. All that being said, however, all modern translators insist that they are not interested in language that is artificial in any way. This central point is taken up in this chapter.

Reality and Artificiality, Directness and Ambiguity

While there is a deep truth in the statement that religion is not about things that are natural, clear, simple and unambiguous (and that truth has enriched discussion about the translation of the Bible), it can be used to skirt around the equally true statement that religion is not about things that are, in any usual sense of the word, artificial. The reality or artificiality of either traditional or modern versions of the Bible is perhaps the basic issue when examining the language in which the biblical material is conveyed. Cecil Day Lewis pinpointed this matter, making a distinction between the right sort of artificiality (i.e. stylization, rhetoric, dramatic figures of speech) and the wrong sort. Writing, in 1966, the foreword to one of his translations of Virgil, he wrote, 'the poet-translator must use the language and rhythms of his own day, I believe, or else he will fall into the wrong sort of artificiality'.[1] On the same principle he translated biblical canticles into modern English. It is not only people of an earlier generation who have spoken of artificiality in this connection. Archbishop Habgood

---

1.   C. Day Lewis, *The Eclogues: The Georgics* (Oxford: Oxford University Press, 1983), p. vii.

draws attention to artificiality as a central issue in religious language. He writes of the need for a language 'that transcends the mundane but which is not so far removed that it creates an inhibiting sense of artificiality'.[1] In the literary field Dr Northropp Frye and Dr Gerald Hammond have encouraged open discussion on this matter by frank acknowledgment that the AV often uses the same sort of well-rounded language for passages that are poetic in the original, and those that are prosaic or conversational.[2] There is a good measure of agreement all round about some traditional words that now sound artificial. In Jas 2.2 the NKJV joins other modern versions in putting 'fine' where the AV had 'goodly', 'a man with a gold ring in goodly apparel'. But there is less agreement on other well-known verses. In Mt. 11.28 the AV reads, 'Come unto me, all ye that labour and are heavy laden'; in the NJB, in place of 'are heavy laden', we find 'are overburdened'. Both translations have power. Some people will want only 'heavy laden', seeing it as the natural language for a solemn word of the Lord such as this. Others may welcome a strong modern idiomatic word such as 'overburdened' here, seeing that as the natural expression, and finding 'heavy laden' a little artificial for modern ears. The word 'over-burdened' retains the literal imagery.

Involved in the GNB statement of its policy is the issue of directness of meaning. This quality has been claimed both by traditionalists for the AV and by innovators for the modern versions. As mentioned in Chapter 3, traditionalists have pointed out euphemistic phrases in modern versions such as the RSV's 'there will be an odour' in Jn 11.39, where the AV has the robust 'he stinketh'. (Happily the NRSV and NKJV have the robust and more suitable, 'there is a stench'.) The charge of excessive paraphrase and loss of subtleties at the edge of the meanings of words, and other forms of indirectness, is often levelled against modern versions. On the other hand, there are verses in the Gospels which are difficult to read nowadays in the AV with any directness of meaning. Mk 14.33 is a central verse, where the AV's rendering that Jesus in Gethsemane 'began to be sore amazed and very heavy' expresses weakly and indirectly for modern ears the terrified

---

1. J. Habgood, *Church and Nation in a Secular Age* (London: Darton, Longman & Todd, 1983), Chapter 8.
2. Frye *The Great Code*, p. 215. Hammond, 'English Translations of the Bible', p. 650.

surprise and dismay (and the consequent theological implications) which the original Greek words convey. The REB has the more direct 'horror and anguish overwhelmed him', and most modern versions are similar.

If there is a right and a wrong sort of artificiality, there is also a right and a wrong sort of ambiguity. Professor C.F.D. Moule, one of the NEB translators, stated the need to recognize multiple meanings in some biblical phrases, and said explicitly that the translator should sometimes use ambiguous terms. He writes,

> Occasionally the Greek seems to be deliberately ambiguous, with the intention of conveying a multiple meaning, a familiar feature of Johannine style. Here the translator may be hard put to it to be ambiguous enough. In Jn 3.8 the (NEB) translators were compelled, like their predecessors, to use both 'wind' and 'spirit' to represent 'pneuma', a single Greek word with both meanings.[1]

Jn 3.8 in the NEB reads, 'the wind blows where it wills; you hear the sound of it, but you do not know where it comes from or where it is going. So with everyone who is born from spirit'. On the other hand, the Introduction to the NEB New Testament is outspoken about what it calls some 'comfortable ambiguities' that have existed in traditional biblical translations where the modern translator may be in a position or may have a duty in the interests of clarity to try and resolve the ambiguity.The NEB New Testament translators say,

> We have conceived our task to be that of understanding the original as precisely as we could, using all available aids, and then saying again in our own native idiom what we believed the author to be saying in his. We have found that in practice this frequently compelled us to make decisions where the older method of translation allowed a comfortable ambiguity. In such places we have been aware that we take a risk, but we have thought it our duty to take the risk rather than remain on the fence.

Moule cites Col. 3.10 as an example of a verse in which the NEB felt bound to clear up an ambiguity where the AV translated the verse in an ambiguous, although literal, way. The AV has, 'ye...have put on the new man, which is renewed in knowledge after the image of him that created him'. The NEB, and the REB, clears up not only the

---

1. C.F.D. Moule, *Cambridge History of the Bible* (Cambridge: Cambridge University Press, 1963), III, pp. 379-82.

awkwardness of the two 'him's but, more importantly, the unnecessary vagueness of 'in knowledge'. The NEB translates, 'you have put
on a new nature, which is being constantly renewed in the image of its
Creator and brought to know God'. These points do not dispose of all
problems of translating ambiguity and breadth of meaning; I noted in
an earlier chapter Hammond's criticism of modern translation where
the AV has 'his heart died within him' for 1 Sam. 25.37. But they do
tackle some of the realities of the problems.

Several aspects of the last chapter and this one meet in the writings
and thinking of C.S. Lewis. Although as conscious as anyone of the
claims of poetic imagination, culture and profundity in the mid-
twentieth century, he championed the cause of those who used natural
and ordinary language in translating the Bible. He said that a style of
biblical translation or theological presentation that was 'rich in
fruitful ambiguities' was not much use when communicating Christian
truth to people who were not familiar with, or who were puzzled by,
the Bible and Christian faith. His thinking was influenced by his
experience in Britain in the Second World War, when he successfully
communicated something of Christian truth and theology in bold,
simple language to servicemen in RAF camps.

In his Introduction to J.B. Phillips's book *Letters to Young
Churches*[1] C.S. Lewis discusses the view held by some of the people
he had met that modern biblical translation is not only unnecessary but
offensive and irreverent. After commenting that this was very like the
objection once felt to any English translation at all, he goes on to say
that much of the New Testament was written originally in the
ordinary language of everyday Greek and that the incarnation was
itself, in a sense 'an irreverent doctrine', telling of God at work in
humble, rough surroundings and of humiliation. Lewis exhorts
readers to look for the real sanctity, beauty and sublimity of the New
Testament, as of the life of Christ himself, to come to them through
an unexpected roughness and simplicity of story and language. He
makes the point that an element of simplicity cannot be excluded
either from Christologies or from biblical translations.

This was, obviously, a very different emphasis and attitude from
that of Prickett a generation later, who, criticizing the language of the
GNB for being too simplified, suggested that it should call itself, 'a

---

1.   London: Bles, 1947.

simplified version, comparable, for instance, with an illustrated childrens Bible'.[1] C.S. Lewis has in recent years sometimes been dismissed as a mere popularizer. Some of his views on the AV, and his argument, as a professor of English literature, that the literary value of the AV came from its religious convictions, and that without these convictions the literary value could not stand on its own, have been somewhat discounted recently. But there have always been some, including scholars, who have returned to his writings and teachings about the paradoxes of profundity and simplicity in these matters of faith and of translation, and who honour his convictions. His viewpoint presents an abiding challenge within the whole debate. He refused to believe that it was only possible to convey the mysteries of faith and biblical truth in language that was sophisticated and literary. We catch in his words more than one echo of what William Tyndale said in his day.

Translating Passages about Hate, Anger and Fear

The charge that modern translations tend to deal in 'euphemisms' or in 'weakened', 'tentative' and 'unconfident' phrases is one that needs further discussion. Many people regard some of the 'natural language' in biblical translation as 'watered-down language'. Those who like the new translations think that it is the AV that contained phrases that sound euphemistic today. For example, in Isa. 13.16 the AV's 'their wives [shall be]...ravished' may sound weaker than 'their wives [shall be]...raped' (GNB and NJB). But those who dislike the new translations think the opposite. Let us examine some passages not previously mentioned.

There are many instances when new translations of concepts such as hate in the New Testament have produced as strong a rendering as the AV or, in some cases, even stronger. In Rom. 12.9 the AV has the words, 'abhor that which is evil; cleave to that which is good'. The NEB and REB, if anything, strengthen 'abhor', since their word 'loathe' comes across very strongly in today's language. The NEB has '[Love in all sincerity], loathing evil and clinging to the good'. (Knox had a strong, though old-fashioned phrase, 'you must hold what is evil in abomination'.) Modern New Testament scholars are at pains to

---

1. Letter to *Theology* 81.681 (May 1978), p. 203.

render the full strength of words such as ἀποστυγεω in modern translations. Professor T.W. Manson considered that even 'hate what is evil' (a phrase used in some modern translations) was too weak. He wrote in the Peake's 1962 Commentary, '"Hate what is evil" is hardly strong enough: the Greek word means to show hatred as well as to feel it, "to recoil with loathing from evil", the exact opposite of embracing what is good'.

The passages which need closest examination are those which contain the AV's uses, in the New Testament, of words such as 'fear', 'wrath', and 'vengeance', where some new versions have considered the AV to have over-translated the original or to have translated it wrongly or misleadingly. In 1 Peter, what the AV translates as 'fear' (φόβος) is mentioned four times. Modern translations tend to vary it in 1 Peter by such words as 'awe' or 'submission', 'respect' or 'deference', and have evidence for the use of the Greek word in this sense at the time when the letter was written. In 1 Pet. 1.17 the AV has, 'And if ye call on the Father, who without respect of persons judgeth according to every man's work, pass the time of your sojourning here in *fear*'. The NEB and REB render this, 'If you say "our Father" to the One who judges every man impartially on the record of his deeds, you must stand in *awe* of him while you live out your time on earth'. In 1 Pet. 2.18 the AV has, 'Servants, be subject to your masters with all *fear*'; the REB has, 'Servants, submit to your masters with all due *respect*'. In 1 Pet. 3.15 the AV translates, 'Be ready to give an answer to every man that asketh you a reason for the hope that is in you with meekness and *fear*'; the NEB has, 'Be always ready with your defence whenever you are called to account for the hope that is in you, but make that defence with modesty and *respect*'. (The REB reads, 'courtesy and respect', the NRSV, 'gentleness and reverence'.) These renderings by the NEB or the REB, following a line found in all modern translations (except for the NKJV which retains 'fear' in all three passages quoted, and in 1 Pet. 3.2), are dictated, not by a desire to water down the wording but by a desire to get as near as possible to what the Greek word meant in the context. Souter's *Pocket Lexicon to the Greek New Testament* says that in the New Testament age φόβος meant 'fear, terror, often fear on the reverential side in reference to God, and such as inspires cautious dealing towards men'. Arndt and Gingrich's *Greek–English Lexicon* gives 'reverence, respect' as the second main meaning of φόβος and cites ten New

Testament passages, including the three already mentioned, in which this is considered to be the right translation.

The translation of the Greek word ὀργή (AV 'wrath') in passages such as Rom. 1.18 raises complex issues and needs discussion. The AV renders, 'For the *wrath* of God is revealed from heaven against all ungodliness and unrighteousness of men'. The word 'wrath' or 'anger' has been used in many modern translations of this passage, but the NEB/REB, the NJB and the NRSV have 'the retribution of God' or 'divine retribution'; the NEB has, 'For we see *divine retribution* revealed from heaven and falling upon all the godless wickedness of men'. The translation 'retribution', while sounding unhappily impersonal to some, tries to cover the total usage of ὀργή in certain Pauline verses (for example, Rom. 4.15 and 12.19) where God's ὀργή is indeed spoken of in a curiously impersonal way according to many people, and where it seems to be a principle that operates rather than a divine emotion. There has been much discussion about how the understanding and translation of ὀργή in Paul's writings can convey both the impersonal way in which the word is sometimes used and also the sense, transmitted at other times, that Paul is talking about a deeply personal divine abhorrence in the presence of evil.[1] The traditional translation 'wrath' has the obvious difficulty of implying, in normal usage, a particular sort of anger that can be impetuous, capricious and irrational. However, the NEB/REB do not rule out the use of the words 'wrath' or 'anger' in their translation of ὀργή in the New Testament (see Jn 3.36 and Heb. 3.11). In addition to the 'retribution' phrase, they give alternative translations that can hardly be described as 'weak'. In Eph. 2.3, as seen earlier, where the AV has 'we were by nature *the children of wrath*, even as others', the REB has 'in our natural condition we lay *under the condemnation of God* like the rest of mankind' (the NEB reads, 'under the dreadful judgement of God'). In 1 Thess. 5.9, where the AV has 'God hath not appointed us to *wrath*', the NEB has 'God has not destined us to *the terrors of judgement*'. And in Rev. 6.16, where the AV has, 'hide us...from the *wrath* of the Lamb', the NEB has, 'hide us...from the *vengeance* of the Lamb'. The REB does not follow exactly the NEB's strongest phrases

---

1. See J.A.T. Robinson, *Wrestling with Romans* (London: SCM Press, 1979), pp. 18-21; C.E.B. Cranfield, *Romans* (ICC; Edinburgh: T. & T. Clark, 1975); and C.H. Dodd *Romans* (Moffatt; London: Hodder & Stoughton, 1932).

in these last three examples. In Eph. 2.3 the REB and the NRSV have 'under the condemnation of God'.

That leads us on to the modern translation of the word ἐκδίκησις. In some places where the AV translates this Greek word by 'vengeance', the NEB gives another word. In Rom. 12.19, a verse much discussed from pulpits during wartime, especially, it seems, from 1914–1918, the AV renders it as follows, 'Dearly beloved, avenge not yourselves, but rather give place unto wrath, for it is written, *Vengeance* is mine; I will repay, saith the Lord'. The NEB has, 'My dear friends, do not seek revenge, but leave a place for divine retribution, for there is a text which reads, *Justice* is mine, says the Lord. I will repay'. (The REB follows the NEB with 'divine retribution, but replaces 'justice' with 'vengeance'.) Lying behind this translation of ἐκδίκησις by 'justice' is the fact that in Hebrew scriptural terminology, which is the background to the thinking behind the verse, there is, confusingly, only one Hebrew word for the concept of both 'vengeance' and 'retributive justice'. The translation also takes into consideration the fact that whereas εκδίκησις normally meant 'vengeance' or 'punishment', it could also mean 'seeing justice done' on behalf of someone else, or what the AV calls 'avenging' someone in need. In the Greek of Num. 31.2 and in Lk. 18.7-8 ἐκδίκησις has the meaning of seeing justice done.

Occasionally modern translations may qualify something in a traditional phrase about anger which raises questions in the minds of readers. Where the AV of Mt. 5.22 has, 'whosoever is angry with his brother', the NEB and REB give, 'Anyone who nurses anger against his brother'. More significance is given to the Greek present tense of the verb, which suggests a continuing activity or state. Such changes are part of the NEB's and REB's total translation activity, which, in relation to human anger and human sin in general, is forthright and definite in its vocabulary. For example, the AV translates Col. 3.8, 'But now ye also put off all these; anger, wrath, malice, blasphemy, filthy communication out of your mouth'; the NEB and REB are no less direct: 'But now you must yourselves lay aside all anger, passion, malice, cursing, filthy talk…have done with them!' (NEB).

It is sometimes said that modern versions put the milder word 'faults' where the traditional translations put 'sins' or 'transgressions'. Certainly in Ps. 51.3 the GNB has 'I recognize my faults' where the AV has, 'I acknowledge my transgressions'. But this is a passage of

poetic parallelism where three or four Hebrew words for wrongdoing
are used in rapid succession, and the GNB includes in its translation of
the passage plenty of strong words such as 'my sin', 'my evil'. It may
also be noted that Coverdale puts 'I acknowledge my faults'. This does
not necessarily mean that 'faults' is the best English word here, but it
does remind us to consider particular isolated words in the context of
a whole passage and its translation.

Little has been said about textual variations and the choice of textual
readings. It is worth noting that, in textual matters, modern translators sometimes may be seen following a harder and less palatable
reading than the more traditional translations which seem to follow a
softer and more comfortable reading. This may be illustrated in
relation to the NEB and REB. In Mk 1.41, when Jesus stretches out his
hand to touch someone suffering from a disease, he does this,
according to some manuscripts of the Gospel, because he is 'moved
with compassion'. But in other manuscripts he does it because he is
'moved with anger' or 'moved with indignation'. Most scholars,
confronted with the perplexing and varied wording in the manuscript
witness to the original text, have considered the first alternative more
likely. It is the most straightforward 'reading', has good manuscript
authority behind it, and gives a sense which can be understood without
difficulty. But the NEB and REB favour the second, harder alternative:
the REB gives, 'Jesus was moved to anger: he stretched out his hand'.
This is a further reminder that modern translators are not interested
in bending the text or translating the text in a way most comfortable
for themselves and others, but are committed to the struggle to be
faithful to the original material.

Translating Passages of Devotion or of Apocalyptic

It may be useful, at the midpoint of this chapter, to examine two
longer quotations from a modern translation, in order to assess
attempts to put biblical words of adoration and apocalyptic vision into
modern English that is both natural and dignified, and in relation to a
whole passage rather than as isolated phrases.

Luke 1.46-55: The Song of Mary or 'Magnificat'
(The printing of the modern version and the AV parallel is here
done with one version following the other, to allow an example to be

given of the particular layout of a contemporary version.)

NJB

1.46   And Mary said:
       My soul proclaims the greatness of the Lord

47   and my spirit rejoices in God my Saviour;

48   because he has looked upon the humiliation of his servant.
       Yes, from now onwards all generations will call me blessed,

49   for the Almighty has done great things for me.
       Holy is his name,

50   and his faithful love extends age after age to those who fear him.

51   He has used the power of his arm,
       he has routed the arrogant of heart.

52   He has pulled down princes from their thrones and raised high the lowly.

53   He has filled the starving with good things, sent the rich away empty.

54   He has come to the help of Israel his servant, mindful of his faithful love

55   —according to the promise he made to our ancestors—
       of his mercy to Abraham and to his descendants for ever.

AV

1.46   And Mary said, My soul doth magnify the Lord,

47   And my spirit hath rejoiced in God my Saviour.

48   For he hath regarded the low estate of his handmaiden: for, behold,
       from henceforth all generations shall call me blessed.

49   For he that is mighty hath done to me great things; and holy is his name.

50   And his mercy is on them that fear him from generation to generation.

51   He hath shewed strength with his arm; he hath scattered the proud in
       the imagination of their hearts.

52   He hath put down the mighty from their seats, and exalted them of low degree.

53   He hath filled the hungry with good things; and the rich he hath sent empty away.

54   He hath holpen his servant Israel, in remembrance of his mercy;

55   As he spake to our fathers, to Abraham, and to his seed for ever.

Notes

Any notes on this passage are bound to be full of references to the LXX. In Luke 1–3, the semitized Greek of the LXX is used by the author, and the writing is full of Old Testament allusions and of echoes or quotations from the LXX.

1.48. The NJB has, 'the humiliation of his servant' (AV 'the low estate of his handmaiden'). The original behind this English translation is a Greek phrase taken directly from the LXX, the words of Hannah's prayer in 1 Sam. 1.11. In that verse the Hebrew word *'oni* is translated by the LXX as 'humiliation' and by the AV as 'affliction'.

1.50. The NJB has, 'his faithful love [extends age after age]'. This is a quotation from Ps. 103.17, where the Hebrew word translated 'faithful love' by the NJB is *hesed*, and the LXX translation of it is ἔλεος which is Luke's word in 1.50. ἔλεος is therefore taken by many translators as representing *hesed* here. *hesed* is usually translated by the AV as 'mercy' or 'lovingkindness', but includes both faithfulness and love, so is translated in most modern translations as the NJB does here.

1.51. The NJB gives, 'the arrogant of heart'; a literal translation of the Greek would be 'those who are arrogant in the thoughts of their hearts'.

1.52. The NJB gives, 'he has pulled down princes from their thrones'. This echoes Job 12.19 where the same Greek word that is used here by Luke (translated 'princes' by the NJB) occurs. It is a word that literally means 'powerful people' and so is used for 'rulers' or 'monarchs'.

1.53. The NJB has, 'he has filled the starving with good things'. Luke's Greek words are taken from the LXX version of Ps. 107.9; the Greek word, translated 'starving' by the NJB and used by the LXX and Luke, was a translation of the Hebrew word *rā'ēb* in Ps. 107.9, meaning both 'hungry' and 'famished'.

1.54. The NJB has, 'he has come to the help of'. The Greek word used by Luke is that used in the LXX of Isa. 41.9.

Revelation 12.7-12
This apocalyptic vision was given to John and the early church in an age which faced appalling cruelty and persecution, injustice and evil. The vision inspired the conviction that where God is with his sacrificial love, the power of evil can never have the last word. The passage contains words of doxology and words about the mystery of evil.

AV	REB
12.7 And there was war in heaven: Michael and his angels fought against the dragon; and the dragon fought and his angels,	Then war broke out in heaven; Michael and his angels fought against the dragon. The dragon with his angels fought back, but he was too weak, and they lost their place in heaven.
8 and prevailed not; neither was their place found any more in heaven.	
9 And the great dragon was cast out, that old serpent, called the Devil, and Satan, which deceiveth the whole world: he was cast out into the earth, and his angels were cast out with him.	The great dragon was thrown down, that ancient serpent who led the whole world astray, whose name is the Devil, or Satan; he was thrown down to the earth, and his angels with him.
10 And I heard a loud voice saying in heaven, Now is come salvation, and strength, and the kingdom of our God, and the power of his Christ: for the accuser of our brethren is cast down, which accused them before our God day and night.	I heard a loud voice in heaven proclaim: 'This is the time of victory for our God, the time of his power and sovereignty, when his Christ comes to his rightful rule! For the accuser of our brothers, he who day and night accused them before our God, is overthrown.
11 And they overcame him by the blood of the Lamb, and by the word of their testimony; and they loved not their lives unto the death.	By the sacrifice of the Lamb and by the witness they bore, they have conquered him; faced with death they did not cling to life.
12 Therefore rejoice, ye heavens, and ye that dwell in them. Woe to the inhabiters of the earth and of the sea! for the devil is come down unto you, having great wrath, because he knoweth that he hath but a short time.	Therefore rejoice, you heavens and you that dwell in them! But woe to you, earth and sea, for the Devil has come down to you in great fury, knowing that his time is short!

Notes

12.7. It is possible that the syntax of the original Greek may imply the meaning 'Michael *and his angels had to* fight against the dragon', but neither the AV nor the REB take it so, nor is it an interpretation widely followed.

12.10. The AV has, 'Now is come salvation, and strength, and the kingdom of our God, and the power of his Christ'. There are a number of possible ways of understanding the original words. The original Greek can mean, 'Now is the salvation, and the power, and the kingdom become our God's, and the authority is become his Christ's' (the REB's way of taking it, though put differently). The words 'our God' early in the verse may be attached either to 'kingdom' only, as the AV, or to 'salvation' and 'power' as well.

12.10. Where the words 'salvation' and 'kingdom' appear in the AV, the REB brings something different out of the important Greek words underlying any translation. The REB has the meaning 'victory' instead of merely 'salvation' and gives 'kingship' ('sovereignty') rather than 'kingdom' here. This happens again in relation to the AV's word 'power' in the phrase 'the power of his Christ'. The REB translates the original Greek word ἐξουσία not just as 'power' but as 'authority' or 'right to rule'. For the Greek word σωτηρία underlying 'salvation' (AV) and 'victory' (REB) in this verse, see Arndt and Gingrich's *Greek–English Lexicon*[1] which states that, underlying the word in this doxology is the Semitic Greek usage of the word meaning 'deliverance'. The word is used, for example, in Lk. 1.71 and in the LXX of the Psalms in the same way.

12.11. The AV has, 'by the blood of the Lamb', the REB, 'by the sacrifice of the Lamb'. The NEB, REB and a number of other modern translations often change from the literal 'blood' when describing sacrificial blood. See Rom. 5.9, where the AV has 'justified by his blood', the REB and others have 'justified by Christ's sacrificial death' or 'justified by his death'.

12.11. The AV has, 'by the words of their testimony', the REB, 'by the witness they bore'. The REB gives an alternative interpretation of the original Greek in a footnote, saying 'by the word of God to which they bore witness'.

12.12. The AV gives, 'to the inhabiters of the earth'; a Greek phrase corresponding to these words was contained in some later, inferior manuscripts of Revelation, followed by the AV here.

12.12. The AV gives, 'great wrath', the REB, 'great fury'. The original Greek word means either 'passion' or 'anger'.

1. Cambridge: Cambridge University Press, 1957.

The first draft of the NEB version of the book of Revelation, of which the REB is a revision, was done by the New Testament scholar and theologian Bishop John Robinson. Although the names of individual NEB translators are not usually revealed, Robinson's contribution was acknowledged in a posthumous work of his.[1] He tells there how he had always been drawn to the last book of the Bible (as indeed his earlier book *In the End God* showed). He was clearly deeply concerned not only to translate the book of Revelation accurately, but also with some sense of its mysteries. About the book and its apocalyptic material he wrote, 'In the terror there is an awful beauty', and he referred to William Blake's profound poetic understanding of it.

Simplicity and Stylization

It is at least arguable that in the two passages examined above the modern translation achieves an effective natural language, marked by a certain simplicity and by dramatic effect. The tension between the simple and direct on the one hand and the stylized and dignified on the other is familiar in many fields of literary and artistic expression. In poetry, drama and music tensions are encountered between the straightforward and the imaginative in presentation, between the simple and the stylized, the realistic and the romantic, and between that which is concerned with the mundane and that which is concerned with the transcendent.

In 1966 Cecil Day Lewis wrote these words, 'the English poet has tended over the last 25 years towards a simplicity of language'.[2] In the same year W.H. Auden, defending modern poetry against the charge of obscurity, compared poetry with riddles, and admitted that, 'in poetry as in riddles one does not always call a spade a spade'.[3]

The same might also be said about drama. A British television programme in 1988 contained a discussion on the degree of artificiality and of 'producing effects' that is inevitable in acting.[4] Sir John Gielgud said that an actor cannot avoid trying to produce certain effects, but Dame Edith Evans was quoted as saying, 'I never make effects' and as championing 'realistic' presentation.

1. *Where Three Ways Meet* (London: SCM Press, 1987), p. 35.
2. In the same foreword to the translation of Virgil noted earlier in this chapter.
3. In a BBC interview, 1966.
4. Channel Four television, July 1988.

It would be a bold person who would claim that all the truth and all the value in such situations lay on one side of this divide. Most would agree that, in many contexts, tensions can be creative, and that the heart of truth and value often lies in both extremes. In diverse fields the imaginative romantics always need, and usually have, the realists and so-called 'non-romantics' to balance them, and vice versa. The dividing line between the two 'sides' is thinner than may first be supposed. The realistic and the romantic, the straightforward and the imaginative, the mundane and the transcendent, are closer to one another than one thinks. Igor Stravinsky was an anti-romantic who turned his back on certain romantic, imaginative patterns from the past. But it is doubtful whether he would want to be told that there was no dimension of the transcendent about his work. Like the romantics, he wanted to 'transcend the mundane', and in 1941, in his so-called 'neo-classical' period, described a symphony of his as 'written to the glory of God'. It is often difficult to label an artistic figure by the single term 'realist' or 'romantic'.

The poet Stevie Smith found inspiration, as mentioned earlier, in E.V. Rieu's modern translation of St Mark's Gospel in the 1940s.[1] She seems to have been attracted to his translation by its combination of directness and imaginativeness of language.

The mixture of elements in any style of language used for biblical translation will always be complex; the REB, in its preface, gives this description of its own mixture, 'care has been taken to ensure that the style of English used is fluent and of appropriate dignity for liturgical use, while maintaining intelligibility for worshippers of a wide range of ages and backgrounds'. However complex the mixture may have to be, the role of natural forms of expression will always be important. Such natural forms of expression cannot be kept for 'childrens' Bibles' or for Bibles intended for the ears of the uninitiated; they are a basic element in any true and deep presentation of the biblical material. True simplicity is surely at the heart of all genuine style.

In this chapter, comparisons of different translations of Luke 1 and of Revelation 12 should enable readers to assess for themselves how

---

1. Stevie Smith's poem 'The Airy Christ' (*Collected Poems* [Allen Lane, 1975]) was sub-titled 'After Reading Dr Rieu's Translation of St Mark's Gospel'. The contents of the poem suggest that by 'airy Christ' she intended to convey a mixture of 'singing Christ' and 'heavenly Christ'.

far such modern versions achieve an effective balance between the simple and the stylized and how far something creative has been fashioned out of abiding tensions between simpler and more complex forms of speech.

Labels are as difficult to apply in the world of biblical translation as in other fields of writing. C.S. Lewis was much involved in discussions about biblical translation and may be said to have had a foot in both 'camps', by his temperament and outlook. He understood the romantics and also, in relation to modern Bibles, the realists. Elsewhere in this volume I examine the significant combination of a realistic 'original-word-meaning' approach and an 'imaginative-literary' approach to biblical translation found in scholars such as Robert Alter, one of the editors of *A Literary Guide to the Bible*. It is hard for anyone involved in twentieth-century biblical translation not to move towards that delicate central ground of articulation where both simplicity and stylization belong together.

The Role of Non-coded Language

The role of coded language will be noted later, particularly in connection with Northropp Frye's writings. The role of non-coded language is also important. At its simplest, the case for natural and non-coded language in the translation of the Bible rests on the need for wording that realistically helps to clarify and communicate the biblical Word in modern times. It is not only the out-and-out popularizers who are exercised over this. Statistics, in their less emotional way, shout loud and clear: in 1987 89 per cent of British teenagers did not read any newspaper except tabloids.[1] As the Church of England's Liturgical Commission said at the beginning of the 1980s about the language which we use in church (including biblical readings), the modern church must give up some of its traditional phrases for everyday use if it is to be a missionary church at a time of a crisis of faith. The Commission stated, 'the cost of the ancient hieratic language, Latin or Tudor English, has to be paid by a missionary Church in a great crisis of faith'.[2]

Many of those who serve in cathedrals, conscious of the claims of

1. Exeter University report, 1987.
2. 'Commentary on the Alternative Service Book 1980'.

imaginative and artistic expression in what is said and sung in cathedrals, have been at the forefront of the encouragement of a true balance between stylized and natural, coded and non-coded language in prayers, hymns and readings. Those who compiled the New Standard Version of *Hymns Ancient and Modern* (1983) put it splendidly in their preface: 'a good hymnbook is necessarily an endeavour in high democracy'. They were referring to the need in any hymnbook to balance the claims of literary and musical tradition with popular needs. Any modern biblical translation is a similar endeavour in democracy, by trying to make the Bible available in language that will always, in some ways, be coded but that should never be artificial. A former Dean of Worcester speaking of religious communication in general in the modern age said, 'the use of antique diction may communicate, to many, a God who is not so much transcendent as remote'.[1] And a sophisticated group of university dons and undergraduates described the style of worship and language that they wanted to have in their college chapel: 'we want in our worship to be taken out of ourselves, but not into another culture: we need to be able to express the mystery and the transcendent in modern language: the world which the worship transcends must be that of the 20th century, not the 16th'.[2]

The case for clear and natural language in religion has never been put more forcefully than by Gerald Priestland in his writings about those who, though truly concerned with the things of the spirit, are put off by the coded language in which religious writing and speaking is generally couched. Writing about his conversations concerning religion with many types of people in Britain in *Priestland's Progress* he says, 'many people were put off religion because it had become a minority hobby in a special coded language. It seemed to me that there was no reason why one should not apply to it that same journalistic motto of "clarify, clarify, clarify" (which is not the same as "oversimplify") that one applied to economics or diplomacy'.[3] He added that when he tried to do just that, with the writing of *Priestland's Progress*, he had more response than he had ever dreamed

---

1. T.G.A. Baker, review of *No Alternative* by D. Martin and P. Mullen.

2. E. James, *John Robinson* (London: SCM Press, 1987), p. 207.

3. G. Priestland, *Something Observed* (London: Deutsch, 1986), p. 271; *Priestland's Progress* (London: Ariel Books, 1981).

of. The publishers of many modern translations of the Bible, speaking from their own perspective, say much the same about the response received (and about the numbers of copies sold). Priestland, while betraying his enthusiasm for clarity, also carefully and definitely warned against unimaginative or oversimplified writing or speaking about religion. To follow Priestland is not to deny the place and importance of coded language in human expression and religious expression. It is simply to recognize its dangers.

Chapter 6

FREEDOM, RHYTHM AND BEAUTY

It is time to look in more detail at the standard of literary style in the new translations, and the charge that there has been a loss of beauty in the English of the modern versions. More particularly, I ask the questions: 'Has there been much imaginative poetic freedom in style?' And, in the combination of dignity and clarity that most of the modern versions have aimed at, 'has there, in fact, been much dignity?'

I begin with three passages from modern translations: one of Old Testament historical narrative, one of Old Testament poetic writing, and part of a Gospel parable. Each passage is famous in English in its AV form. Readers may compare the literary styles and aesthetic sensitivities of the AV with a modern translation. Perhaps I may recommend that the translations be read aloud, to test the effectiveness of the translation as spoken as well as written word.

1 Samuel 16.6-13
Samuel calls Jesse and his sons to him, and David is anointed.

	AV	GNB
16.6	And it came to pass, when they were come, that he looked on Eliab, and said, Surely the Lord's anointed is before him.	When they arrived, Samuel saw Jesse's son Eliab and said to himself, This man standing here in the Lord's presence is surely the one he has chosen.
7	But the Lord said unto Samuel, Look not on his countenance, or on the height of his stature; because I have refused him: for the Lord seeth not as man seeth; for man looketh on the outward appearance, but the Lord looketh on the heart.	But the Lord said to him, 'Pay no attention to how tall and handsome he is. I have rejected him, because I do not judge as man judges. Man looks at the outward appearance, but I look at the heart.'

8	Then Jesse called Abinadab, and made him pass before Samuel. And he said, Neither hath the Lord chosen this.	Then Jesse called his son Abinadab and brought him to Samuel. But Samuel said, 'No, the Lord hasn't chosen him either.'
9	Then Jesse made Shammah to pass by. And he said, Neither hath the Lord chosen this.	Jesse then brought Shammah. 'No, the Lord hasn't chosen him either', Samuel said.
10	Again, Jesse made seven of his sons to pass before Samuel. And Samuel said unto Jesse, The Lord hath not chosen these.	In this way Jesse brought seven of his sons to Samuel. And Samuel said to him, 'No, the Lord hasn't chosen any of these'.
11	And Samuel said unto Jesse, Are here all thy children? And he said, There remaineth yet the youngest, and, behold, he keepeth the sheep. And Samuel said unto Jesse, Send and fetch him: for we will not sit down till he come hither.	Then he asked him, 'Have you any more sons?' Jesse answered, 'There is still the youngest, but he is out taking care of the sheep.' 'Tell him to come here,' Samuel said. 'We won't offer the sacrifice until he comes.'
12	And he sent, and brought him in. Now he was ruddy, and withal of a beautiful countenance, and goodly to look to. And the Lord said, Arise, anoint him: for this is he.	So Jesse sent for him. He was a handsome, healthy young man, and his eyes sparkled. The Lord said to Samuel, 'This is the one—anoint him!'
13	Then Samuel took the horn of oil, and anointed him in the midst of his brethren: and the Spirit of the Lord came upon David from that day forward. So Samuel rose up, and went to Ramah.	Samuel took the olive-oil and anointed David in front of his brothers. Immediately the spirit of the Lord took control of David and was with him from that day on. Then Samuel returned to Ramah.

Notes

16.6. This verse is four words longer in the GNB than in the AV, but this may be to avoid the ambiguity of who is meant by 'he' in the AV. (See 'And he said' in vv. 8 and 9.) In the passage as a whole, the GNB uses fewer words than the AV.

16.11. Note the GNB's 'we won't offer the sacrifice' as compared with the AV's 'we will not sit down' (the Hebrew is literally 'we will not gather round'). The NAB further spells it out, 'we will not begin the sacrificial banquet'.

16.12. The AV has 'ruddy', the GNB, 'healthy' (Hebrew literally 'red'). Many modern translators retain the word 'ruddy' or 'with ruddy cheeks'. In the past readers have sometimes taken the Hebrew, and the word 'ruddy', to mean 'red-haired', but all translators make it clear that they see the reference to be to complexion. The Shorter Oxford English Dictionary says that ruddy means 'with a fresh or healthily red complexion'.

The AV has 'of a beautiful countenance', the GNB, 'his eyes sparkled'. There is uncertainty about the meaning of the Hebrew. The literal translation of the Hebrew was traditionally taken to be 'fair of eyes'. Some modern translators think, with the GNB, that it means 'with fine, bright eyes'. Others use phrases such as 'with a fine appearance'.

16.13. The AV has, 'took the horn of oil', the GNB simply, 'took the olive-oil'. It is hard to see why the GNB omits 'horn'; it is not a complex word and is a good symbol, conveying something of the ancient setting of this saga-like story.

The AV has, 'came upon David', the GNB, 'took control of David' with the word 'immediately' preceding. The Hebrew word here probably means some powerful movement causing David to be possessed by the Spirit's power. The NIV has 'was with David in power', the NJB, 'seized on David'. But the REB is as mild as the AV and has simply 'was with him'.

The AV has, 'rose up, and went to', the GNB condenses the two verbs into one and says 'returned to'. Most other modern translators give force to the first verb. The NEB gives 'set out on his way to', the NAB, 'when Samuel took his leave, he went to Ramah'.

Isaiah 32.1-5
A message of hope about a time when a leader will come, when the needy will find fulfilment, and when the false promises of insincere leaders will be shown up. Sir Arthur Quiller Couch, early in the twentieth century, spoke of the 'glorious sentences' of this passage in the AV as one of the glories of English literature, and said, 'when a nation has achieved this manner of diction, and these rhythms for its dearest beliefs, a life is surely established'.[1] But most modern translations are also striking, and, for example, have succeeded in giving new force and clarity to vv. 1 and 2, where the AV's 'a man' can be misleading. Verse 2 is about one of the 'just kings and princes'

1. *On the Art of Reading* (Cambridge: Cambridge University Press, 1920), p. 155.

mentioned in v. 1 and not a new figure; the AV has often added confusion here.

	AV	NJB
32.1	Behold, a king shall reign in righteousness, and princes shall rule in judgement.	There will be a king who reigns uprightly and princes who rule with fair judgement;
2	And a man shall be as an hiding place from the wind, and a covert from the tempest;	each will be like a shelter from the wind, a refuge from the storm,
	as rivers of water in a dry place, as the shadow of a great rock in a weary land.	like streams on arid ground, like the shade of a solid rock in a desolate land.
3	And the eyes of them that see shall not be dim, and the ears of them that hear shall hearken.	The eyes of seers will no longer be closed, the ears of hearers will be alert,
4	The heart also of the rash shall understand knowledge, and the tongue of the stammerers shall be ready to speak plainly.	the heart of the hasty will learn to think things over, and the tongue of the stammerers will speak promptly and clearly.
5	The vile person shall be no more called liberal, nor the churl said to be bountiful.	The fool will no longer be called generous, nor the rascal be styled bountiful.

Notes

32.2. Notice the NJB's strong alliteration, 'streams', 'shade', 'solid'. And the AV's beautiful 'weary land' is well matched by the NJB's similar 'desolate land'.

As already noted, it has never been certain in the AV what 'a man' means here, and for the sake of clarity and the force of the passage the ambiguity needs to be tackled. The GNB, NAB, NIV and NRSV all put 'each of them', like the NJB.

32.3. The AV translates this in a literal way. Its rhythm is fine, but it is hard to receive any meaning from the second half. It may be justifiable to sharpen up the meaning in both parts. For the AV's 'them that see', the NJB has 'seers'. The GNB sharpens up the meaning by a different interpretation and by using considerable freedom, making the verse refer to the leaders mentioned earlier: 'their eyes and ears will be open to the needs of the people'.

32.4a. The word 'rash', in the AV's 'the heart also of the rash shall understand knowledge', has the Hebrew verb *māhar* lying behind it. This has the literal meaning of being hasty or hastened, often used in the Old Testament of people 'making haste'. The AV translates it as 'fearful' in Isa. 35.4 ('Say to them that are of a fearful heart, be strong') and as 'rash' here. When not used in its literal sense of hastening on a journey, the Hebrew word seems to be a mixture of hastiness, fear and panic. The NJB puts 'the hasty', the NAB, 'the flighty' ('the flighty will become wise and capable') and the REB has 'the impetuous' (the impetuous mind will understand and know').

The NJB has the bold phrase, '[the heart of the hasty] will learn to think things over', compared with the AV's more general, 'shall understand knowledge'. The REB's 'will understand and know' and the NRSV's 'will have good judgement' are two more interpretations of the original words in the context, narrowing the meaning somewhat. In connection with the NJB's phrase 'will learn to think things over', it is interesting to note that George Adam Smith in the nineteenth century said that the literal meaning of the Hebrew would be 'shall learn to know'.

32.5. The AV's 'vile', 'liberal' and 'churl' are no longer found in most modern translations, for obvious reasons of obscurity, changed meaning or inaccuracy.

Luke 15.11-24

AV	REB
15.11 A certain man had two sons, and the younger of them said to his father,	There was once a man who had two sons; and the younger said to his father,
12 Father, give me the portion of goods that falleth to me. And he divided unto them his living.	'Father, give me my share of the property'. So he divided his estate between them.
13 And not many days after the younger son gathered all together, and took his journey into a far country, and there wasted his substance with riotous living.	A few days later the younger son turned the whole of his share into cash and left home for a distant country, where he squandered it in dissolute living.
14 And when he had spent all, there arose a mighty famine in that land; and he began to be in want.	He had spent it all, when a severe famine fell upon that country and he began to be in need.
15 And he went and joined himself to a citizen of that country; and he sent him into his fields to feed swine.	So he went and attached himself to one of the local landowners, who sent him on to his farm to mind the pigs.

16 And he would fain have filled his belly with the husks that the swine did eat: and no man gave unto him.

He would have been glad to fill his belly with the pods that the pigs were eating; but no one gave him anything.

17 And when he came to himself, he said, How many hired servants of my father's have bread enough and to spare, and I perish with hunger!

Then he came to his senses: 'How many of my father's hired servants have more food than they can eat', he said, 'and here am I, starving to death!

18 I will arise and go to my father, and will say unto him, Father, I have sinned against heaven and before thee,

I will go at once to my father, and say to him, "Father, I have sinned, against God and against you;

19 And am no more worthy to be called thy son: make me as one of thy hired servants.

I am no longer fit to be called your son; treat me as one of your hired servants".'

20 And he arose, and came to his father. But when he was a great way off, his father saw him, and had compassion, and ran, and fell on his neck, and kissed him.

So he set out for his father's house. But while he was still a long way off his father saw him, and his heart went out to him; he ran to meet him, flung his arms round him, and kissed him.

21 And the son said unto him, Father, I have sinned against heaven, and in thy sight, and am no more worthy to be called thy son.

The son said, 'Father, I have sinned, against God and against you; I am no longer fit to be called your son'.

22 But the father said to his servants, Bring forth the best robe, and put it on him; and put a ring on his hand, and shoes on his feet.

But the father said to his servants, 'Quick! fetch a robe, the best we have, and put it on him; put a ring on his finger and sandals on his feet.

23 And bring hither the fatted calf, and kill it; and let us eat, and be merry:

Bring the fatted calf and kill it, and let us celebrate with a feast.

24 For this my son was dead, and is alive again; he was lost and is found. And they began to be merry.

For this son of mine was dead and has come back to life; he was lost and is found'. And the festivities began.

Notes

15.13. The AV has, 'gathered all together', the NEB and REB 'turned the whole of his share into cash'. There is evidence that the Greek verb used here sometimes had the technical meaning of realizing assets as well as the general meaning of 'gathering together'. Either could be right.

15.15. The AV has, 'a citizen', the NEB and REB, 'one of the local landowners'. Although 'landowners' is a free addition, the word 'local' is precisely right for the Greek word, which signifies the opposite of a foreigner. And 'local' needs a noun with it.

15.18. The AV has, 'I have sinned against heaven', the NEB and REB, 'I have sinned against God'. 'Against heaven' was of course a Jewish, roundabout way of saying 'against God', used out of reverence.

15.20. The AV has, 'and had compassion', the NEB and REB, 'and his heart went out to him'. The latter catches the idea of being inwardly moved which the Greek verb carries.

15.22. The AV has, 'Bring forth the best robe', the REB, 'Quick! fetch a robe, the best we have'. All the earliest manuscript, and other, evidence for the Greek text includes the word 'quickly' here.

The Authorized Version's Rhythms and Cadences

The first comment on these passages must be on the strengths and beauties of the AV's language.[1] Anyone brought up to know the AV well hardly needs persuading of the beauty. And the English language is full of its splendid phrases. It was, perhaps, Sir Arthur Quiller Couch who best described the treasures and skills of language found in the AV. He drew attention to the importance of its vowel sounds at the

---

1.   It is true that the sixteenth- and seventeenth-century translators' English style appeared rather foreign-sounding at first, and not particularly beautiful, to their contemporaries, because of the translators' fairly literal reproducing of much of the syntax, idiom and cadences of the original biblical languages. In one sense the translators brought something new into English literature, helping an emerging beauty of language to be fashioned. It was not simply a case of them being fortunate to coincide with the maturing of the English language, and having an easy vehicle of language to hand (see M. Roston, *16th Century English Literature* [London: Macmillan, 1982], pp. 30-31). Their translations eventually were recognized as having great beauty, being a merging not only of a biblical pattern of language but also a merging of the translators' lively use of contemporary English idiom and poetic nuance with existing features of English literary style (e.g. Ciceronian traditions of speech).

beginning of its translation of Isaiah 60.[1] In Isa. 60.1, 3 there recurs many times what Quiller Couch called 'that noble i', which expresses a lift of vigour and delight, either as a long 'i' or a short 'i' or an 'ee':

> Arise, shine; for thy light is come, and the glory of the Lord is risen upon thee... And the Gentiles shall come to thy light, and kings to the brightness of thy rising.

The same 'i' sound occurs in the second half of v. 2, but, by contrast, in the first half there is the more solemn 'o' sound:

> For behold the darkness shall cover the earth, and gross darkness the people

Later, T.R. Henn, Cambridge scholar and poet, wrote that the AV often achieved a striking sense of finality by the subtlety of its final cadences, or by its climax of strong monosyllables in the final lines.[2] He said that the AV translators built on what their predecessors had already worked on in 'blending the phonetic and the dramatic'; they caught the exaltation of a particular passage through 'strange and definite rhythms'. He instances the last few words of 1 Kgs 19.12, commenting that, 'a still small voice' as a cadence was a great improvement on 'a small still voice' given by earlier translators in the John Rogers and Matthew Bible of 1537. In the AV, Henn notes, 'the vowels i-a-oi drop in a descending scale' in a magical way. It is in such intricate and imaginative matters that much of the freedom of style of the AV has been exercised.

More recently, Bishop Richard Harries pointed out the remarkable use of alliteration through the repeated letters 'ab' in the AV of Eph. 3.20: 'Now unto him that is *able* to do *abundantly above* all that we ask or think according to the power that worketh in us, unto him be glory'. He describes the threefold 'ab' as 'a steady downbeat', and continues, 'each word adds, in both sound and sense, to what has gone before. "Able" is short and decisive; "abundantly" indicates the richness, profusion and generosity of God's grace; whilst "above" lifts us to the source of all'.[3]

Another, and simpler, example of alliteration (quoted by Henn) is the description of Wisdom in Prov. 3.17: 'her ways are ways of

1. *On the Art of Reading*, p. 155.
2. 'The Bible as Literature', p. 14.
3. *Church Times*, August 1988.

pleasantness, and all her paths are peace'. The AV, it is true, had its troubles over the use of monosyllables, as do all translations; for example, in Lk. 14.33 the AV 'whosoever he be of you that forsaketh not' makes for difficult listening and reading today. But clearly the almost unfailing beauty of the AV's alliterations, monosyllables and vowel sounds is a major part of the glory of its style. The A V translators were experienced in the public reading of Scripture, and had a sure instinct for setting down exactly what would sound well, and be well remembered.

Emphasis on the Bible as spoken word, and on translation as translation of spoken word, has been the mark of much recent discussion on styles of language for English Bibles. This emphasis was stimulated by the success of the 'performances' on stage of the reading of St Mark's Gospel by the British actor Alec McCowen. It is an emphasis especially articulated in works such as Northropp Frye's book *The Great Code*. Frye says that he uses the AV rather than modern versions not just because of the decorative beauty of its cadences, but because of its emotional and creative power to move the mind; he says that this power springs from its base in the spoken word and its closeness to the roots of the English language.[1] He stresses the fact that the AV was itself 'appointed to be read in churches', and sees that as the secret of 'its immense literary success'. He writes, 'it is sensitivity to one's own language, not scholarly knowledge of the original, that makes a translation permanent'. Frye, as mentioned previously, is honest about the weaknesses and unevennesses of the AV, but he emphasizes the great strength of its oratorical power, and of its achievements in authoritative and repetitive resonance. He considers that a modern age that uses more descriptive, analytical and scientific language rather than the poetic and mythological is not a good age for biblical translation.

Peter Levi, too, puts great emphasis on the spoken word. He criticizes most modern English translations of the Bible as coming from people more accustomed to the written than the spoken word, and lacking a foundation or special skill in spoken English.[2] In commending styles of poetry, translation and other writing that may

---

1. A main theme of Frye's book is that the roots of the language, in an earlier phase of culture, were spoken, poetic, mythological and metaphorical roots.
2. Levi, *The English Bible*, p. 12.

be said to have simplicity and strength, Levi clearly has in mind the simplicity and strength belonging to dramatic and rhetorical grandeur in the spoken word. He writes of 'lost thunders and lightnings' in an age of modern writing.

For some writers and poets, and for many others, the AV's use of 'thee' and 'thou' and '-est' and '-eth' is part of its preciousness as a translation. The poet John Heath-Stubbs, judging from his poem 'Use of Personal Pronouns', likes 'thou' to be retained as giving a sense of intimacy.

> Beginning as an honorific, the unaffectionate 'you',
> For English speakers, has put 'thou' out of business.
> So, in our intimate moments,
> We are dumb, in a castle of reserve.
>
> And he alone
> From Whom no secrets are hid, to Whom
> All hearts be open,
> Can be a public Thou.[1]

Northropp Frye likes 'thou' to be retained as usefully 'lending distance'; for modern times, he says, 'the antique colouring of "thou hast" and of the southern "-eth" ending of verbs greatly increases the sense of the oracular and the distant'.[2]

Nearly all modern translations have left behind such usages, though Moffatt, the NEB and the NKJV have kept them in addressing God. The REB and the NRSV both adopt 'you', 'your's' and corresponding terms throughout. The NIV, in its preface, defends its use of 'you' throughout on the grounds of faithfulness to the original, 'neither Hebrew, Aramaic nor Greek uses special pronouns for the persons of the Godhead', it says.

Literary Awareness among Modern Translators

Some of these points need careful consideration. On the matter of alliteration and the spoken word, it has to be said that many new versions are alive to these points and use alliteration vigorously, often

1. In D. Wright (ed.), *The Mid Century English Poetry* (Harmondsworth: Penguin Books, 1965).
2. *The Great Code*, p. 215.

in passages where there is not alliteration in the traditional versions.
In Jer. 2.22 the GNB has powerfully alliterative words for God's word
to his people, 'even if you washed with the *s*trongest *s*oap, I would
*s*till *s*ee the *s*tain of your guilt' (cf. the AV 'for though thou wash thee
with nitre, and take thee much soap, yet thine iniquity is marked
before me'). It is also true that in the AV, at times, considerations of
alliteration seem to take priority over poetic phrasing. In Job 26.14
the AV has, 'Lo, these are the *p*arts (*qaṣâ*) of his ways, but how little a
*p*ortion (*dābār*) is heard of him? but the thunder of his *p*ower who can
understand?' The REB conveys more of the imagery without any
alliteration, yet in a translation that reads very well indeed: 'These are
but the fringes of his power, and how faint the whisper that we hear
of him! Who could comprehend the thunder of his might?'

In general, modern translators have responded to attacks on their
literary style by saying,

> We are not unconcerned with style and beauty of language, and we con-
> sider that our versions are not colourless. But it is true that in the final
> analysis our aim has not been beauty of language but clarity and the com-
> munication of meaning, and faithfulness to the original biblical material.

The claim by modern translators to be concerned for beauty of style
is not an empty one. It is perhaps surprising that in the NIV's official
volume about the making of its translation great emphasis is put on
producing a version that sounds good when read aloud. Professor
Calvin Linton, Professor Emeritus of English Literature at George
Washington University, says that the translator's first job is to ensure
that the biblical material is made clear and intelligible to Tyndale's
'ploughboy' in every generation; but the second job is to clothe the
content in a form or style which enables it to be aesthetically appreci-
ated, enjoyed, deeply absorbed, and received in ever-greater depth as
time goes on. Linton's rule is 'first information, then ever-expanding
appreciation'.[1] (This may be compared with David Martin's maxim,
already mentioned, 'first incantation, then comprehension'.) Linton
says unhesitatingly, 'The Bible is literature, that kind of writing which
attends to beauty, power and memorability as well as to exposition. It
is like a rich chord compared to a single note'. He adds that, 'the Bible
requires profound attention to style when it is translated'. He quotes

1. *The Making of Contemporary Translation*, pp. 42, 20-21.

from another NIV volume, *The Story of the NIV*,[1] for another NIV
policy indication: 'when the original is beautiful, its beauty must shine
through the translation; when it is stylistically ordinary, this must be
apparent'. At one point Linton describes how, in the NIV, care has
been taken to translate Hebrew poetry in a poetic way and with a
sensitive rendering of rhythms, not by attempted imitation of the
terseness of Hebrew poetry but by something singable or recitable in
English, just as the original was singable and recitable in its day. The
scansion adopted (called by Linton 'accentual scansion' as, distinct
from 'syllable scansion') works on the principle, not of a set number
of syllables each time supplying a regular beat, but on the freer
method of relying on the natural accent and stress of any emotionally
charged syllable. In between those natural accents are different
numbers of syllables, in the manner of the free verse found in much
modern poetry. Linton urges the reader to speak aloud two verses
from Job 29 in the NIV, being careful to give full value to the
difference between stressed and unstressed syllables:

	NIV	AV
29.2	How I long for the months gone by, for the days when God watched over me,	Oh that I were as in months past, as in the days when God preserved me;
3	when his lamp shone upon my head and by his light I walked through darkness!	When his candle shined upon my head, and when by his light I walked through darkness;

Although the AV wording is poetic prose, and there may not seem to
be a great difference between old and new versions here, yet the more
definite poetic lilt in the NIV may be noted, especially in the first line
of each verse (for example, 'How I long for the months gone by' as
compared with 'Oh that I were as in').

Pre-dating that American, NIV policy by perhaps a decade, some of
the JB (first edition) translators in Britain experimented with a similar
approach to the translation of Hebrew poetic writing. In translations
where a team has been at work, it is not customary for publishers to
give the names of the main translators of individual books, but
Dr Anthony Kenny described in his autobiography how he translated
the book of Job for the 1966 JB, and how he tried to copy Gerard

---

1.   New York: New York International Bible Society, 1978.

Manley Hopkins's so-called 'sprung rhythm' or 'abrupt rhythm'.[1] Verbally, the JB version of Job is generally freer, and further from the AV wording, than is the later NIV, but the principle of poetic translation is similar. Special attention was given to the 'spoken word' aspect of translation (the British actor Robert Speaight was one of those who did drafts for the JB). Kenny's idea was that each couple of lines in English, matching the Hebrew parallelisms, would have an equal number of strong stresses, usually three or four, which would be emphasized when the passage was read aloud. But the number of unstressed syllables would be flexible and, in one sense, immaterial, provided that the number of stresses was constant. It is interesting to note that Hopkins's rhythmic structures have sometimes been described as closer to the beat of Anglo-Saxon verse than the more regular beat and metrics of most English poetry of his time.

In addition to marked emphasis of that sort on literary style, a distinctive feature of modern translations is attractiveness of format and layout of the written pages of the Bible. The traditional AV layout crowded the page with words, with no sense of spaciousness or aesthetic beauty of layout. Most new versions, in an imaginative way, have printed poetic or hymnic material in an appropriate form. The inspired line drawings by Annie Valloton in the GNB, depicting people and scenes that are historically accurate but that also include gestures and movements with universal significance, introduce a new dimension into the presentation of the biblical Word.

But Clarity Comes First?

The second point made by most modern translators, should also be considered: in the final analysis, clarity and communication of meaning must come first in the order of priority for the translator. This point was put most forcibly by C.S. Lewis and William Barclay.

C.S. Lewis's words about how beauty of style can blunt the impact of the biblical material are fairly well-known.[2]

> We must sometimes get away from the Authorised Version if for no other reason, simply because it is so beautiful and so solemn. Beauty exalts, but

---

1. *A Path from Rome* (Oxford: Oxford University Press, 1986), p. 120.
2. Introduction to J.B. Phillips, *Letters to Young Churches* (London: Bles, 1947), pp. viii-ix.

beauty also lulls. Early associations endear but they also confuse. Through that beautiful solemnity the transporting or horrifying realities of which the Book tells may come to us blunted and disarmed and we may only sigh with tranquil veneration when we ought to be burning with shame or struck dumb with terror or carried out of ourselves by ravishing hopes and adorations. Does the word 'scourged' really come home to us like 'flogged'? Does 'mocked him' sting like 'jeered at him'?

C.S. Lewis was far from being uninterested in the Bible as literature, nor did he want its translation to be denied all beauty. When he wrote *Reflections on the Psalms*,[1] his love of the Old Testament poetry was quite clear: 'in beauty, in poetry, Coverdale and St Jerome, the great Latin translator, are beyond all whom I know'. He even makes the explicit statement: 'the Bible, since it is after all literature, cannot properly be read except as literature: and the different parts of it as the different sorts of literature they are'. But he believed passionately that the Bible was to be read first for its faith and message; and, as a professor of Mediaeval and Renaissance English, he made some specialized and radical comments about the place of the AV in English literature.[2] Lewis suggested that much popular admiration for the beauty of the AV as something timeless was misplaced. Although he agreed that, through its imagery, the AV's influence on the English language was central and integral, he did not think that its influence on the actual style of the English language in general had been as great as was usually presumed. He argued that, although in the nineteenth century, during the romantic movement with its 'taste for the primitive and the passionate', there had been immense admiration for the AV, this was not true of earlier times. He believed that 'only a particular period in the history of taste' has really applauded the AV and taken it to its heart. In his view, people in the twentieth century often applauded the AV from nothing deeper than a sort of sentimental feeling that it was good to have it around. Lewis did not consider that the AV would continue to be read as literature, nor did he see it as a timeless biblical style; regarded from a literary angle he saw it as a museum piece. 'I predict that the Bible will in the future continue to be read as it always has been read, almost exclusively by Christians,

---

1. London: Bles 1958.
2. C.S. Lewis, *The Literary Impact of the Authorized Version* (Philadelphia: Fortress Press, 1963).

that is, as sacred truth not as literature.'[1] Lewis's views on this matter did not commend themselves to literary scholars, although Peter Levi criticized the style of the AV along different lines. It may be that several scholars would agree with adverse criticism if accompanied by the statement that although the AV's strength lay in its accuracy when compared with earlier English versions of the Bible, yet in style it was less flowing or rhythmically beautiful than the Great Bible of 1539 and its antecedents. By and large, however, not many people would not fail to salute the AV's majesty of style.

The abiding point in C.S. Lewis's views on the language of biblical translations, old and new, does not lie in these detailed matters of literary criticism, but in his warnings about 'timeless translations' and about the sad tendency of the language of all familiar translations to act as an anodyne rather than as an invigorator. On those points he presents an uncompromising challenge, with fiercely worded comments, never more so than in his letter to J.B. Phillips in 1943 encouraging him to go on from the initial translation of the Letter to the Colossians to translate other books of the New Testament. Lewis wrote, 'of course you will be opposed tooth and nail by all the "cultured" asses who say you're spoiling the "beauty" of the AV'.

A quarter of a century after Lewis wrote those words, William Barclay put his convictions into uncompromising language. In his essay 'On Translating the New Testament',[2] he wrote,

> It is a simple fact that anything which makes the New Testament sound stately and dignified and archaic, or even beautiful, in style gives precisely the wrong impression of what it originally was. It is not slang, and to make it sound like slang is bad translation; but it is colloquial and to make it sound like ordinary speech is good translation.

Or again, 'No true translation of the New Testament can be made so long as the dominating desire is for beauty of literary style rather than plain and challenging lucidity of meaning'. Barclay, as a Greek and classical scholar, was well aware that some parts of the New Testament were written in more elegant Greek than others; he knew about the more literary style of, for example, the Letter to the

---

1. *The Literary Impact of the Authorized Version* (Piladelphia: Fortress Press, 1963).

2. Appendix to his translation, *The Gospels and Acts of the Apostles* (London: Collins, 1968), p. 312.

Hebrews and parts of Luke and Acts, and about dramatic and apocalyptic writings such as the book of Revelation. He would have been well aware that to call the main style of the Greek of the New Testament 'colloquial' was over-simplification, since among its language of the market place are to be found some keywords and characteristics of a different sort taken from Jewish backgrounds. But he was concerned to emphasize the predominantly non-literary character of New Testament Greek.

Another New Testament scholar, John Robinson, wrote about a related area of discussion. He said that the trouble with the AV style was that it sounds literary throughout, whether a literary style is required or not. He called this the 'unevenness' of the AV, and said that the NEB attempted to avoid such unevenness. In a tribute to C.H. Dodd, director of the NEB translation, Robinson commented that Dodd's profound learning, combined with a remarkable gift for simplicity of thought and expression, had helped the NEB to achieve a balance between different styles and different books. He added, 'Even King James' men had no such director, or the AV might have been less uneven than it is'.[1] Other scholars had similar views earlier in the century. Dr Goodspeed, the American scholar and translator, used stronger language. He wrote that the effect of the centuries-old monopoly of the AV was

> to submerge completely the styles of Matthew, John and Paul under...
> 16th century diction, which covers them all so thickly that their distinctive
> qualities of style are almost invisible. Not only are the individual styles
> lost and blurred together, but the general colloquial tone of the Greek New
> Testament disappears. To crown all, this literary disaster, which in
> exchange for the Greek New Testament has given us a literary curiosity of
> the 16th century, is defended in the name of English literature and liberal
> culture.[2]

Does all this (written mainly about the New Testament and not about the Bible as a whole) answer the demands for more literary elegance, more dramatic panache, and more resonance of phrasing? Would all modern translators agree with, say, Barclay's points? The answer is

---

1. Foreword to C.H. Dodd, *The Founder of Christianity* (London: Collins, 1971).

2. E. Goodspeed, *The Making of the English New Testament* (Chicago: University of Chicago Press, 1925), p. 118.

that most probably would, but some would want to qualify them. Professor Kenneth Grayston, like Barclay, a NEB translator, while thoroughly in favour of clear modern translation, and emphasizing the inevitable obscurity of much of the AV, since 'the AV was a translation made by men who knew far less than we know', still has doubts about the ability of modern English to convey the full force and clarity needed in biblical translation. He looks back with longing to the English of Elizabethan days, writing bluntly, 'Modern English, it seems to me, is slack instead of taut, verbose and not concise, infested with this month's cliché, no longer the language of a proud and energetic English people, but an international means of communication'.[1]

That is weighty testimony coming from a skilled translator of long experience. But E.V. Rieu on one occasion warned against too much inveighing against the inadequacies of modern English. Writing about the translation of Homer into modern English he said, 'If there are some occasions when a translator of Homer may justly inveigh against the shortcomings of modern English, there are many more, I fear, when it is his own that are to blame'.[2] Honesty about the shortcomings of modern English and honesty about its strengths seem to be necessary. William Tyndale was involved in similar discussions about contemporary English; in his situation he was right to refute his contemporaries who said that the English of their day was 'too rude' and too uncouth to be the vehicle of a worthy biblical translation. When one looks back to a magnificent AV phrase such as 'Be strong and of a good courage' in Josh. 1.9, it is encouraging to notice that modern English equivalents compare well with it for resonance: 'Be strong, be resolute' (NEB, REB). 'Resolute' seems not only accurate, but a word with a long history in the English language, and much used in modern speech.

Consideration of Particular Criticisms of New Versions

Several comments cited earlier seem incomplete or misleading. When David Martin quotes W.H. Auden as saying that we should not 'spit on

---

1.   K. Grayston, 'Confessions of a Bible Translator', *New Universities Quarterly* 33 (Summer 1979), p. 288.

2.   Introduction to *The Odyssey* (Harmondsworth: Penguin Books, 1946), p. 20.

our luck' or cease using at the centre of our worship the old
translations and liturgies, he is telling only half the story. True,
Auden was an enthusiast for traditional Anglican, Orthodox and Latin
forms of worship; in the end he even seems to have wanted the Book
of Common Prayer said in Latin. It is true also that he was defensive
about traditional language, writing, 'the only duty a writer has as a
citizen is to defend language'.[1] At the same time, in St Mark's in the
Bowery church in the Lower East Side of New York, where he
worshipped when he was living in New York in the 1960s, he entered
fully into the spirit of modern liturgy, and contributed phrases to the
orders of service. In their prayer of confession the following words
occur: 'Holy Spirit, speak to us. Help us to listen, for we are very
deaf'. We are told that the last five words were one of Auden's
contributions.[2] Traditional liturgical wording obviously appealed to
his sense of poetry and ritual, but at the same time, modern liturgical
wording and freedom of expression appealed to his human, social and
political sense. This would fit in with hints which he gave when he
wrote to a friend that he was 'politically liberal, I hope...and theologically and liturgically conservative, I know'.[3] That two-sided need
in Auden is revealing, perhaps reflecting some comparable two-
sidedness in many people today. If there is to be life, we need to have
roots in past experience and also to be moving and reaching out in
new ways. A biblical translation, in the end, has to strike a balance
between past and future, between timeless beauty and present
meaning.

The mention of Latin wording raises more interesting points. Many
of us have been attracted to certain Latin wordings and translations of
verses of Scripture that go back far into history and have been much
treasured through the centuries. 'Sic Deus dilexit mundum' has a ring
about it that the AV's 'God so loved the world' does not, by some
strange alchemy of the power of wording not used by us in everyday
life; the alliteration, vowel-sounds and rhythm give the Latin a special
resonance. Another such phrase is the couplet from the Psalms:

1.   Quoted in S. Spencer (ed.), *W.H. Auden: A Tribute* (London: Weidenfeld &
Nicholson, 1975).

2.   E. James, *A Life of John Robinson* (London: SCM Press, 1987),
pp. 155-56.

3.   C. Osborne, *W.H. Auden* (London: Eyre Methuen, 1980), p. 294.

Non nobis, Domine, non nobis,
sed nomini tuo da gloriam.   (Ps. 113, Vulgate; Ps. 115, Hebrew)

Historically, internationally and culturally, these are famous words.
But I treasure, alongside them, not only Coverdale's great rendering:

Not unto us, O Lord, not unto us,
but unto thy name give the praise

but also some of the modern versions of this verse. The wording of
this verse used in worship by the Taizé Community for their version
in English is especially striking and seems close to the original
(although the translation 'never' is a bold one).

Never to us, O Lord, never to us:
to you alone let glory be given.[1]

Mention has been made of some losses when English becomes an
international language. But this Taizé translation shows another side to
this. The Taizé-style beginning of this psalm is a good example of how
English can be used, alongside other languages, in a modern living
way, in the international setting of a centre such as Taizé, without
losing resonance and beauty of style.

The Guardian leader's words about Philip Larkin and how his
comments on drafts sent to him by the NEB were ignored by the NEB
makes unhappy reading, but are also somewhat puzzling. He was
never one of the consultants appointed by the NEB committee, nor a
member of the literary panel. His comments may have been the result
of informal approaches to him by individuals linked with the project,
taken by him to mean that an official request for comment had been
made. Some years later he was officially consulted by the REB translators about aspects of the style of the NEB, and his contributions,
though few, are on record as having been valued and acknowledged. It
had been planned to send drafts for his comment, but, sadly, he had
died by this time.

Some critics have objected to the new versions for being a sort of
'rewriting' of the AV,[2] which, though not explored earlier in this
book, may be mentioned here, since it raises important issues, and is

1.   *Psalms from Taizé.*
2.   For example, J. Bowden in the brief preface to his *By Heart* (London: SCM
Press, 1984)

linked with the question of periodic retranslations of the Bible
previously touched on. The issue is simply whether translations of the
Bible into English after the AV can be taken seriously at all, and if so,
what the relationship between versions is to be.

I have always thought of the relationship between a classic version
of the Bible and a modern version not in terms of one being a
rewriting of the other but more like the relationship between a
twentieth-century musical setting of biblical words and a classic
seventeenth-century setting of the same words. Henry Purcell, in the
seventeenth century, composed a great anthem on the words 'Rejoice
in the Lord always'; Henry Ley, early in the twentieth century,
composed his own anthem on the same words. Both are sung in
cathedrals today, but Ley is not seen as trying to 're-write' Purcell.
My analogy cannot be pushed too far: Purcell's anthem was never an
'authorized version' musically. But even so great a classic as the AV
translation of the Bible cannot be so solid as to make us forget that it
was in fact a 'setting' in English of an original in Hebrew and Greek.
In the translation of secular classics, we are accustomed to periodic
re-translations and to seeing well-known translations followed by
other settings. Dryden translated Chaucer into the English of his own
day ('to refresh memory', he said). Nevil Coghill did the same in the
twentieth century. In 1940 Cecil Day Lewis translated Vergil's
Georgics (and later the *Aeneid* and *Eclogues*) not into classical or
archaic English but into modern English. In the Penguin Classics
series are translations of Homer's *Odyssey* and *Iliad* by E.V. Rieu,
Walter Sherring and Martin Hammond. These do not follow what one
reviewer called 'an authorized sort of translation', nor do they follow
the nineteenth-century styles of translation used by the famous teams
of Butcher and Lang, or Lang, Leaf and Myers; but they have caught
the Homeric material and atmosphere in modern rhythms and
vocabulary for a new century.

Patterns of Beauty, New and Old

These considerations of a few detailed criticisms of modern
translations inevitably lead to the consideration of a common criticism
underlying most of these comments: the charge of aesthetic bleakness.
This in turn leads on to the most fundamental question of all: 'what
does the term "beauty" mean in relation to biblical translation?' To

many modern translators the alleged bleakness of their language appears as straightforwardness and realism, and as the avoidance of traditionally ornate, well-rounded biblical English in passages where ornate formal language is obviously out of place.

When the RSV was published in 1946 there were discussions on the type of beauty that was desirable in a modern Bible. In an article on the use of the New Testament in worship, Dr Walter Russell Bowie (the noted American preacher and member of the RSV's New Testament panel) wrote that modern translators were not uninterested in beauty of language, but suggested that what they sought might be best called 'functional beauty'.

> There can be a new kind of beauty as the creators of the best modern music and of the sheer upsoaring and triumphant lines of modern architecture have made evident—a functional beauty which is the expression of purpose in the most vital and therefore the most fitting form.[1]

I am not quite happy with the phrase 'functional beauty' if it is used to suggest that there is no longer a place in modern biblical translation for the lyrical and the poetic. But if it means that there must be an element of realism in the beauty of language fashioned for use in translation, then the phrase is a welcome one. In Mt. 11.28 the AV has the wording: 'Come unto me, all ye that labour and are heavy laden, and I will give you rest'. The aesthetic, classical beauty of the language, fashioned sensitively with planned alliteration and vowel sounds, is beyond dispute; and there is no obscurity of meaning for the modern reader. When set alongside a modern version, there is not a huge difference in the wording, but 'heavyladen' has become the perhaps more functional 'overburdened', as noted earlier.

In Bowie's words we find, once again, the analogy between modern music and modern translation. There is about much modern music a certain bleakness, associated with, amongst other characteristics, dissonance and discord; and (critics are quite right) there is a certain bleakness in modern biblical translations compared with the more rounded and ceremonious English of the AV. But does this mean that the heart of the beauty in the language has disappeared? I attended a Palm Sunday service in an English cathedral recently where one piece

1. L.A. Weigle (ed.), *An Introduction to the Revised Standard Version of the New Testament* (USA: International Council of Religious Education, 1946), p. 63.

of 'passion music' sung was by the sixteenth-century composer
Victoria. The music was passionate but harmonious and almost
without dissonances, even when it came to 'Let him be crucified'. In
contrast, another piece of music at the same service was a Poulenc
motet from the twentieth century with an atmosphere of serenity,
assurance and peace about it, but there were other more dissonant and
astringent elements there; something that could be described as bleak.
A twentieth-century changed emphasis in tonal expression was
present. I liked both the classic style of Victoria and the modern style
of Poulenc, as expressions of what we were concerned with that day,
just as I also accepted the combination of classic and modern in some
varied styles of language used in biblical readings and prayers during
the service.

Tonal systems in music change and evolve. In about 1200 AD the
musical interval called the third was regarded as dissonant, but later
came to be accepted as part of what could be called beauty, and even
came to be regarded as a consonance. Increasingly, perhaps, tension,
and the generation and relief of tension, has become more marked or
found more frequently in musical styles. By the twentieth century
distinguished musicians in Britain were beginning to discuss the
importance of including ugliness in music. In 1911 even Sir Hubert
Parry, who has been associated mainly with sonorous and ceremonial
music for national occasions, gave a talk to the International Music
Society on the value of ugliness.

> Ugliness would seem to be one of the most beneficent provisions of
> nature. It is an incitement to attention, to grapple with something that may
> reward thinking about. A work which avoids everything ugly is soothing,
> but it does not enlarge men's lives much.[1]

The parallels with a more bleak and astringent type of language
in biblical translation are apparent. Language that is modern
(C.S. Lewis's example of 'flogged' instead of 'scourged') may shock
or disturb the reader by its directness, but still has an important place
within the light and shade of the whole beauty of language in a
passage. In the present day, with its spirit of realism, questioning and
honest exploration, musicians and readers of the Bible often desire a

---

1. Cited in P. Scholes (ed.), *Oxford Dictionary of Music* (Oxford: Oxford
University Press).

style of expression that is not too grandiloquent but that has a down-to-earth quality about it.

Clearly, critics such as Peter Mullen would not like my analogy between modern translation and modern music. It is the discovery of links between the AV and modern music that he prefers. When he says that, 'the form of religious expression must change from age to age', he does not mean that modern biblical translations should be seen to follow on the work of the AV, but that it is in modern literary and musical works that we should look for the AV's allies in the task of expressing God's truth. He is aware of the combination of consonance and dissonance in modern music, but this he links with what he sees as a similar combination in the AV, not with anything in modern biblical translations (which are regarded as shallower). The AV's words, he says, 'are at once familiar and strange, they attract and they repel'.[1] Oddly, he does not seem to have experienced what I call the anodyne quality of much of the AV's well-rounded, familiar language; he finds it uniformly invigorating, a good mixture often of grandeur and earthiness. 'Just as a modern symphony makes whole music out of cacophonies and dissonances, so the verbal symbols of the AV give meaning to the flux of life's events', he writes. I have found more resemblance between the realism of modern music and the realism of modern translations, and have found that to be the significant analogy.

Beauty and Ordinariness in Biblical Translation

It would be tedious to try and spell out further my idea of a modern biblical translation as comparable with a modern musical setting. However, by way of a further analogy to the artistic world, I examine the work of the painter Rembrandt, who used a certain ordinariness and simplicity of style in presenting religious truth, and who was keen that beauty of style should truly accompany and not eclipse the truth that he was presenting. From the age of forty he turned his back on the classical, decorative ideal of heroic beauty which was fashionable in late Renaissance or Baroque art. His painting came to be characterized by realism and simplicity. It was not that his paintings had no mystical beauty in them; they did. But the beauty lay in the

1. Mullen, *The New Babel*, pp. 52-53.

ordinariness of the people and figures he painted, although it was an ordinariness transfigured by something beyond itself. The Jews in the etching *Christ Healing* were painted from people in the Jewish quarter in Rembrandt's own neighbourhood. Those who know his pictures well say that, as time went on, he ceased to depict Christ resplendent in human glory, and portrayed him as one who was present, incognito, in the human scene, without great beauty. Professor John W. Dixon writes of how, in Rembrandt's later painting, 'the humbling of the Word in the ordinary' is to be discerned. Dixon adds that in the early Christian times beauty was expressed more exclusively in terms of an icon-like presentation of religious truth, but that by the seventeenth century beauty was beginning to be expressed also in terms of human personality and persons.[1] And W.A. Visser T'Hooft spells out Dixon's point about Rembrandt explicitly:

> From this time the beautiful ceased to be an end in itself for him. He realised that beauty must serve something higher, namely truth, or else it is in danger of becoming an empty shell, falsifying the reality of life. If beauty accepts this part, it acquires a new substance through which the eternal shines.[2]

Where modern biblical translation achieves the right sort of 'ordinariness' it is not simply a manifestation of transient modern trendiness, but is showing an aspect of aesthetic style with a long Christian history and tradition behind it. In fact, of course, the tradition goes back at least five centuries earlier than Rembrandt. When St Bernard of Clairvaux, in the twelfth century, wrote about plainsong and Gregorian chant, he said that the beauty of the music should accompany the words and not dominate them: 'it is no slight loss of spiritual grace to be distracted from the profit of the sense by the beauty of the chant, and to have our attention drawn to a mere vocal display, when we ought to be thinking of what is sung'.[3] He was writing about (non-popular) monastic recitation of the psalms in mediaeval times; but the principle enunciated by him is relevant to any

1.   J.W. Dixon, 'Aesthetics and Theology', in A. Richardson and J. Bowden (eds.), *A New Dictionary of Christian Theology* (London: SCM Press, 1983), p. 8.

2.   *Rembrandt and the Gospels* (London: SCM Press, 1957), p. 13.

3.   Quoted in A. Robertson, *The Interpretation of Plainchant* (London: Collins 1937).

discussion of the relationship between artistic things and the things of faith. The beauty of language that expresses, communicates the things of God, and the cries of the human heart should, above all, never 'draw our attention away' from the sense of the words that it accompanies. Those who, in general, favour modern biblical translation are conscious of the dangers if, in the English-speaking world, we take as our only version of the Bible something written in undoubtedly beautiful Shakespearian language. There is a danger of having our attention drawn away from meaning by the beauty of the words.

During the eighteenth and nineteenth centuries the romantic emphasis which focused on the AV and its style of language was an important one. But it is only one emphasis within the wider world of Christian thought and creative art and should be balanced by other emphases which focus on realism, and which are conscious of the need to see that truth is not eclipsed by beauty.

Although critics say that the new translations have not held truth and beauty together well, and although, as has been seen, critics doubt whether modern English is the language in which such a holding together can be achieved, one should not be too despairing. Just as in the world of literature, some twentieth-century poets have achieved a remarkable blend of imaginativeness and unaffected realism,[1] so the new versions, in their own field, have often achieved a richer blend than has been acknowledged by the critics. Most would agree that the style of language needed for a good modern translation should have two characteristics above all. It should be language that is sufficiently 'transparent' (a term much used by translators to describe the language they aim for) to allow the original Hebrew or Greek to shine through without too much overlay of added English beauty. While for much of the time it may be natural, unsophisticated, unsentimental, undecorative and unpretentious, yet it should also have the capacity to become lyrical, lively or apocalyptic when the occasion demands.

---

1.   See Kenneth Allott's magnificent sentence about Kathleen Raine, in the *Penguin Book of Contemporary Verse 1918–1960* (Harmondsworth: Penguin Books, 1962), p. 215 that 'she writes musically in unaffected language and...can express an apocalyptic element in feeling without inflation'.

Beauty, Communication and Freedom

Roy Hattersley's words about 'the Church Beautiful' have been quoted
earlier. I respect those words, spoken from the heart, which echo
John Keats's lines:

> 'Beauty is truth, truth beauty'—that is all
> Ye know on earth, and all ye need to know.[1]

They echo too a Christian tradition reaching much further back than
Keats, to Augustine of Hippo. Augustine, theologian, mystic,
musician, was emotionally and spiritually drawn to the beauty and
proportion of form as inseparable from clarity of truth, and he
approached many theological and biblical truths in aesthetic terms. He
called the incarnate Christ 'Beauty ever ancient, ever new'. He was
deeply concerned with the relationship between figurative language
and reality, and, partly through early philosophical influences,
described theological concepts such as providence in aesthetic terms
such as 'the chiaroscuro of light and darkness'.[2] Religion and beauty,
religion and poetry, belong together.

Alongside that, one cannot help placing the fact of the biblical
translator's continuing commitment to wide-ranging communication.
The case for the honouring and use of the great classic English
versions (whether William Tyndale's translations, the Great Bible of
1539, or the Authorized Version), with their majestic and sonorous
language, is unanswerable. Difficulties do arise when the case is
presented in exclusive terms, which suggest that these classic versions
are the only real forms of the English Bible. If this happens and if
beauty of language becomes too dominating a consideration, great
problems arise in the effective transmission of biblical material to a
full range of readers and hearers.

This is a hard truth and one in which issues of freedom of language
are central. Undoubtedly, the freedom of imaginative translators may
be limited if they have to be balanced against considerations of other
factors in effective communication. Freedom in translation is never
absolute. Idiomatically imaginative translators (for example, modern

---

1. Ode 'On a Grecian Urn'.
2. A phrase quoted from H. Chadwick, *Augustine* (Past Masters; Oxford:
Oxford University Press, 1986), p. 46.

translators who are drawn to the use of paraphrase and a clarifying expansion of words) in their turn see freedom subjected to constraints.

Jerome, often acclaimed as a biblical translator with outstanding gifts of language, put his finger on the main points of principle in this matter, when he wrote,

> a translation made for the Church, although it may indeed have some literary merit, ought to conceal and avoid it, so as to address itself, not to the private schools of the philosophers, with their handful of disciples, but rather to the whole human race.[1]

---

1. Quoted in H.F.D. Sparks, in *The Cambridge History of the Bible*, (Cambridge: Cambridge University Press, 1970), I, p. 524; and in Prickett, *Words and the Word*.

Chapter 7

Translating Poetic Imagery

Some of the strongest criticism of modern versions of the Bible has been about the translating of poetic imagery and figurative language generally. A British lecturer in Old Testament studies made this comment to me on the GNB:

> Its language is banal and flat. It removes much of the poetic imagery of the original. Instead of 'The Lord is my strength and shield' (Ps. 28.7) we get 'The Lord protects and defends me'. I use the New Revised Standard Version in my classes. As a version, the Good News Bible may be all right for evangelistic purposes, but not as an all-round replacement of more literal versions.

Modern Generalizing Tendencies

Professor David Frost, although in favour of new language in church services and biblical translation, is critical of what he regards as inadequate treatment of poetic imagery by modern versions generally. He writes, 'Every modern Bible translation tends to render the vivid, concrete images of poetry into grey abstractions'.[1] And the late Dr George Caird commented on the way in which biblical translators, in the interests of greater clarity, sometimes 'unpack metaphors' in an unnecessary manner and in passages where the metaphor's meaning is clear. He cites the translation of 1 Cor. 15.20 in the TNT, a verse which we have already looked at in Chapter 1. He is unhappy that the TNT removes the 'firstfruits' imagery there. (And the TNT is in general a far less expansive translation than the Living Bible previously quoted.) The AV translates the verse, 'now is Christ risen from the dead, and become the firstfruits of them that slept'. The TNT has, 'Christ has been raised from the dead. This is the

---

1. Frost, *The Language of Series 3.*

guarantee that those who have died will be raised also' (the GNB rendering is similar). Caird says that surely the metaphor of 'firstfruits' and the harvest language is understood everywhere and needs no unpacking.[1]

This comment is heard not only on the lips of academic figures, but also from ordinary churchgoers, who miss, in many modern versions, the 'rocks', the 'shields' and the 'crowns' which are such a feature of the older, more literal translations. I take some further examples from the GNB; it certainly has a policy of frequently turning a piece of poetic imagery into more general terms, turning a metaphorical noun into a generalized verb for example, or dropping some concrete image entirely.

The well-known words of Ps. 95.1 in the AV read, 'Let us make a joyful noise to the rock of our salvation'. The GNB translates it, 'Let us sing for joy to God, who protects us!' Similarly, in Ps. 18.2 the AV has an accumulation of poetic images beginning with, 'The Lord is my rock' (Coverdale, 'The Lord is my stony rock'). The GNB translates it, 'The Lord is my protector'. To translate several Hebrew words for 'rock', the GNB uses a variety of words in English including 'refuge', 'defender' and especially 'protector' (or the verb forms of these words).

In the Isa. 55.12 text about the coming time of deliverance, the GNB removes the literal image of trees clapping their hands. The AV has, 'The mountains and the hills shall break forth before you into singing, and all the trees of the field shall clap their hands'. The GNB translates it, 'The mountains and the hills will burst forth into singing, and the trees will shout for joy'.

In Josh. 7.5 the AV says that, after a defeat, 'the hearts of the people melted and became as water'. The GNB has, 'the Israelites lost their courage and were afraid'.

Similar points arise in the New Testament. In Phil. 4.1 Paul, addressing Christians in Philippi, says that they are a sign of the success of his work. His words in the literal AV translation are, 'my brethren...my joy and crown...stand fast in the Lord'. The Greek word for 'crown' is στέφανος, and the reference is to the crown or wreath placed on the head of a victorious general or athlete. The GNB does not use this concrete image; instead of the literal translation of

1. Caird, *Language and Imagery*, p. 91.

'joy and crown' it has the phrase, 'How happy you make me and how proud I am of you!'

Modern Renderings Newly Catching the Imagery

I would like now to give a broader picture of the treatment of poetic imagery in translations old and new. Alongside what we have just examined it is also necessary to look at some of the many passages where the original poetic imagery is translated in the modern versions more literally, and rather better, than in the AV.

In Isa. 1.8 a piece of colourful Palestinian imagery is brought out better in the modern versions, in my view, than in the AV. The AV, translating this passage about Jerusalem's troubles, has 'the daughter of Zion is left as a cottage in a vineyard, as a lodge in a garden of cucumbers, as a beseiged city'. The GNB translates it, 'Jerusalem alone is left, a city under siege—as defenceless as a watchman's hut in a vineyard or a shed in a cucumber field'. The GNB's 'hut' and 'shed' convey the vivid imagery better than the AV's 'cottage' and 'lodge' which give an impression of old-world charm and permanence, not relevant to the metaphor of a rough shelter in a field in Palestine during the growing season which the context requires.

Again, in Ps. 31.1 (and similarly in Ps. 71.1) the AV's well-known and lovely words do not bring out as well as the GNB and other modern versions the full imagery lying behind the first Hebrew verb here (*ḥāsâ*, which is about taking refuge). The AV has, 'put my trust', where the GNB has, 'come for protection'. The AV translates the verse, 'In thee, O Lord, do I put my trust: let me never be ashamed'. The GNB translates it, 'I come to you, Lord, for protection; never let me be defeated'. The REB has, 'In you, Lord, I have found refuge; let me never be put to shame'. The Jewish Publication Society Version has, 'I seek refuge in you, O Lord; may I never be disappointed'. The AV may have had reasons for not using 'refuge' or some similar word to bring out the poetic imagery of the original: rock and fortress imagery come in the next two verses, and the full imagery is there brought out by the AV. But the fact remains that the modern versions go out of their way to see that all the imagery is caught at the beginning of this psalm. There are many other examples of places where the AV, and Coverdale, do not leave metaphors and imagery in the original literal and concrete form, but use more general terms. In

Ps. 19.14 the AV and Coverdale have, 'Let the words of my mouth, and the meditation of my heart, be acceptable in thy sight, O Lord, my strength and my redeemer'. Who would want to argue with the AV's magnificent rendering here? But the Hebrew word translated as 'my strength' means literally 'my rock', and it is the modern versions that bring out that imagery.

In the AV at Ps. 53.4 (and in Coverdale similarly) the Hebrew imagery is reproduced literally, but the modern translations both reproduce the imagery here and convey it vividly. Knox was wordy, but gives a stronger translation than the AV, in my view. The AV translates it, 'Have the workers of iniquity no knowledge? who eat up my people as they eat bread'. Knox has,

> What, can they learn nothing,
> all these traffickers in iniquity,
> who feed themselves fat on this people of mine,
> as if it were bread for their eating.

The AV is more poetic on another occasion, when in Job 24.8, in a couplet about the needy and the oppressed, there are words of great beauty, 'they are wet with the showers of the mountains, and embrace the rock for want of a shelter'. But a modern version, the REB, tackles the 'embracing' imagery even more effectively: 'drenched by rainstorms from the hills, they cling to the rock, their only shelter'.

Ps. 51.8 gives us the fine and well-known words: 'Make me to hear joy and gladness; that the bones which thou hast broken may rejoice'. But it is modern translations such as the REB and the NJB that bring out the real imagery lying behind the Hebrew word translated 'rejoice' by the AV. The Hebrew word means 'to spring about', 'to dance', and not only 'to be joyful'. The NJB has, 'Let me hear the sound of joy and gladness, and the bones you have crushed will dance'.

In the New Testament the new versions bring out colourful underlying meaning in a number of places where the language of the AV tends to be flat and prosaic. In Gal. 3.1 Paul writes, 'O foolish Galatians, who has bewitched you...before whose eyes Jesus Christ hath been evidently set forth, crucified among you?' The Greek word translated by the AV's phrase 'evidently set forth' has the imagery of a picture or a placard lying behind it; it is more adequately rendered as 'clearly portrayed' or 'publicly placarded'. Hence the NJB's 'You

stupid people in Galatia! After you have had a clear picture of Jesus
Christ crucified, right in front of your eyes, who has put a spell on
you?' This last translation also deals firmly with the Greek word
βασκανία, translated by the AV as 'bewitched' and by the NJB with
'cast a spell'; the English word 'bewitched' is a strong one, and several
modern translations retain it. But in modern Greek βασκανία means
'the evil eye', and so 'cast a spell on' is also good.[1]

It is even arguable that in Jn 10.9 (AV, 'I am the door') the imagery
is best caught in English by the rendering, 'I am the gate' which many
modern versions give (NRSV, NIV, GNB, NJB). The image of the
gateway is stronger in English literature than the imagery of the door,
from the days of John Donne onwards, and 'gate' may perhaps give
better equivalence here. It is true that the Greek word used in Jn 10.9,
θύρα, has usually been translated 'door', and that the word 'gate' has
been reserved for the translation of another Greek word, πύλη. But
there may be less distinction between θύρα and πύλη than has
traditionally been supposed: Mt. 7.13 speaks about the narrow πύλη
into the kingdom, and Lk. 13.24 about the narrow θύρα into the
kingdom. The NIV in Jn 10.9 has, 'I am the gate; whoever enters
through me will be saved'.

Two Translators and their Comments

Rather than lengthening the list of such examples, I turn to what
Eugene Nida says about the GNB's policy over the translation of
figurative expressions. In his book *Good News for Everyone*[2] he
writes as someone closely linked to the whole GNB enterprise of
translation. He recognizes that 'rendering of poetry constitutes one of
the most difficult of all problems in the preparation of a common-
language translation', but states that where possible the GNB retains
figurative expressions that are in the original text, for instance 'your
shepherd's rod and staff protect me' in the GNB at Ps. 23.4. However,
he points out that, since in the international cosmopolitan setting in

1.   A.M. Hunter, in *Galatians to Colossians* (Layman's Bible Commentaries;
London: SCM Press, 1959) took seriously the 'evil eye' background to the word,
linking it up with the phrase 'before your eyes' in the verse, and reinforcing, as
Paul's overall message here, the sense of 'keep your eyes on Christ crucified', p.26.

2.   Nida, *Good News for Everyone*, Chapter 5.

which English is read and spoken today figurative expressions often leave the reader or hearer unclear as to meaning, the GNB sometimes does not give a literal translation of such expressions or inserts additional explanatory words in the translation; this, he says, is part of the GNB's policy of striving to achieve the 'closest natural equivalent' in English. Among his examples of how this works in practice are the following:

1. Ps. 16.7, where, as Nida says, a literal translation would be, 'in the night my kidneys warn me' or, as the AV literally had, 'my reins also instruct me in the night season', 'reins' being a word used for 'kidneys' in those days. The GNB, along with other modern versions, does not reflect the imagery literally but renders it, 'in the night my conscience warns me'. Many modern versions use words such as 'heart' for the GNB'S 'conscience'.

2. In Ps. 23.5 the AV has, 'thou annointest my head with oil'. The GNB removes the imagery and renders it, 'you welcome me as an honoured guest'. Nida remarks that '"annoint my head with oil" seems entirely strange to the present day reader, for "oil" would only be understood as some kind of lubricant for engines and motors'. Even 'pouring olive oil on the head', he says, would seem inappropriate; scarcely the way to honour a guest at a banquet. Therefore the GNB brings out the equivalent meaning by describing the honouring of a guest. Nida adds that this was 'something which on one occasion a man who invited Jesus to his house failed to do'. But it is noticeable that the GNB firmly retains the imagery in the clause immediately following which is easily understood, 'my cup runneth over' are the words in the AV; the GNB has, 'you fill my cup to the brim'.

3. In Ps. 60.8 the AV has 'Over Edom will I cast out my shoe'. Nida is surely right in saying that this might well be interpreted by the average reader as meaning that God simply despises Edom and is content to use it as nothing more than a box in which to toss dirty shoes or sandals. He points out that the real meaning of the phrase is to take over ownership of something (see Ruth 4.7), and says that the GNB, while wanting to retain the imagery but not use many footnotes, clarifies by expanding the translation. The GNB translates, 'I will throw my sandals on Edom, as a sign that I own it'.

4. Mt. 6.3 (AV) has, 'when thou doest alms, let not thy left hand know what thy right hand doeth'. Nida comments that this piece of imagery, which originally signified unostentatious giving, has

unfortunately come to mean that 'in doing something underhand or illegal, it is important to keep no records'. The GNB renders it, 'When you help a needy person, do it in such a way that even your closest friend will not know about it'.

It is useful to examine what modern translators such as William Barclay have written about the translation of imagery. He largely shared Nida's approach. He wanted imagery translated directly and literally where this was possible, and in Mt. 13.3 put simply, 'A sower went out to sow his seed'. But he regarded some of the farming metaphors used in the New Testament as too obscure nowadays to be translated literally. In Mt. 25.24 (the parable of the talents) he did not feel able to give a literal translation such as the AV had, where the 'lord' who gave the talents to his servants was described as 'reaping where thou hast not sown, and gathering where thou hast not strawed'. Barclay wrote, 'This passage as it stands is in terms of agricultural practice which is quite strange to a modern urban man. It is better therefore to modernize the picture.' In other words he considered this to be one of those rare occasions when the translator is forced to give an amplified translation, and he renders it, 'I know that you have a habit of letting someone else do the work and of then taking the profits. I know you often step in and appropriate the results of some enterprise which you did not initiate'. Barclay added,

> In some very few cases the whole New Testament metaphor is obscure, because it comes from a society and from activities which are now quite strange. On some few occasions it is... better to go the whole way with Hilaire Belloc's principle, and to ask, not, how can this be put into English, but, how would an Englishman of the middle twentieth century have said it.[1]

This is an example of Barclay's passion for clarity, and how he sometimes protested violently at people's glib assumption that traditional biblical phrases are easily understood. Most modern translators are content to give a literal translation of the clause in question.

One thing which Barclay cannot be accused of is putting abstractions in place of poetic images (a charge sometimes levelled at translators, as we have seen). As a human being, a musician, a Scot with a Highland background, and as a communicator, he wrote these

---

1. W. Barclay, 'On Translating the New Testament', in *The New Testament*. I. *The Gospels and Acts* (London: Collins, 1968), p. 341.

words, 'I cannot think in abstractions at all: I think in pictures'.[1] He quoted Regine Pernoud: 'There is a world of difference between learning to repeat "God is an omnipotent being", and learning to address oneself to God saying "Thou art my rock"'.[2] If Barclay refrained sometimes from giving a piece of biblical imagery a literal translation, it is certain that the motive was clarity, and nothing else.

Barclay goes out of his way in his translation of Mk 10.38 to bring out the full meaning and vivid imagery of the word 'baptized', which is used figuratively in that verse. For the words of Jesus to James and John, the AV has, 'Can ye be baptized with the baptism that I am baptized with?', and most modern translations also give the word 'baptized'. But Barclay, conscious of the figurative way in which the word was sometimes used of the experience of being overwhelmed or submerged in life, translated the verse as follows, 'Can you be submerged in the sea of troubles in which I must be submerged?' (The NAB similarly has, 'Can you...be baptized in the same bath of pain as I?' And the earlier translator Charles Kingsley Williams rendered it, 'Can you...pass through the waters that I am passing through?') Barclay translated the Greek word βαπτίζω by the single English word 'baptize(d)' in passages where the reference is to literal baptism in Jordan, but was keen to convey the metaphorical aspect of the word. As he wrote,[3] the Greek word βαπτίζω (literally meaning 'to dip in water') not only had behind it the imagery of religious rituals such as baptism and of secular and religious washings of hands, but also the imagery of idiomatic expressions and metaphors about bitter experiences of suffering. In the secular Greek of those times a ship sunk at sea was said to have been 'baptized' in the water. People who were hopelessly in debt were described as being 'baptized' in debt. It must have been similar to the modern English phrase, used of a person in a dilemma or describing some crisis, 'I was completely sunk'. The metaphorical usage of the word βαπτίζω was closely linked with pieces of Hebrew imagery such as the psalmist's phrase about his suffering, 'all thy waves and storms are gone over me'

1. W. Barclay, *Testament of Faith* (London: Mowbrays, 1975).

2. Pernoud, *Heloise and Abelard*, p. 35, as quoted in Barclay, *Testament of Faith*.

3. Barclay, 'On Translating the New Testament', p. 321.

(Ps. 42.9 in Coverdale's version), and the phrases about 'being overwhelmed in the Red Sea'.

Finally I refer to one of the passages mentioned earlier, Phil. 4.1, where the GNB and others do not translate 'crown' literally (AV, 'my joy and crown') but read, 'my pride' or 'my sign of success' (the GNB, 'How proud I am of you!'). I think that the translation of the Greek word here is as perfect an example as one can find of the agonizing dilemma facing translators. On the one hand, how can one put anything except 'crown', a colourful and central image and metaphor in the Mediterranean world of those days? Many modern translators retain 'crown'. On the other hand, how can one retain 'crown' literally, when the metaphor is neither close in meaning to any 'crown' metaphors that we have in English (not even to 'crowning achievements'), nor is it an example of an AV phrase that has passed into common English usage. Perhaps one should follow the few translators who, like the GNB, put in place of 'my joy and crown' renderings such as 'you give me joy and you are the sign of my victory' (TNT) or who have Paul greeting his readers here as 'all my delight and my prize' (Knox). My own view is that this is a phrase which still awaits an appropriate translation in English, one that will, in a brief compass, include both the imagery of something that goes on the head and a clearer indication than 'crown' gives of Paul's meaning. Something less impossibly colloquial is needed, not unlike, 'You are a delight for me, a real feather in my cap'. It seems to be true, in relation to biblical translation for the modern cosmopolitan English-speaking world, that the more traditionalist translators stick too often to the precise and literal old image, while more innovative translators, in moving on to something new, too often tend to discard any related imagery, and fall too easily into a generalized and paraphrased mode of expression.

Translating Biblical Body Language

The large and interesting topic of how Hebraic imagery of body, face, eyes and mouth is translated in modern Bibles must be discussed only briefly here. In Philemon 12 Philemon is told that Onesimus, 'that is mine own bowels' (AV), is being sent back to him; the NIV has 'I am sending him—who is my very heart—back to you'. In Lk. 1.70 the AV has, 'he spake by the mouth of his holy prophets'; the REB gives, 'he proclaimed by the lips of his holy prophets'. In Lev. 19.32 the AV has, 'thou shalt honour the face of the old man'; the NJB gives, 'you will honour the person of the aged'. Opinions differ on whether the freer translations give adequate equivalence to the original meaning and flavour of the passage. There are particular complications with the literal translation of some 'face' imagery. In Ps. 95.2 (the 'Venite') the Hebrew phrase which is literally 'Let us come before his face with thanksgiving' is not so translated by Coverdale and the AV but as 'Let us come before his presence with thanksgiving'. Phrases suggesting an anthropomorphic idea of God have often, though not entirely, been avoided by scriptural authors and translators. Some modern versions boldly bring out a full and literal face imagery: the Psalter of the Church of England's Alternative Service Book has the rendering 'Let us come before his face with thanksgiving and cry out to him joyfully in psalms'.[1] And Peter Levi, in the *Penguin Classics Psalms*, attempts a new solution with 'Come into his sight with praise, and cry out to him with music'.

The translation of the word given as 'loins' in the AV presents the modern translator with its own problems. When Elijah girds up his flowing robes around his waist (1 Kgs 18.46) there is a difference between the AV's literal 'he girded up his loins and ran' and the REB's non-literal 'he tucked up his robe and ran'. However, the real challenges come with 'loins' phrases used figuratively. The Semitic idiom 'gird up your loins' carries the sense not only of stripping off encumbrances, but also of being disciplined or ready for action, and of summoning up all one's energies. The difficulty here is to get English phrases that are both resonant and more than merely decorative, and also that capture the breadth of meaning.

In Job 40.7 the AV has, 'Gird up thy loins like a man: I will demand of thee, and declare thou unto me'. Job is being challenged by God to defend himself. Modern translators have found a useful modern phrase, with a strong claim to possess equivalent imagery, in 'brace yourself'. The NEB and REB give, 'Brace yourself and stand up like a man; I shall put questions to you, and you must answer' (cf. the NIV similarly, and the NJB's 'Brace yourself like a fighter'). 'Bracing oneself', like girding up one's loins, is concerned with binding things together, but also, like 'girding up the loins' in its day, carries the

---

1. *The Psalms: A New Translation for Worship* (London: Collins, 1977).

developed idiomatic meaning of 'summoning up energies for a task' and generally 'getting ready for action'.

In 1 Pet. 1.13 the readers, as newly baptized people, are urged to stand firm against the pull of their old way of life. The AV has, 'gird up the loins of your mind, (be sober, and hope)', a resounding phrase, but perhaps too vague for a modern ear to catch the sort of vivid meaning that the original phrase must have had in its day. Moffatt first put here, 'Brace up your minds, then', instituting the use of 'brace yourself' in this connection. Knox had, 'Rid your minds of every encumbrance', the NRSV has, 'Prepare your minds for action'.

In Lk. 12.35 the AV translates the phrase, 'Let your loins be girded about, and your lights burning'. The wording is strong with some powerful rhythm, alliteration ('let', 'loins', 'lights') and monosyllabic words. The word 'about' gives a picture of clothes gathered or belted round the waist. Modern translators have not found it easy to find expressions to set alongside the AV's great words. The NAB's 'Let your belts be fastened around your waists and your lamps be burning ready' finishes well, but is long, and does not seem to do justice to imagery which was concerned not only with the fastening of belts but also of having loose clothing fastened in to enable movement. Some other modern versions are less literal. William Barclay had, 'Always be ready stripped for action, with your lamps lit', the GNB has, 'Be ready for whatever comes, dressed for action and with your lamps lit', the NRSV gives, 'Be dressed for action and have your lamps lit'. Perhaps this is another of those biblical verses that is still searching for a modern translator. Something like, 'Keep your bodies clothed for action, belts secure' seems to be the line to follow, with the merit of getting some alliteration with 'bodies' and 'belts'. But it is not succinct enough, and needs a poet to condense metaphor and meaning into a more dramatic compass.

Two Passages of Imagery: Poetic and Apocalyptic

For some extended passages in this chapter I have chosen Eccl. 12.1-7, as a lyrical passage with much poetic imagery in it, and Isa. 63.1-6, as a typical passage containing apocalyptic imagery. The GNB's rendering of the first has a certain directness and terseness about it, but seems to be one of the very best examples of lyrical quality in a 'common-language translation'. The fact that the passage is open to different interpretations makes the accompanying notes here somewhat longer than usual, but does not prevent its style and language from receiving attention.

Ecclesiastes 12.1-7

The passage is about old age and the approach of death, as v. 1 makes clear. The imagery depicts old age in three ways: first, as the winter of life (v. 2), when storms threaten and the clouds hardly lift, secondly, as a house or household under threat, with activity failing and breaking down, and 'the keepers of the house trembling' (vv. 3-5). These opening verses are often taken, even in rabbinical interpretation, as an elaborate allegory in which the house stands for the human body and the failing powers of its various parts; for example, 'those that look out of the window' and are 'darkened' (12.2 in the AV) are taken to be the old man's eyes. The third way in which old age is depicted is through imagery about lamps and wells, with the light of life and the water of life failing, because the chain by which the lamp hangs breaks, and the oil-bowl, water-jar and rope-wheel all break (12.6).

In 12.3-5, where old age is pictured as a household breaking down, modern translations follow one of two policies, either following the AV in translating the symbolism of the Hebrew directly or, taking the verses as a definite allegory of the ageing body, spelling out the assumed meaning of the symbolism. The REB, on the whole, follows the first of those. For example, in 12.3 it gives, 'those who look through the windows can see no longer'. In a sense the REB is less literal than the AV here, since in 12.4 where the AV speaks of the 'daughters of music brought low', the REB has the more interpretative phrase, 'the song-birds fall silent'. On the whole, the REB, like the AV, does not spell out the allegory's meaning. The GNB, on the other hand, follows the alternative approach and, in an interpretative way, spells out the meaning of the imagery. In 12.3 it does not describe people looking out of windows, but speaks of 'eyes too dim to see clearly'.

In general, among commentators and translators there is huge variation in the interpretation of the significance of the symbolism. What the AV renders as 'the sound of the grinding is low' in 12.4 is taken by some to mean simply that those in the house can hardly hear the mill outside as it grinds; by others it is taken to be an allegorical reference to the diminished sounds of human conversation in the aged man's life.

Several literary figures have expressed the view that only the AV's translation of this passage catches the poetry of the original. T.R. Henn expressed the view that the phrase in 12.5 (AV, 'they shall be afraid of that which is high') is spoilt in modern versions by the attempt to narrow down and spell out the meaning, making it refer to the aged man's fear of steps, or whatever. Henn defended the use of a wide phrase, such as the AV's, which covers terrors of storm, sky or divine vengeance. By comparing the AV and the GNB translation that follows it will be possible to judge the merits of the two translations. I find that the AV translation remains fine and moving, the classic translation. But I find the GNB's version possesses not only clarity of meaning but also a remarkable lyrical and poetic quality. Although radical in its restructuring, many parts of the symbolism at the beginning and end of the passage (about lamp and well, for example) are direct translations, not altered interpretatively or 'spelt out'. The language is vivid throughout; I believe that the GNB's version could, in its own way, become as historic a piece of English writing about human life and old age as the classic AV translation is today. Recently that impression was confirmed in the writings of Bishop John Robinson. Examining Ecclesiastes 12 he wrote, 'The only translation I know which supplies the reader with the clue to the symbolism is that of the Good News Bible, for which I have come to have an increasing regard, especially in the livelier parts of the Old Testament. (It is superb on Proverbs)...'[1]

Ecclesiastes 12.1-7

	AV	GNB
12.1	Remember now thy Creator in the days of thy youth, while the evil days come not, nor the years draw nigh, when thou shalt say, I have no pleasure in them;	So remember your Creator while you are still young, before those dismal days and years come when you will say, 'I don't enjoy life'.
2	While the sun, or the light, or the moon, or the stars, be not darkened, nor the clouds return after the rain:	That is when the light of the sun, the moon, and the stars will grow dim for you, and the rain clouds will never pass away.

---

1. From a sermon printed in *Where Three Ways Meet*, p. 168.

3 In the day when the keepers of the house shall tremble, and the strong men shall bow themselves, and the grinders cease because they are few, and those that look out of the windows be darkened,

Then your arms, that have protected you, will tremble, and your legs, now strong, will grow weak. Your teeth will be too few to chew your food, and your eyes too dim to see clearly.

4 And the doors shall be shut in the streets, when the sound of the grinding is low, and he shall rise up at the voice of the bird, and all the daughters of musick shall be brought low;

Your ears will be deaf to the noise of the street. You will barely be able to hear the mill as it grinds or music as it plays, but even the song of a bird will wake you from sleep.

5 Also when they shall be afraid of that which is high, and fears shall be in the way, and the almond tree shall flourish and the grasshopper shall be a burden, and desire shall fail: because man goeth to his long home, and the mourners go about the streets:

You will be afraid of high places, and walking will be dangerous. Your hair will turn white; you will hardly be able to drag yourself along, and all desire will have gone. We are going to our final resting place, and then there will be mourning in the streets.

6 Or ever the silver cord be loosed, or the golden bowl be broken, or the pitcher be broken at the fountain, or the wheel broken at the cistern.

The silver chain will snap, and the golden lamp will fall and break; the rope at the well will break, and the water jar will be shattered.

7 Then shall the dust return to the earth as it was: and the spirit shall return unto God who gave it.

Our bodies will return to the dust of the earth, and the breath of life will go back to God, who gave it to us.

I do not intend to examine the reasons behind every variation of wording between the two above versions, but it may be helpful to take just one Hebrew poetic phrase, 'the daughters of music' in 12.4, as typical of such phrases and examine its translation in the GNB. While the AV has, 'All the daughters of music shall be brought low', the GNB has, 'You will barely be able to hear...music as it plays'.

Few modern translators (RSV and NAB) retain the literal 'the daughters of music' (the NRSV has 'the daughters of Song'). Most follow the GNB and express it differently. In the REB the wording is 'the songbirds', in the NJB 'the singing', in the NIV 'their songs'. The accompanying Hebrew verb (translated in the AV as 'shall be brought low') does not reveal the meaning of 'the daughters of music', especially since there is some textual uncertainty about it. The traditional word in the text means 'will sink low'; the LXX translated it in the

sense of 'all the daughters of singing will be humiliated'. Modern emendations of the Hebrew suggest that a similar Hebrew word meaning
'have stopped', 'fall silent', 'grow faint' may be the true reading.

Is it necessary to retain 'the daughters of music' in the interests of
poetry and poetic 'width of reference'? Should so traditional and
beautiful a phrase, carrying such a distinctive Hebraic flavour,
disappear in modern versions? Or is the phrase, poetic as it is, somewhat misleading in this context? Modern scholars have interpreted it
variously as meaning 'songbirds' (G.R. Driver), 'songsters' (i.e. those
who produce music or song) (John Bright) or 'things that produce
music' (such as a human throat that produces music till old age sets
in). There is also the suggestion among modern scholars that the
Hebrew idiom translated 'daughter of' or 'daughters of' does not
really mean that in English idiom. In Isa. 1.8 'the daughter of Zion',
personifying Jerusalem and its population as a young maiden, means
in English idiom, according to John Bright, 'daughter Zion' (perhaps
'precious little Zion'). Perhaps this leads towards something like 'you
will barely be able to hear the precious sound of music as it plays' in
Eccl. 12.4. In a similar phrase in Jer. 8.19, where the AV has, 'Behold
the voice of the cry of the daughter of my people' (a dramatic,
rhetorical accumulation of several pieces of Hebrew periphrasis),
many modern versions (NIV, REB, GNB) have no 'daughter of' and no
'voice' in their translations putting instead 'Hark, the cry of my
people', the idiomatic English equivalent.

Isaiah 63.1-6

This passage is about the judgment of the nations, and uses strong
imagery about God the warrior. The imagery is the basis for such
well-known hymns as Julia Ward Howe's 'Battle Hymn of the
Republic' with the words 'Mine eyes have seen the glory of the
coming of the Lord: He is trampling out the vintage where the grapes
of wrath are stored...his truth is marching on'. This imagery forms
the basis for John Steinbeck's novel *The Grapes of Wrath*, and is also
found in Rev. 14.19, 20, which tells how 'the vine of the earth' was
gathered by the angel and 'cast into the great winepress of the wrath
of God' (AV).

Northropp Frye[1] writes of the 'resonance' of the AV translation, 'I

1.   *The Great Code*, p. 217.

have trodden the winepress alone, and of the people there was none with me; for I will tread them in mine anger and trample them in my fury; and their blood shall be sprinkled on my garments'. (63.3). In the third stanza of the Julia Ward Howe hymn this passage is linked with the cross of Christ, where the blood was his own, not his enemies'. Frye calls Isaiah's words a 'tremendous vision of a blood-soaked deity', and says that in their original context they were 'little more than a ferocious celebration of a prospective massacre of Edomites'. But the words have achieved a universal significance by the resonance of their imagery and phrasing.

For the purpose of this chapter, it is of particular interest to note that, in translating the words about the winepress in Isaiah 63, the GNB conveys the meaning by the word 'grapes', which does not occur in the AV (it does occur once in the AV with this type of imagery in Rev. 14.18). Where the AV has, 'travelling in the greatness of his strength' (63.1), the GNB has, '*marching* along in power and strength'. These two words, 'grapes' and 'marching', are two of the most prominent in Julia Ward Howe's hymn, composed a century before the GNB. The RV, published in 1885, was the first English version to put 'marching' in Isa. 63.1.

	AV	GNB
63.1	Who is this that cometh from Edom, with dyed garments from Bozrah? this that is glorious in his apparel, travelling in the greatness of his strength? I that speak in righteousness, mighty to save.	'Who is this coming from the city of Bozrah in Edom? Who is this so splendidly dressed in red, marching along in power and strength?' 'It is the Lord, powerful to save, coming to announce his victory'.
2	Wherefore art thou red in thine apparel, and thy garments like him that treadeth in the winefat?	'Why is his clothing so red, like that of a man who tramples grapes to make wine?'
3	I have trodden the winepress alone; and of the people there was none with me: for I will tread them in mine anger, and trample them in my fury; and their blood shall be sprinkled upon my garments, and I will stain all my raiment.	The Lord answers, 'I have trampled the nations like grapes, and no one came to help me. I trampled them in my anger, and their blood has stained all my clothing.

4   For the day of vengeance is in mine heart, and the year of my redeemed is come.

I decided that the time to save my people had come; it was time to punish their enemies.

5   And I looked, and there was none to help; and I wondered that there was none to uphold: therefore mine own arm brought salvation unto me; and my fury, it upheld me.

I was amazed when I looked and saw that there was no one to help me. But my anger made me strong, and I won the victory myself.

6   And I will tread down the people in my anger, and make them drunk in my fury, and I will bring down their strength to the earth.

In my anger I trampled whole nations and shattered them. I poured out their life-blood on the ground.'

Notes

63.1. There is uncertainty about the precise Hebrew reading at the point where the AV has 'travelling' and the GNB has 'marching along', and about the meaning of the underlying Hebrew word. The AV was probably following the general line of the Vulgate which used a Latin word giving the meaning 'stepping forward'. The LXX gives the sense of someone 'pressing forward forcibly'. Some modern translators follow the Massoretic text reading for the Hebrew which gives the difficult meaning 'stooping' or 'bowing down'. (The commentator Delitzsch quoted a related term in Arabic and saw in it 'a gesture of proud self-consciousness'.)[1] But most give 'marching', following various ancient translations or an emendation of the Massoretic text.

63.1. Where the AV has, 'I speak in righteousness', the GNB has, 'coming to announce victory'. The Hebrew word here translated 'righteousness' in the AV has, in the Old Testament (and especially in prophecies towards the end of Isaiah), the sense of God's active, righteous vindicating of his people and of his victory over enemies.

63.3. The word translated 'will tread' in the AV is given in the past tense ('trampled') in the GNB. The change from future to past tense is not a whim, but due to two possible ways of taking a particular Hebrew verb form.

1.   See J. Skinner, 'Isaiah', in *Cambridge Bible for Schools and Colleges* (repr.; Cambridge: Cambridge University Press, 1951).

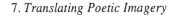
The Benefits and Dangers of Unpacking Metaphors

Perhaps my enthusiastic words about the GNB version of Ecclesiastes 12 should be balanced with the mention of some critical remarks from Dr Anthony Thiselton on the way in which that same version translates several pieces of New Testament imagery. He begins with comments on Gal. 3.27, which in the AV reads, 'For as many of you as have been baptized into Christ have put on Christ', taking up the phrase 'put on Christ'.[1] He writes,

> Today's English Version [GNB] consistently softens the force of biblical metaphors, because it aims above all else at clarity of meaning. Thus 'put on Christ' becomes 'take upon themselves the qualities of Christ'. Readers are no longer left to ask the question for themselves: how does one 'put on' not new clothes but a person? The ambiguity has been removed, but so has the self-involvement and appeal for a reaction. Even normally dead metaphors like 'hand of the Lord' (Acts 11.21), which may not be dead to everyone, are rendered 'power of the Lord'. The powerful metaphor 'pass from me this cup' (Lk. 22.42) is flattened for the sake of clarity into 'free me from having to suffer this trial'.

Clearly, Thiselton is keen to emphasize the way in which metaphor challenges the hearer or reader and makes them think. He gives a warning against the excessive unpacking of metaphors in the interest of clarity. But two or three further sentences in the same passage (which is primarily examining the use of Scripture in liturgy) show that his warnings are not only directed at the GNB and other modern translations, but also at those who take the opposite view and retain complex metaphorical language not understood by the average person. Thiselton wants both the power of metaphor and the power of meaning to shine out from any translation. He writes, 'In liturgy it is probably necessary to attempt a middle course between the two extremes' (between the power of metaphor and of meaning). Although admitting that 'if language is so metaphorical as to be naturally unintelligible to the average worshipper, it defeats its own ends', he emphasizes the importance of retaining as much as possible of the metaphorical language.

It is easy to find examples of passages where the traditional

---

1. *Language, Liturgy and Meaning* (Nottingham: Grove Books, 2nd edn, 1986), p. 26.

translations leave complex metaphorical language which is hard to understand, but it is often difficult to see the solution. In Deut. 10.16 the AV has, 'Circumcise therefore the foreskin of your heart, and be no more stiffnecked'. The meaning of the metaphor of circumcision is explained, to an extent, by the second clause, but the metaphor remains a difficult one. How is the power of metaphor balanced against the power of meaning here in such a strong phrase? The GNB removes the imagery radically and gives, 'So then, from now on be obedient to the Lord and stop being stubborn'. The REB, while reproducing the first metaphor about circumcision, gives the second in non-metaphorical language: 'So now you must circumcise your hearts and not be stubborn any more'. Most modern translations follow the REB, but a problem exists in such verses; perhaps it will be solved one day.

Old Testament phrases about prostitution, harlotry, fornication are another case in point. To 'go whoring from thy God' (AV), 'to play the harlot' or 'to commit fornication' are basic Old Testament metaphors for idolatry and unfaithfulness to Yahweh and the covenant, especially used when turning towards old Canaanite gods or foreign gods in harvest or fertility rites. The use of these metaphors is made more complex by the fact that sometimes these rites included cultic prostitution, and sometimes the prophetic writers and prophets were referring both to metaphorical 'harlotry' (i.e. unfaithfulness) and to actual harlotry. In many passages the GNB does not remove or paraphrase any of the strong imagery (see especially Ezek. 16.23-34 in the GNB), but on many occasions it makes sure that the wording delivers clearly the meaning of metaphorical phrases about religious unfaithfulness. In Hos. 9.1 the AV has, 'Rejoice not, O Israel, for joy, as other people: for thou hast gone a whoring from thy God, thou hast loved a reward upon every cornfloor'. The GNB has the longer translation (47 words for the AV's 26),

> People of Israel, stop celebrating your festivals like pagans. You have turned away from your God and have been unfaithful to him. All over the land you have sold yourselves like prostitutes to the god Baal and have loved the corn you thought he paid you with!

We may not like the lengthy and interpretative style of the latter translation, but the GNB does not gloss over the original imagery. The REB's rendering (31 words) likewise combines metaphor and meaning: 'Do not rejoice, Israel, or exult like other peoples; for you have been unfaithful to your God, you have been attracted by a prostitute's fee on every threshing-floor heaped with grain'.

In the New Testament one of the most difficult pieces of imagery for the translator is the well-known phrase at the solemn point, in Jn 1.18, where Christ 'the Son' is described as 'in the bosom of the Father' (AV). Most modern versions find the best English equivalent to be 'close to the Father's heart' or 'at the Father's side'. These are good and accurate translations; the original Greek phrase occurs again at Jn 13.23 where 'the disciple whom Jesus loved' is said to have been 'leaning on Jesus' bosom' (AV). The phrase was a technical one, used at a formal meal in the Mediterranean world to describe the guest who was lying on a couch next to the host. (Some modern attempts to go back to a more literal English translation of Jn 1.18 are less than happy: Levi's 'on the Father's lap', for example.) But even 'close to the Father's heart' may not be the final modern idiom for this metaphor. Is there no English term that lies closer to the original Greek phrase? Could the noun 'bosom' be turned into a verb that is related to its sense of intimacy and oneness? 'Enfolded in the Father's love' (or even 'enfolded in the Father's arms'?) may approach the meaning but is not quite right and needs working at.

These passages are another reminder that the task of translating some biblical imagery in a way that takes the retention of metaphor and the communication of meaning seriously is a task still to be completed.

Chapter 8

FREEDOM AND ACCURACY

Points concerning freedom versus accuracy of translation have been taken up and discussed already. Considerations of accuracy affect freedom of translation in two very different ways. In some passages they may curb excessive novelty and freedom, but in other passages, equally usefully, they act as factors demanding novelty and freedom.

In Chapter 2 I mentioned the GNB translation of Isa. 11.1: 'The royal line of David is like a tree' ('And there shall come forth a rod out of the stem of Jesse', AV). Gains achieved in the GNB's free style of translation were acknowledged, but the suggestion was made that the GNB's total omission of the name of Jesse could be changed in the interests of accuracy.

On the other hand, considerations of accuracy and new knowledge often make it necessary to break away from traditional English wordings for the passage. In 1 Pet. 2.2 the AV has, 'as newborn babes, desire the sincere milk of the word'. The phrase 'sincere milk' was accepted as strange but presumably with a biblical meaning: then some papyri were discovered in Egypt dating from New Testament times and it became known that the Greek word ἄδολος, while normally meaning 'sincere', was sometimes used colloquially for 'unadulterated' or 'pure' corn or wine. Now all modern translators, including the NKJV, put 'the pure milk' in 1 Pet. 2.2. A more complicated, but similarly significant case is the new wordings in the well-known sentence of Paul in Rom. 1.17. The AV has, 'For therein is the righteousness of God revealed from faith to faith', in a passage about the gospel. Many modern versions translate the Greek word, rendered 'righteousness' in the AV, in new and free ways, either as 'a righteousness from God' (the NIV) or 'God's way of righting wrong' (the NEB) or 'the saving justice of God' (the NJB). The REB returns to the use of the traditional 'the righteousness of God'. This passage will be looked at more fully later in this chapter. These new translations, which have moved away from the AV wording, have been prompted by the desire to bring out more accurately and clearly the meaning of the phrase in the original context. It would be wearisome to recall in detail changes of translation in the interests of accuracy that came in with the modern age of biblical studies. Many of these changes, once fiercely fought over, have long been accepted by everyone. The Revised Version in 1885 put 'the tent of meeting' in place of the AV's 'the tabernacle of the congregation' in Exodus, bringing out clearly that what was spoken of was God's meeting with his people, not just the people coming together. In the New Testament apostolic sermons in Acts, the RV, in its 1881 New Testament translation, spoke of God glorifying 'his *servant* Jesus' in place of glorifying 'his *son* Jesus' as the AV has it. This conveys more accurately the meaning of the word παῖς ('son' or 'servant' or 'child' in Greek) as used in the LXX of Isaiah 40–55, material much quoted in Acts. Rather than these matters of past history, I am more concerned here to explore three or four basic questions that underlie current discussions about freedom and accuracy, freedom and literalism. First, how free is it necessary to be, to be accurate and clear? (This takes up the NRSV's maxim about making its revision 'as free as necessary'.) Secondly, is it 'word for word' translation or 'sense for sense' translation that delivers the more accurate translation? Thirdly, is any accurate translation possible today of documents that originated in the ancient world and in a different culture? And fourthly, is the attempt to reflect accurate word meanings from ancient times more important than studying the AV's imaginative translation which has a life of its own?

More About Paraphrase and Literal Translation

'Sense for sense' translation, expanded translation, and paraphrase have already been mentioned in previous chapters. Arguments between traditionalists and innovators have always been concerned with the establishment of what constitutes acceptable paraphrase within a translation and what, on the other hand, constitutes the outright paraphrase which is no longer translation. Added to this discussion is the issue of whether translators should make clear their own interpretation of the original when passages are condensed or generalized, or whether this should be left to the commentaries. I believe that the only possible definition of acceptable paraphrase is 'non-literal words needed for bringing out the full meaning of the original, but expressing only what is present in the original'. 1 Tim. 2.6 is a good example of a highly condensed, doctrinal verse of 13 words in the AV, 16 in the REB, and 23 in the TNT. The footnotes to the TNT translation make a case for considerable freedom and expansion in translation here.

	AV	REB	TNT
2.6	who gave himself a ransom for all, to be testified in due time.	who sacrificed himself to win freedom for all mankind, revealing God's purpose at God's good time.	He gave himself to set all men free, and so he bore witness, at times of his own choosing, to God's saving purpose.

Greek phrases of this complexity do not occur on every page of the New Testament, but it is typical of the problems of obscurity faced by literal translation and the problems of length faced by free translation. The TNT footnote to the last clause in the verse (AV, 'to be testified in due time') points out that the completely literal translation would be, 'the evidence at own times', a phrase that all translators have worked hard to make clear. The TNT's note states,

> This needs expanding to be clear: (1) a full sentence is required; (2) the nature of the 'evidence' needs to be stated; (3) the meaning of 'own times' needs to be brought out: it could mean the proper, right or fitting time; but this, perhaps rightly, ignores the plural 'times', which could refer to different times in the life of Jesus. If so, then 'own' will not mean 'proper', etc., but Christ's own chosen times.

It is true that expanders and clarifiers may arrive at the wrong interpretation in such a passage. However, in verses which are not part of a poetic passage, which require not a broad impressionistic treatment but some precision of meaning, most people would prefer a version that has taken the risk of achieving some clarity than one which reproduces the original word for word but which means very little. Just as the broad impressionistic treatment involves a risk of inaccuracy as an equivalent expression of the original, so the second alternative runs a corresponding risk: namely, that of expressing as obscure what surely had meaning for the author.

Again, I look back at the modern pioneers in free translation who tackled basic issues in a thorough way. It was Ronald Knox and William Barclay who argued most for the rightness of an element of paraphrase and interpretativeness in modern biblical translation, and C.S. Lewis who supported the same cause with his blunt statement that 'The AV has ceased to be a good (that is, a clear) translation'.[1] Knox wrote, 'The translator must never be frightened of "paraphrase": it is a bogey of the half-educated...When St Paul describes people as "wise according to the flesh", the translator is under an obligation to paraphrase'.[2] (Knox's own paraphrase of that Pauline phrase in 1 Cor. 1.26 was 'wise in the world's fashion'.)

William Barclay was conscious of the dangers of the wrong sort of paraphrasing, writing that 'paraphrase is only safe and effective when the mind and heart of the translator are married to the mind and heart of the author', but he was no less committed to the rightness of the use of strong elements of paraphrase. 'However impossible it may be to achieve it', he wrote, 'the aim of the translator must be to produce a translation which can stand by itself, and which needs no commentary to make it intelligible'.[3] Barclay has been criticized for using an excessive amount of paraphrasing. His biographer says that, as a member of a NEB panel of translators for the Apocrypha and of a panel for the TNT, he wanted to go further in expansion and paraphrase than his colleagues.[4] However, in the case of one phrase from Mt. 20.2, where the same biographer says that Barclay did not 'provide a pure translation' and was excessively interpretative, Barclay was in line with many other translators. In Mt. 20.2 Barclay wanted the translation 'a normal day's wage' where the Greek literally said 'a denarius' (cf. the AV 'a penny a day'). But the NEB has something almost identical ('the usual day's wage'), as do the NRSV, the REB, the GNB and the NAB.

It is well known that the whole discussion about free translation and literal translation has a history going back many centuries. Stretching beyond John Purvey[5] in the fourteenth century, who edited the second edition of Wyclif's Bible and who wrote, 'The best translating out of Latin into English is to translate after the sentence and not only after

1. Introduction to Phillips, *Letters to Young Churches*.
2. Knox, *On Englishing the Bible*, p. 12.
3. 'On Translating the New Testament', pp. 319, 317.
4. C. Rawlins, *William Barclay* (Grand Rapids: Eerdmans, 1984), p. 626.
5. Although Tyndale particularly stressed the value of word-for-word translation for many biblical passages, he too combined with that a 'meaning-for-meaning' approach.

the words', that is sentence for sentence, to Jerome in the fourth century who wrote, 'I render sense for sense and not word for word'. And half a century before Knox and Barclay in Britain, R.F. Weymouth wrote, 'with a slavish literality, delicate shades of meaning cannot be reproduced'.[1]

Further Passages for Consideration

Does the modern translator translate literally the Greek phrase in Mk 2.19: 'the sons of the bridechamber'? I know of none who does, though it is not absolutely clear what the original phrase meant. Modern versions refer variously to wedding-guests, or bridegroom's friends and attendants; Knox rendered it, 'the men of the bridegroom's company'. In Lk. 16.8 the literal phrase 'the sons of light' (AV, 'the children of this world are in their generation wiser than the children of light') presents even more problems to the translator. Several modern versions, including Moffatt, the NRSV and the NJB, keep some literal translation (GNB, 'the people who belong to the light'); others change the literal rendering for modern terms such as 'unworldly' or 'otherworldly'. The TNT gives, 'in their dealings with those of their own kind worldly people are more shrewd than the unworldly'. One of the problems in this parable is that of how to describe the figure who has given the parable its traditional name. There are no poetic undertones here (as there are with the splendid phrase 'the sons of light') and modern versions work away freely at the meaning. Leaving on one side the AV's 'unjust steward', modern translators vary between 'dishonest steward' and 'dishonest manager'.

The translation of other types of genitives, some of them similar to 'the sons of light', can be difficult. A word-for-word literal translation of 2 Thess. 3.5 gives, 'May the Lord direct your hearts to the love of God and to the steadfastness [or "patience"] of Christ'. How far should the translator try to make clear whether it is God's love for us and Christ's steadfastness that is meant, or whether it is our love for God and a Christ-centred endurance in human beings? The original Greek construction covers both senses. The AV takes the second meaning, making that quite clear in the final clauses: 'And the Lord direct your hearts into the love of God, and into the patient waiting for Christ'. But the REB takes the first sense, and makes that quite clear: 'May the Lord direct your hearts towards God's love and the steadfastness of Christ'. Some modern versions prefer to leave the phrases with some ambiguity, that is with a word-for-word translation as given above. But it is interesting to note that the AV feels that it has to try and be interpretative and explanatory in this verse. Even the literal AV is often fond of freedom!

In Mt. 11.7 a convincing case has been made for some slightly expanded translation. The traditional, word-for-word translation of Jesus' words about John the Baptist are: 'What went ye out into the wilderness to see? A reed shaken with the wind? But what went ye out for to see? A man clothed in soft raiment?' (AV). This has suggested to many readers and listeners that it refers to an unstable person, tossed this way and that by every breeze. But Barclay wrote of that understanding of it, 'this is very far from the meaning: in Palestine "a reed shaken by the wind" would be a phrase to describe the most ordinary and everyday sight, something that no-one could help seeing every day of the week, if he went out into the desert'.[1] He suggested, 'What did you go out to the desert to see? Was it to see what you can see any day there...the long grass swaying in the wind?' The NEB seems to convey a similar meaning, with its interpretative rendering of the word κάλαμος, although without the same expansion, showing that the reed or grass referred to was a real reed or reed-bed, not a human being compared to a reed, 'What was the spectacle that drew you to the wilderness? A reed-bed swept by the wind? No? Then what did you go out to see? A man dressed in silks and satins?' There is room for further discussion here. How easily can the Greek word κάλαμος ('reed') be represented as a 'reed-bed' or 'long grass'? The REB has 'a reed swept by the wind?', removing the AV's 'shaken' but also the NEB's 'reed-bed'. And in the Qumran writings 'a reed shaken by the wind' mans a 'desert holy-man'. The interesting point to note is that in some passages quoted above, all translations, including the AV, come across as fairly interpretative.

Barclay's bold exploring in translation, in the interests of accuracy and clarity, went even further. He felt so strongly that traditional translations of the clause in Mt. 5.41 (AV, 'And whosoever shall compel thee to go a mile') were inadequate and inaccurate that he

1.   Barclay, 'On Translating the New Testament', p. 339.

translated the clause by fifteen words where the AV has nine, putting, 'If a Roman officer commandeers you to act as a baggage porter for one mile'. He pointed out that if the Gospel writer had wanted simply to say 'compel' here, he would have used the normal Greek word for 'compel'; the word actually used was very specific, taken from a Persian word, naturalized in Greek, used for requisitioning or commandeering people and animals for public service. Barclay saw more than an issue of linguistic precision here; he saw a keypoint of Jesus' teaching obscured if the force of the word was generalized. Jesus said that even if one's rights are flouted and one is commandeered by foreign soldiers at a moment's notice, one must act positively and generously, and 'go with him two miles'. Though Barclay's translation is too long, his point was made and has been incorporated into many modern versions. The NAB uses no more words than the AV but conveys Barclay's idea with 'Should anyone press you into service for one mile, go with him two miles'.[1]

The issue of free experiments in translation is still a live one especially in this era when revised editions of some of the major translations of the 1960s are being published. Changes made in the name of increased accuracy of content feature prominently in these revised editions. The REB, for example, has made changes in some of the NEB's free renderings in the Old Testament, particularly those based on conjectural emendations. The REB's introduction to its Old Testament section in 1969 says that it has only 'sparingly' resorted to conjectural emendation of the Hebrew text, and has been 'aware of the dangers of an over-zealous use' of possible clarifications of the Hebrew text coming from modern study of Semitic languages cognate with Hebrew, and from modern discoveries such as the Ras Shamra texts in Syria. One of the simpler examples of a prudent reversion by the REB, from an NEB position to more traditional wording (retained by almost all modern translations), is its return to 'humbly' in the well-known verse Mic. 6.8. In the AV this reads, 'What doth the Lord require of thee, but to do justly, and to love mercy, and to walk humbly with thy God?' The NEB puts 'wisely' instead of 'humbly'. This interpretation was discussed in the 1962 Peake's Commentary, where Dr Winton Thomas wrote that, according to a 1949 article in

---

1. Barclay, 'On Translating the New Testament', p. 324.

the Journal of Jewish studies,[1] the Hebrew phrase really means 'to walk carefully, circumspectly, guardedly'. In matters of idiom and paraphrase rather than of emendation or Jewish word studies, the REB's approach may vary. Sometimes it seems to retain all of the NEB's best and boldest wordings, for example, in what must surely be one of NEB's very best passages, Lk. 15.11-24, already quoted at the beginning of Chapter 6. But at other points the REB's changes away from the bolder NEB wording are more controversial. I am not convinced that some reversions to traditional wording (though made on the grounds that suitability for public reading demands such changes) are an improvement; some of the NEB phrases certainly came within the area of acceptable freedom of expression. Rom. 1.17, appears to many people to be a case in point.[2]

Is Accurate Translation of Ancient Material Ever Possible?

To answer the question 'Is any accurate translation possible today of documents that originated in the ancient world and in a different culture?', many biblical scholars and theologians would say that the task is an almost impossible one. If Professor Nineham is right and the culture gap between ancient and modern times is almost unbridgeable,[3] that must be the conclusion. (If, however, the culture gap is seen to be less completely unbridgeable,[4] a less despairing conclusion may be reached.) Dr John Bowden, as a theologian and a distinguished modern religious translator, gave formidable backing to the view that modern translations of the Bible can never really be successful.[5] He

1. *Journal of Jewish Studies* 1.4 (1949).
2. One has to add that others have expressed themselves unconvinced and questioning over aspects of change in other revised editions of modern translations: see Roger Tomes's comments on the NJB in the *Times Literary Supplement* for 11 July 1988, which include the remark that the NJB has tended to 'iron out' many of the JB's pieces of 'acceptable paraphrase'. While I have not given any comparisons between original and revised editions of particular translations, I trust that readers will be able to judge for themselves, in the longer passages quoted from the REB and the NJB, the general approach of those translations to issues of freedom of wording.
3. D.E. Nineham, *The Use and Abuse of the Bible* (London: Macmillan, 1976).
4. See A.T. Hanson and R.P.C. Hanson, *The Bible without Illusions* (London: SCM Press, 1989), pp. 101-104.
5. *Jesus: The Unanswered Questions* (London: SCM Press, 1988), pp. 133-47.

believes that it is presumptuous for anyone in later centuries (including the AV's seventeenth century) to think that it is possible to express in English the authentic meaning of Aramaic, Hebrew or Greek idioms in the original biblical material. The translators have an impossible task, he says. He does not consider that the AV gives a particularly accurate impression of the biblical material, but he considers it to be more accurate than modern translations, because it is more literal and less interpretative. Although Bowden makes a distinction between moderate and radical modern translators, he thinks that all of them make difficult tasks impossible by excessive attempts at clarification of meaning; these attempts only widen the gap between modern and ancient ways of thinking. He admits that the NEB, in its introductory comment, faces squarely the major problem of the rendering of ancient material into modern English, but he does not see that the attempt can be successful. More than that, he sees dangers in the fact that modern translations modernize much but not all of the text. For example, they do not modernize the conceptuality and the thought world of, say, the New Testament. By giving the reader familiar words, tailored to modern understanding, 'they gloss over the inevitable strangeness of the world of the first century AD and give it the semblance of familiarity'.[1]

I am puzzled by the last part of that criticism. It must be an inevitable part of the delicate bridging and balancing activity associated with any translation, ancient or modern, to modernize some of the original but not all. And it is not clear to me that modern translators, in altering the idiom, have been so destructively modernizing as critics such as Bowden suggest. Earlier I mentioned how some modern versions (e.g. REB) have the translation 'Long live the King!' in Dan. 2.4, in place of the literal 'O king, live for ever!' of the AV. The Hebrew idiom has, in the REB, been deorientalized but not modernized; 'long live the king!' is idiomatic English but matches the more formal etiquette of older, even mediaeval, times. Idiom is one thing, style another. Idioms may have to alter, but certain continuing elements of style and content can maintain continuity across the centuries, making translation, if not perfect, at least viable. At the end of the day, to despair of the possibilities of translation seems to exaggerate the dangers of over-translation and play down the dangers of

---

1. Bowden, *Jesus: The Unanswered Questions*, pp. 136-37.

under-translation. Modern versions of the Bible are certainly open to the charge of over-translation at many points; but traditional versions, correspondingly, are open to the charge of under-translation to the modern ear.

Philological Meanings and Literary Meanings

Together with the questioning of the possibility of accurate translation across the centuries, some mention should be made of the questioning, in modern times, of scholarly attempts to continue to explore precise historical word meanings from ancient times. Can we ever get back accurately and objectively to the original? Is it not more important, other 'poet-translators' say, to explore the AV's imaginative poetic translation, which, within the whole European tradition, has an authority and life of its own, which should not be cast into the shadows by endless talk about Hebrew and Greek word meanings? Stephen Prickett voiced this criticism in his book, describing the GNB approach to interpretation and translation as made on the false presupposition that the scriptural text 'has a meaning that is finally independent of our cultural presuppositions' or made on the false assumption that the text can be seen 'as an objective entity over and above any debilitating niceties of cultural relativity and academic debate'.[1] Although modern hermeneutics have led to several good subjective approaches (not least in relation to intercultural under-standings), there remains a wrong sort of subjective approach which ignores, almost entirely, historical word meanings, as well as distinctions between similar original words in a passage.

An example of this was a comment in *The New Babel*.[2] Mullen says that where the word 'thief' or 'thieves' resonates significantly throughout the Gospels in the AV ('fell among thieves', 'are ye come out as against a thief', 'two thieves crucified with him', and 'thief in the night'), modern versions have introduced the alternatives 'brigand' or 'bandit' in most of these cases, destroying the resonances and echoes in the language. Certainly for the AV's 'thieves' in Lk. 10.30 Barclay gives, 'he fell into the hands of brigands', and the NJB gives 'bandits'. In Mt. 26.55, too, for the AV's 'are ye come out as against a

1. Prickett, *Words and the Word*, p. 6
2. Mullen, *The New Babel*, p. 59.

thief?', the REB and NEB have 'do you take me for a bandit?', and the NIV has, 'am I leading a rebellion that you have come out with swords and cudgels to capture me?' But what is not mentioned by these critics is that, in the New Testament, the AV uses 'thief'/'thieves' for two different words in the Greek original. κλέπτης ('thief in the night') means simply 'thief', but ληστης (the Greek word in all the other instances above) means primarily 'robber', 'highwayman', 'bandit' or 'revolutionary insurrectionist', according to Arndt and Gingrich's *Greek–English Lexicon of the New Testament*. Such word meanings cannot be said to lack objectivity. The claims of accuracy prompt new and freer translation than 'thief'/'thieves' every time. That does not mean that all new ideas about historical original word meanings should be put indiscriminately into new versions. The idea of putting 'wisely' into the NEB in Mic. 6.8 ('to walk wisely before your God') has, largely, been dropped. However, it does mean that philological disciplines are not discarded.

It is impossible to be brief when examining the new literary approach to biblical language and its translation, without appearing to be unfair, since there are so many modern literary approaches and the new literary movement as a whole has brought its own understandings into biblical interpretation.[1] But some forms of literary approach seem to sit uncomfortably with philological considerations and accurate word meanings, and have been less fruitful than others. Structural exegesis, mentioned earlier in connection with some imaginative biblical interpretation, seems, to many people, to claim too much.[2]

It is encouraging that the editors of *The Literary Guide to the Bible*, while commending the riches of the AV, have not used exaggerated language about it. They write,

> We have as a rule used the King James version in translations... It is the version most English readers associate with the literary qualities of the

1. See, for example, T.R. Wright, *Theology and Literature* (Oxford: Basil Blackwell, 1988); and D. Jasper, *The Study of Literature and Religion* (London: Macmillan, 1989).

2. Note the comments of C.F.D. Moule at the beginning of the 1980s in the Preface to *The Birth of the New Testament* (London: A. & C. Black, 3rd edn, 1980), p. x. Writing on the possibility of dangers in structuralism, he said, 'in so far as structuralism plays into the hands of treating the New Testament documents on a purely literary level, without regard to historical questions, it tends to eliminate a vital factor in the study of Christian origins'.

Bible, and it is still arguably the version that best preserves the literary effects of the original languages. But it has serious philological deficiencies and its archaism may at times be misleading: accordingly our contributors have sometimes felt obliged to revise it... or to provide their own translations.[1]

Subtle literary qualities of language convey important and delicate shades of meaning; but the lexicon, too, has its functions, contributing to important subtlety and precision.

A Detailed Look at One Key Phrase and its Translation

I close here with further consideration of the well-known phrase in Rom. 1.17, which is translated 'the righteousness of God' in the AV, but is translated with much freedom by many modern translators on the grounds of both clarity and accuracy. Perhaps the most important contribution of the new versions to clarity and accuracy has been their tackling of fresh translation into English of some of the biblical keywords such as δικαιοσύνη and *ḥesed*. For *ḥesed*, in a passage such as Ps. 100.5, where the AV has 'mercy' ('the Lord is good: his mercy is everlasting'), new versions have translated the word by 'faithful love' or something similar. Here we concentrate simply on the translation of δικαιοσύνη.

Rom. 1.16-17 reads as follows in the AV:

> For I am not ashamed of the gospel of Christ: for it is the power of God unto salvation to every one that believeth; to the Jew first, and also to the Greek. For therein is *the righteousness of God* revealed from faith to faith: as it is written, The just shall live by faith.

This is, in effect, the letter's major introductory statement of its theme. James Moffatt, who used many bold new phrases in translation, kept to 'the righteousness of God' in this passage, considering it a concept whose meaning was hard to unpack in any other words. More recently scholars have said that, at the beginning of a profound theological letter such as Romans there should not be too much initial unpacking of the big phrase which Paul does later in the letter, but something with a broad range of meaning is necessary. Reference has already been made to more recent translations, such as the REB and

1. Alter and Kermode, *The Literary Guide to the Bible*, pp. 7, 11, 32.

the NEB. Where the AV has 'the righteousness of God', the REB has 'in it [the gospel] the righteousness of God is seen at work'. In other words, although it puts 'is seen at work' where the AV has 'is revealed', the noun phrase is the same as the AV. The REB appears to have decided that the NEB, with its 'here is revealed God's way of righting wrong', spells out the phrase too explicitly.

But the difficulty about leaving 'the righteousness of God' here is that it confronts the reader or hearer, expectantly listening for the phrase in which Paul will describe the essence of the Christian gospel, with a phrase that does not do justice to Paul's theme of God's judgment and mercy. It may leave the reader (such was my own experience when first I read the letter) asking some questions such as, 'Of course God is righteous, but where is the saving good news there?' Many people find the bolder new versions have helped the reader to get a genuine feeling for and sense of what Paul is saying in this verse.

We should not underestimate the difficulties of translating Rom. 1.17 accurately and clearly. One difficulty is that inside Paul's great concept and phrase about 'God's δικαιοσύνη' is packed the profound paradox of both law and grace, the divine judgment and justice, and also the divine grace and acceptance of the sinner. As Karl Barth wrote, what is revealed in the gospel is Christ as both the pronouncing of God's verdict on sin and also as the effecting of God's work of salvation: 'God's verdict is God's work of salvation'.[1] The δικαιοσύνη of God means that he is both goodness and right, and that he sets things right and saves. The paradox in Jewish words and thinking about divine judgment and mercy had existed for centuries, and Paul was merely taking over these expressions, and using them in a new way. Far back in Jewish history was the notion of a 'judge' both as one who punishes sin and as one who positively, actively and savingly champions the cause and rights of the oppressed and the voiceless. The very phrase in Rom. 1.17, 'the righteousness of God', had been used in many passages in Second Isaiah and the Psalms as synonymous with the concept of salvation; for example, in Isa. 56.1, the AV gives, 'my salvation is near to come, and my righteousness to be revealed'.

Modern translations have addressed this paradox, tackling the job of

---

1.   K. Barth, *A Shorter Commentary on Romans* (trans. D.H. van Daalen; London: SCM Press, 1959 [1956]), p. 22.

bringing out with some clarity the heart of the paradox of grace as Paul proclaimed it, and as the earlier Jews had glimpsed it. Some modern translators have been reluctant to leave behind traditional English phrases in the translation of 1.17. Ronald Knox held to a literal approach, using the technical, legal term of 'justification' and 'acquittal': 'it [the gospel] reveals God's way of justifying us, faith first and last'. This kept close to the juridical background of the Hebrew word ṣᵉdāqâ which underlies δικαιοσύνη. But most modern translators have not found it easy to use those terms in 1.17, especially in our age when the words 'justify', 'righteous', and others are used predominantly in the pejorative sense of 'self-righteousness' and 'self-justification'. These days translators have tended to keep the connotation, from the original word δικαιοσύνη, of something to do with what is right, keeping the word 'right', but putting it into phrases about God 'righting wrong' or making people 'right with himself'. The GNB translates it, 'the gospel reveals how God puts people right with himself: it is through faith from beginning to end'. The TNT has, 'For it is now being revealed through the Good News that the beginning and end of the process by which God puts men right with himself is faith'. And the NEB translates it as follows: 'here is revealed God's way of righting wrong, a way that starts from faith and ends in faith'. For many people the NEB's phrasing here (especially 'God's way of righting wrong') is a very fine moment, a superb phrasing that is likely to stay for many generations as the best English translation of this central Pauline phrase about the Christian faith. For those who take this view it not only catches the meaning but also has a style with new freedom, rhythm and resonance about it. With the same aim of conveying something of the Pauline paradox of law and grace are both the NJB's strong wording, mentioned earlier, 'in it [the gospel] is revealed the saving justice of God', and the freedom of the phrase favoured by Kenneth Grayston, 'God's saving goodness'.[1] The heart of the saving good news is seen clearly in these versions as a δικαιοσύνη of God (accepted through faith) that is both a divine quality and activity.

All the translations mentioned here follow, broadly, the same line of interpretation, taking 'God's δικαιοσύνη' as an activity of God.

---

1.   In *Dying, We Live: A New Enquiry into the Death of Christ in the New Testament* (London: Darton, Longmann & Todd, 1990).

This interpretation may be said to have a majority following today. But I would like to examine one other major translation which follows a different interpretation and, while retaining the word 'righteousness', gives 'a righteousness from God' instead of 'the righteousness of God'. The NIV takes δικαιοσύνη to be a righteousness that the believer has by faith from God, and gives, 'For in the gospel a righteousness from God is revealed, a righteousness that is by faith from first to last'. This is a return to Tyndale's approach: he translated the verse, 'for by it [the gospel] the righteousness which cometh of God is opened from faith to faith'.

The discussion about the merits of these two main interpretations is well explained in Professor C.E.B. Cranfield's commentary on Romans.[1] He follows the Tyndale (and NIV) line, although admitting that there is a case for taking God's δικαιοσύνη here to be an activity of God. He writes, 'The expression "God's righteousness" had come to be used in some Jewish circles for God's saving justice'. Cranfield also acknowledges the relevance of nearby phrases in Romans 1 about 'the power of God unto salvation' (1.16) and 'the wrath of God is revealed' (1.18) to that understanding of the phrase. But he sees the Tyndale line of interpretation as fitting in best with the main theme of Romans, and takes the following words in Romans as supporting that view: 'he who is righteous by faith shall live' (1.17b), the words of 1.17a about 'from faith to faith', and verses such as Rom. 10.3 about those 'who go about to establish their own righteousness' and 'have not submitted themselves unto the righteousness of God' (AV).

With these differing interpretations of the phrase in Rom. 1.17, one may conclude that the whole matter is too complicated, and that it may be best to stick with the AV's general and ambiguous phrase which allows several interpretations. Others remain open to the width of the discussion, and salute fresh translations that are willing to take the risk of committing themselves to one side or the other, and offer some clarity of meaning.

1.   *Romans: A Shorter Commentary* (Edinburgh: T. & T. Clark, 1985) (based on his earlier International Critical Commentary series volume).

Chapter 9

Freedom and Taking Risks

Readers may see that both traditionalists and innovators in the field of biblical translation and its language have used many phrases about taking risks and about boundaries and frontiers.

In an earlier chapter I drew attention to a significant and honest point made in the Introduction to the New Testament section of the NEB (written over the signature of C.H. Dodd), that the translators' work involved the taking of risks. Frequently, he wrote, they had felt it necessary, somewhat boldly, to translate phrases in the Greek into English 'native idiom', in passages where they might have got by with a literal word-for-word translation and with what he calls 'a comfortable ambiguity'. 'We have been aware', he said, in relation to such passages, 'that we take a risk, but we have thought it our duty to take the risk rather than remain on the fence'.[1] Elsewhere Dodd echoed this emphasis on modern translation as a venture frequently demanding a decisive tackling of difficult boundaries, frontiers and barriers of language. He said that the NEB attempted to be 'above all, a translation which may in some measure remove a real barrier between a large proportion of our fellow-countrymen and the truth of the Holy Scriptures'.[2]

That seems to reflect the language used by English biblical translators about biblical translation centuries ago. In the main preface to the AV of 1611, entitled 'The Translators to the Reader', attributed to Myles Smith one of the 1611 translators and later Bishop of Gloucester, the debt to pioneer translators of previous generations is acknowledged, and the early pioneerings described as like new discoveries across the world's oceans and icefloes, in language that

1.   Introduction to the New Testament section in the NEB, p. vii.
2.   Quoted from F.F. Bruce, *The English Bible* (London: Lutterworth, 1961), p. 228.

might have come straight out of Hakluyt's chronicles twenty years earlier. The passage reads, 'Blessed be they...that break the ice, and gave the onset upon that which helpeth forward to the saving of souls'.

Modern talk of risk-taking and the crossing of barriers in relation to biblical translation is obviously not confined to the so-called innovators in modern translation. The so-called traditionalists also use these figures of speech. Stephen Prickett's remarks about 'the odd boundary-breaking quality of the Hebrew' in 1 Kgs 19.12, a quality which the AV catches well, he says, and which all translators in English should attempt, have already been cited. Significant also, in this connection, is Prickett's emphasis on what has been called 'liminality' in Wordsworth, defined as 'the sense of being on a margin or threshold of something further'.[1] Prickett warns of the danger of modern translators being filled with a belief that they can, analytically, master the Word of Scripture, instead of standing, vulnerable and in awed contemplation on the threshold of its supernatural world of mystery.

The thresholds, boundaries and frontiers on which the translator may be found need no detailed recalling. They are described in various ways in Dodd's and Prickett's writings, and others like them. Sometimes the frontier between ancient and modern times is referred to, or the frontiers and barriers between Hebrew and English idiom, or barriers and thresholds between literary and non-literary language. At other times the reference is to the barriers and boundaries between meaning and mystery, to the barely definable frontiers between that which is expressible and that which is inexpressible, or to the thresholds between time and eternity, the factual and the symbolic. The language used runs in similar patterns, and is all about frontiers on which translators can find themselves exposed and at risk.

Lying behind this intriguingly common language and emphasis is the equally intriguing phenomenon that both traditionalists and innovators in biblical translation are fond of using the language of the imagination and are both centrally concerned with imaginativeness in language. The distinctions within the term 'imaginativeness' are valid ones; in the language of clarity that appeals especially to the innovators the emphasis is on good idiomatic imaginativeness, whereas

---

1. Prickett, *Words and the Word*, p. 224. The quotation is from the literary scholar J.R. Watson.

in the language of resonance that appeals to the traditionalists, the emphasis is on good poetic imaginativeness. These distinctions cannot be pressed too far. Poetic imaginativeness is not absent from the language of translation used by the innovators, as may be seen by reading lyrical passages in some of the new versions. And neither is idiomatic imaginativeness absent from traditional styles of translation, judging by some of the resonant phrases from the older English versions which have passed into the English language and still light a spark in people's minds.

It goes without saying that dangers cannot be avoided in any risk taking or imaginative moving along frontiers. The innovators' risk-taking, in the interests of clarity and directness of speech, can all too easily lead them into the sort of arrogant brashness of language that treads clumsily across intricate and sensitive areas of meaning. The traditionalists' type of risk-taking, in the interests of spiritual and poetic resonance, can too easily lead them into the sort of literary snobbishness that ignores the requirements of wide communication. These real dangers cannot destroy the validity of the emphases that are being made, nor remove the validity of the whole idea of running risks.

Frontier Talk and Modern Theologies of Communication

It is useful to look at the task of biblical translation against the background of the overall task of Christian communication. For the emphasis on risk-taking and of freedom in translation is not an idea produced by translators to legitimize their fancies and whims of language. It is built into the very heart of all true and deep communication, and into the heart of all deep theologies of communication and mission.

In an article on the theology of mission[1] Bishop Simon Barrington-Ward uses this same language of 'gulfs' and barriers, of boundaries and frontiers, and of Christian presence in risky, exposed places. The 'gulf-situations' to which he refers are those areas of human existence, spiritual, material, personal or public, where people find themselves between hope and reality. Writing about divisive gulfs

1. 'Mission, Theology of', in A. Richardson and J. Bowden (eds.), *The New Dictionary of Christian Theology* (London: SCM Press, 1983).

between God and humanity and between different groups, brought about by sorrow, sin and oppression, he speaks of gulfs 'between heaven and earth, between ideal and reality, and between a spiritual depth on the one hand and, on the other, the hard inconsequential surface of mundane life'. He says that it is in these gulf situations, across the world, north or south, that tasks of mission and communication have to take place. In writing about those who are caught in some of the world's 'gulfs', he remarks that for many of them it is to the figure of Christ, 'a wounded man alongside them', that they are drawn and attracted. He includes in these divisive gulfs those brought about by differences of language, culture and religion. He touches on the cultural gulfs in Western civilization through the centuries where Christian mission and communication has found itself placed on the frontier between the claims of reason and emotion, rationalism and romanticism, and has had to communicate in the middle of these complex and intricate patterns of human life.

Even this brief digest may remind us that some of the almost impossibly complex but vital frontiers on which biblical translation finds itself are a small part of the almost impossibly complex but vital frontiers on which all deep communication has to take place.

Future Risk-Taking

Some think that there will not be so much risk-taking in biblical translation in the future, with two huge centuries of translation (the sixteenth and the twentieth) behind us. But there are still plenty of translational tough nuts waiting to be cracked; many biblical passages or phrases where an English wording that has both resonance and clarity has not yet emerged, or where some such wording that seemed to possess these qualities has run into difficulties. I have examined a number of such passages or phrases in previous chapters, for example, the phrase in Jn 1.18 about the Son, with the literal meaning of 'in the bosom of the Father'. Another phrase, 'the poor in spirit', is literally rendered in Mt. 5.3 ('Blessed are the poor in spirit: for theirs is the kingdom of heaven'). The fact that this comes in such a well-known verse, engraved on the hearts of many, makes attempts to explore seriously any alternative translations particularly hazardous and unpopular. I take up the latter verse here.

Mt. 5.3, like all the 'Beatitudes' verses, is a verse which, in its traditional form is much loved, used and full of meaning for the committed. It has been described as an icon phrase with huge depth of meaning in it, from which each person can take their own requirements. The literal word-for-word rendering is succinct, in common with most of the other Beatitudes. Perhaps this rendering should never have any alternative laid beside it. However, icon phrases, like all coded phrases, have their difficulties. 'Poor in spirit' is not without them. A 'poor-spirited' person in modern parlance is someone who sulks when they are not put in the football team. Again, 'spiritual poverty' is a phrase with a particular meaning in modern times, used, for example, by Mother Teresa on occasions when she has come to Britain and has said challengingly, 'Remember us in India with our problems of material poverty, as we remember you in western countries with your problems of spiritual poverty'. It becomes ever harder to stick only with 'the poor in spirit' and to offer no alternative.

Of course, modern translators since the beginning of the twentieth century have boldly tackled the question of a fresh, alternative translation. James Moffatt put, 'Blessed are those who feel poor in spirit!' Edgar Goodspeed had, 'Blessed are those who feel their spiritual need'. William Barclay gave,

> O the bliss of those who realize
>   the destitution of their own lives,
> for the blessings of the Kingdom of Heaven
>   are theirs here and now.

The NEB has, 'How blest are those who know their need of God; the kingdom of Heaven is theirs'. The GNB renders it, 'Happy are those who know they are spiritually poor; the Kingdom of heaven belongs to them!' These translations, following a similar approach and wording, have taken the risk of breaking the monopoly of 'the poor in spirit', and have made clear a central interpretation of the original words. Their approach has seemed to some people too paraphrasing, too lengthy, or too narrowing, and in one case, got put aside in a time of revision without any other fresh translation being offered. One hopes that the experience of these twentieth century translators will not deter other risk takers in the future.

Future translators of this verse might conceivably be following one or two fresh lines of wording already hinted at, including suggestions by some scholarly translators. The first of these approaches says in effect, 'We need something blunt, simple, and maybe as naive as the original must have been: something like "Blessed are the modest. It is to them that the kingdom of heaven belongs"'. Secondly, there is the more complex and radical approach that would attempt a phrasing which combines more of the varied aspects of meaning lying behind the word πτωχοί (and so behind πτωχοὶ ἐν πνεύματι 'poor in spirit') in later Jewish usage. This refers to the use of πτωχοί in the LXX translation of Isa. 61.1 (quoted in Lk. 4.18), where the Hebrew word *ᵃnāv* is translated and where the AV has, 'the Lord...hath anointed me to preach good tidings to *the meek*'. πτωχοί seems to encompass a sense of the whole affliction of God's people, not only in their material poverty and religious humility, but in the sense of their being defenceless, oppressed and disillusioned. Such suggestions may be drafted as follows:

1.　'Blessed are those whose spirit has been trampled on, for theirs...' This, though very free, takes πνεῦμα ('spirit') seriously as does the second translation (below).
2.　'Blessed are those who feel diminished/humiliated in spirit, for theirs...' This uses words sometimes heard today on the lips of those whom life has treated cruelly.
3.　'Blessed are the poor and vulnerable. It is for them God's kingship reigns.' This radical suggestion turns the literal 'in spirit' into 'vulnerable'. It raises the possibility that those words, 'in spirit', with their signalling of an inwardness of meaning, might be so transformed.

These unusually risk-taking explorations are experimental sketches, but they show the way in which some translators have tried to move along the barriers of language.

Expectations

The stimulation of experimental translating, it is true, does not reduce complexity in the field of modern biblical translation. Nor can the effort to take seriously, as this book has done, both the traditionalist and the innovative emphasis in the modern scene remove complexity. Good biblical translation is seldom fashioned or sustained through the centuries by smooth processes of straightforward evolution. Tensions can be creative tensions.

The twenty-first century will not see so many official new translations of the Bible come into being as have emerged in the twentieth, presumably. But we may look forward to two things. First, to continuing ventures in individual translating, both from those following in the footsteps of figures like William Barclay, with special skills and boldness in communicating with ordinary people, and from poet-translators like Peter Levi, who bring distinctive blends of dignity and liveliness of style. Secondly, we look forward to some real dialogue between traditionalists and innovators, in the hope that the so-called traditionalists, with their stress on glory and spiritual resonance of wording, and the so-called innovators, with their stress on clarity and directness of wording, are not diverted into viewing their own particular insights in a polarized or militant way, but may see them as part of an undivided truth about the communication of the biblical Word.

Speaking about the glory and clarity of language, it is interesting that John Wyclif translated Jesus' words in Jn 12.28 (familiar to many in the AV form 'Father, glorify thy name') as 'Father, clarify thy name'. In those days 'to clarify' and 'to glorify' both had a similar meaning of 'to make clear', 'to make known', 'to make honoured'.[1] Clarity and glory have always belonged together, and do so today. It is becoming ever clearer that where there is true clarity, glory is never far away, and vice versa. The task of holding them together in biblical translation is an ongoing and unfinished task.

---

1. George Macleod pointed this out in *Only One Way Left* (Edinburgh: Iona Community, 1956), p. 62. No attempt is made here to discuss what in 'Wyclif's translation' came from his own hand and what from that of his assistants or successors.

BIBLIOGRAPHY

Bible Versions and Translations

Authorized Version of the Bible/King James Bible (Cambridge: Cambridge University Press; Oxford: Oxford University Press; London: Collins, 1611).

The Bible in Basic English (Cambridge: Cambridge University Press, NT 1941, OT 1950).

Fifty Psalms: An Attempt at a New Translation (London: Burns & Oates, 1968).

Good News Bible (London: Collins for United Bible Societies, 1976).

Jerusalem Bible (London: Darton, Longman & Todd, 1966).

Knox, R.A. (trans.), *The New Testament* (London: Burns, Oates & Washbourne, 1946).

—*The Old Testament* (London: Burns, Oates & Washbourne, 1949).

Levi, P. (trans.), *The Holy Gospel of John: A New Translation* (Worthing: Churchman, 1985).

—*The Psalms* (Harmondsworth: Penguin, 1976).

Moffatt, J. (trans.), *The New Testament: A New Translation* (London: Hodder & Stoughton, 1913).

Mowlvey, H. (trans.), *The Psalms for Today's Readers* (London: Collins, 1989).

New American Bible (Nashville: Nelson, 1983).

New English Bible (Oxford: Oxford University Press; Cambridge: Cambridge University Press, 1970).

New International Version (New York: International Bible Society, 1978).

New King James Version of the New Testament (Nashville: Nelson, 1979).

New Jerusalem Bible (London: Darton, Longman & Todd, 1985).

New Revised Standard Version (Nashville: Nelson, 1990).

Phillips, J.B. (trans.), *Letters to Young Churches* (London: Bles, 1947).

—*Four Prophets* (London: Bles, 1963).

—*The Book of Revelation* (London: Bles, 1957).

—*The Gospel of Luke* (London: Collins, 1973).

The Book of Psalms: A New Translation according to the Traditional Hebrew Text (Philadelphia: Jewish Publication Society of America, 1972).

The Psalms: A New Translation for Worship (London: Collins, 1977).

Revised English Bible (Oxford: Oxford University Press, 1989).

Revised Standard Version (New Jersey: Nelson, 1946, 1952).

Rieu, E.V. (trans.), *The Four Gospels* (London: Lane, 1951).

Taizé Community, *Psalms from Taizé* (ET; London: Mowbray, 1983).

Translator's New Testament (London: Bible Society, 1973).

Wand, J.W.C., *The New Testament Letters Prefaced and Paraphrased* (Oxford: Oxford University Press, 1946).

Weymouth, R.F., *The New Testament in Modern Speech* (London: James Clarke, 1902).

Other Sources and Related Writings

Allen, W. (ed. and trans.), *Translating for King James: Notes Made by a Translator of King James Bible* (Nashville: Nelson, 1969).

Alter, R., and F. Kermode, *The Literary Guide to the Bible* (London: Collins, 1987).

Barclay, W., 'On Translating the New Testament', in *The Gospels and the Acts of the Apostles* (London: Collins, 1968).

Barker, K. (ed.), *The Making of a Contemporary Translation: New International Version* (London: Hodder & Stoughton for the International Bible Society, 1987).

Barr, J., *The Semantics of Biblical Language* (Oxford: Oxford University Press, 1961).

Beekman, J., 'Idiomatic Translations and Some Underlying Theological Questions', in *Notes on Translation 1968* (Dallas: SIL), pp. 8-17.

Beekman, J., and J. Callow, *Translating the Word of God* (Grand Rapids: Zondervan, 1974).

Benjamin, W., 'The Task of the Translator', in H. Arendt (ed.), *Illuminations* (London: Collins, 1973).

Bruce, F.F., *The History of the Bible in English* (London: Lutterworth, 1979).

Caird, G.B., *The Language and Imagery of the Bible* (London: Gerald Duckworth, 1980).

Chomsky, N., *Syntactic Structures* (The Hague: Mouton, 1957).

Commentary on the Alternative Service Book (London: Central Board of Finance of the Church of England, 1980).

Cotterell, P., and M. Turner, *Linguistics and Biblical Interpretation* (London: SPCK, 1989).

Daiches, D., *Literary Essays* (1956).

Dixon, J.W., 'Aesthetics and Theology', in A. Richardson and J. Bowden (eds.), *A New Dictionary of Christian Theology* (London: SCM Press, 1983), p. 8.

Dodd, C.H., 'Introduction to the New Testament', in the New English Bible.

Driver, G.R., 'Introduction to the Old Testament' in the New English Bible.

Duthie, A.S., *The Bible Translations and how to Choose between them* (Exeter: Paternoster Press, 1985).

Ebeling, G., *A Theological Theory of Language* (ET; London: Collins, 1973).

Eliot, T.S., *Notes Towards a Definition of Culture* (London: Faber & Faber, 1948).

Ellingworth, P., 'Modern Translations', in R.J. Coggins and J.L. Houlden (eds.), *The Dictionary of Biblical Interpretation* (London: SCM Press, 1990).

Emmerson, G.I., 'Problems of Translation', in Coggins and Houlden (eds.), *The Dictionary of Biblical Interpretation*.

Fitzgerald, R., 'The Art of Translation', *The Paris Review* 94 (1984).

Frost, D., *The Language of Series 3* (Nottingham: Grove Press, 1973).

Frye, N., *The Great Code: The Bible as Literature* (London: Routledge & Kegan Paul, 1982).

Gibson, J., 'Hebrew and Modern Linguistics', *Expository Times* (July 1991).

Goodspeed, E., *The Making of the English New Testament* (Chicago: Chicago University Press, 1925).

Grayston, K., 'Confessions of a Bible Translator', *New Universities Quarterly* (Summer 1979), p. 288.

Habgood, J., 'Alternative Worship', in *Church and Nation in a Secular Age* (London: Darton, Longman & Todd, 1983).

Hammond, G., 'English Translations of the Bible', in Alter and Kermode (eds.) *The Literary Guide to the Bible*, pp. 647-66.

—*The Making of the Bible* (Manchester: Carcanet, 1980).

Henn, T.R., 'The Bible as Literature', in *Peake's Commentary* (London: Nelson, 1962), pp. 8-23.

Hunt, G., *Introduction to the New English Bible* (Cambridge: Cambridge University Press, 1970).

Jasper, D., *The Study of Literature and Religion: An Introduction* (London: Macmillan, rev. edn, 1992 [1989]).

Jasper, D. (ed.), *The New Testament and Literary Imagination* (London: Macmillan, 1987).

Jenkins, D., *The British: Their Identity and Religion* (London: SCM Press, 1975).

Knox, R.A., *On Englishing the Bible* (London: Burns & Oates, 1949).

Kubo, S., and W.F. Sprecht, *So Many Versions? Twentieth Century English Versions of the Bible* (Grand Rapids: Zondervan, 1983).

Larson, M.L., *Meaning-Based Translation* (Lanham, MD: University Press of America, 1984).

Levi, P., *The English Bible* (Grand Rapids: Eerdmans, 1974; repr.; Worthing: Churchman, 1985).

Lewis, C.S., *Reflections on the Psalms* (London: Bles, 1958).

—*The Literary Impact of the Authorised Version* (Philadelphia: Fortress Press, 1963).

Lyons, J., *Language and Linguistics* (Cambridge: Cambridge University Press, 1981).

McFague, S., *Speaking in Parables* (Philadelphia: Fortress Press, 1975).

McIntyre, J., *Faith, Theology and Imagination* (Edinburgh: Handsel, 1981).

Martin, D., and P. Mullen, *No Alternative* (Oxford: Basil Blackwell, 1981).

Metzger, B., R. Denton and W. Harrelson, *The Making of the New Revised Standardd Version of the Bible* (Grand Rapids: Eerdmans, 1991).

Meyer, C.S., *Cranmer's Selected Writings* (London: SPCK, 1961).

Morris, B. (ed.), *Ritual Murder* (Manchester: Carcanet, 1980).

Moule, C.F.D., 'The New English Bible', in *Cambridge History of the Bible* (Cambridge: Cambridge University Press, 1963), III, pp. 379-82.

Mullen, P., *The New Babel* (London: SPCK, 1987).

—'The Religious Speak-Easy', in D.J. Enright (ed.), *Fair of Speech* (Oxford: Oxford University Press, 1985).

Nida, E.A., *Good News for Everyone* (Waco, TX: Word Books, 1977).

—'Poetry and the Bible Translator', *Bible Translator* 33 (1982), pp. 435-38.

Nida, E.A., and C.R. Taber, *The Theory and Practice of Translation* (Leiden: Brill, 1969).

Phillips, J.B., *The Price of Success* (London: Hodder & Stoughton, 1984).

Porter, S.E., 'Greek Language and Linguistics', *Expository Times* 103.7 (April 1992), pp. 202-208.

Prickett, S., *Words and the Word: Language, Poetics and Biblical Interpretation* (Cambridge: Cambridge University Press, 1986).

—'What Do the Translators Think they Are up to?', *Theology* 80.678 (November 1977), pp. 401-403.

Quiller Couch, A., *On the Art of Reading* (Cambridge: Cambridge University Press, 1920).

Richards, I.A., and C.K. Ogden, *The Meaning of Meaning* (United Kingdom, 1923).

Rieu, E.V. (trans.), *The Odyssey* (Harmondsworth: Penguin 1946).

Robinson, E., *The Language of Mystery* (London: SCM Press, 1989).

Salevsky, H., 'Theory of Biblical Translation and General Theory of Translation', *Bible Translator* 42.1 (January 1991), pp. 101ff.

Schutz, R., *The Power of the Provisional* (ET; London: Hodder & Stoughton, 1969).

Schwarz, W., *Principles and Problems of Biblical Translation* (Cambridge: Cambridge University Press, 1955).

Shehan, P.W., G.W. MacRae and R.E. Brown, 'The English Bible', in *Jerome Biblical Commentary* (Englewood Cliffs, NJ: Prentice-Hall, 1968), II, §§69.151ff.

Silva, M., *Biblical Words and their Meaning* (Grand Rapids: Zondervan, 1983).

—*God, Language and Scripture* (Grand Rapids: Zondervan, 1990).

Sisson, C.H., 'The Poet and the Translator' (Jackson Knight Memorial Lecture, Exeter University, 1984).

Sjölander, P., 'Expressing Religious Terms in Simple Language', *Bible Translator* 34 (1983), pp. 426-31.

Thiselton, A.C., *Language, Liturgy and Meaning* (Nottingham: Grove Press, 2nd edn, 1986).

Waddell, H., *Mediaeval Latin Lyrics* (London: Constable, 1929).

Wendland, E., 'Receptor Language Style and Bible Translation', *Bible Translator* 32.1 (January 1981), pp. 107-24.

Weigle, L.A. (ed.), *An Introduction to the Revised Standard Version of the New Testament* (USA: International Council of Religious Education, 1946), p. 63.

Wiener, A., *The Prophet Elijah and the Development of Judaism* (London: Routledge & Kegan Paul, 1978).

Wright, T.R., *Theology and Literature* (Oxford: Basil Blackwell, 1988).

INDEX OF BIBLICAL REFERENCES

OLD TESTAMENT

INDEX OF SUBJECTS

INDEX OF NAMES